Foresighted Leading

Yunxian Chen

Foresighted Leading

Theoretical Thinking and Practice of China's Regional Economic Development

北京大學出版社
PEKING UNIVERSITY PRESS

Springer

Yunxian Chen
Foshan
People's Republic of China

The Chinese edition was originally published by Peking University Press. This translation is published by arrangement with Peking University Press, Beijing, China.

ISBN 978-3-642-35367-3 ISBN 978-3-642-35368-0 (eBook)
DOI 10.1007/978-3-642-35368-0
Springer Heidelberg New York Dordrecht London

Library of Congress Control Number: 2013930233

Printed on acid-free paper

Springer is part of Springer Science+Business Media (www.springer.com)

A truly successful economic system implies that government must exercise foresighted leading by the aid of the foundations of market economy, its mechanisms and rules and employ the “visible hand” to overcome the defects and make up the margins caused by the “invisible hand”.

Natural economy is contingent upon the capricious sky
Market economy is contingent upon the invisible hand
Knowledge economy is contingent upon the intelligent mind

Foreword

China's reform and opening up in more than 30 years has paved a unique road of economic development with Chinese characteristics in the economic world. The reason for my use of "road" of China's economic development rather than the conventionalized term "Chinese mode" is simple. Modes tend to be ossified, and ossified modes and dogmatism will harm courage to make explorations and hinder progress. That will be fatal for China's economic development, whose past, present, and future is contingent upon practical explorations. The previous 30 years' reform and opening up has been based upon such explorations, and so will the current transformation of economic development mode.

In terms of economic theories, what are needed are not the empty talks, which sound like grand views and look like the moon in the water or the flowers in the mirror, but the down-to-earth theoretical perceptions that are acquired from practical explorations and can guide practical economic work. Over the past 30 years, Chinese economists have done their bit, and looking into the future, they are supposed to continue their contributions in the twenty-first century. Dr. Chen Yunxian is one of those economists who work at the forefront of economic development and at the same time keep thinking about economic issues.

One of the focal points of reform in the transition from planned economy to market economy is government behavior, in other words how to define government functions. In fact, the notions of government functions under planned economy are still exercising influence upon today's reform, for instance, government is almighty, government should keep everything under its control, whatever government can do should all be done by government, etc. Such notions have become shackles for the development of market economy. What economists should do is to define government functions and roles. It will turn out to be of primary importance to break away from conventionalized ways of thinking about government behavior and look at the function of government under market economic system from more foresighted perspectives.

Over the recent years, I have repeatedly pointed out that the success in China's economic transformation resides in breaking out of the vicious cycle of investment stimulus and its resultant cycle of capital bubble. Government should not stop at "post-process" intervention and should take measures to exercise "anticipatory intervention" and establish early-warning mechanisms. Dr. Chen Yunxian sees eye to eye with me in his theory of "foresighted leading".

As for the economic transformation under way all over China, I persist in the principle of "development in transformation and transformation in development". "Development in transformation" means creating conditions for economic development in the transformation of economic development mode, and what turns out to be the most crucial and challenging in this process is the restructuring of microeconomic foundations from macroeconomic perspectives and the revitalizing market forces. "Transformation in development" means strengthening capabilities to shoulder the strong impacts from violent institutional transformation in economic development and intensify wide-ranging social support and understanding of reforms so as to enhance market-oriented economic system reform.

Therefore, I have always emphasized that efforts must be made to restructure microeconomic foundations from macroeconomic perspectives and revitalize market forces. As Dr. Chen Yunxian points out in this book, under the context of market economy, government is an independent economic entity that not only provides services and administers public affairs but also coordinates, facilitates, and leads economic development. The dual role of local government represents its functions at both micro-level of market economy and macro-level of government leading, regulating, and adjusting economic development. As far as I can see, his idea of government as major market entity is of vital importance.

As indicated in my book *Unbalanced Chinese Economy*, as far as economic operations (including resources allocation) are concerned, macro goals come before micro goals in terms of operational objectives, and market regulation comes before government regulation in terms of operational mechanism. Government regulation aims to coordinate micro and macro economy. To be more specific, government regulation aims to achieve through effective government intervention the macro objectives that cannot be realized merely through market regulation on condition that market mechanism ensures the sound operations of micro economy. Government regulation does not intend to constrain enterprise or market vitality but to consider social marginal benefits of resources investment from the macroeconomic perspective of resources allocation. Government regulates economy through as much force of market mechanism as possible to influence decision making on the part of microeconomic units and facilitates the optimization of resources allocation through their adjustment and transfer of resources investment.

All in all, government intervention aims to make macro and micro economy develop in the coordinating way rather than disconnected. In addition, government intervention cannot fall behind and cannot stop merely at "post-process". "Foresighted leading", which Dr. Chen Yunxian advocates, aims to promote "anticipatory regulation" rather than "post-process" intervention so that government can fill with the "visible hand" the deficiencies and blanks left by the "invisible hand" of market. He points out that if "enterprises" stand for micro economy, then "state" stands for macro economy, and "regions" stand for meso economy. I consider this a rewarding economic exploration in the development of regional economy.

After reading the first draft of this book, I feel compelled to hope that Dr. Chen Yunxian's concept of "foresighted leading", which is derived from his practical work in Shunde, a frontier county-level city of China's reform and opening up, together with the notion of "Intelligent Foshan via Fourization", which is being implemented, will bear substantial fruit in Foshan, where he is working as a major member of government leadership, and open a new road for China's regional economic development.

In addition, Chen Yunxian, a scholar and government official, also made insightful remarks relating to reform of urban-rural dual system and urban-rural integration. There is also justification to believe that admirable achievements will be made in these aspects as well. I have also conducted a lot of follow-ups concerning the reform of urban-rural dual system. I have made repeated mention that China's planned economy has state-owned enterprise system and urban-rural dual system as its two major underpinnings. What has been transformed over the past 30 years since reform and opening up has been mainly limited within the state-owned enterprise system, and almost no change has been made in the urban-rural dual system. As a frontier city of economic development and reform, Foshan enjoys unparalleled superiority over other cities and is highly likely to provide rich experience for China's regional economic development and social progress in both theoretical explorations and practical work.

I am extremely delighted to see the book *Foresighted Leading* meet its readers. It will certainly provide illuminating insights into the development and transformation of China's regional economy and offer practical guidance for those involved in theoretical researches and practical work in this regard.

Li Yining

Preface

> There is a sail in the south of the southern world,
> I will venture out into the south of the southern world,
> I will have my destiny reoriented in the south of the southern world.

These lines are taken from a song entitled "South of the Southern World". The south of the southern world refers obviously to Guangdong. Reading these lines, I can sense mingled feelings surge inside me. It has been nearly 20 years since I came to settle in Guangdong, and how time flies, just like a second. When I drive on the Guangzhou-Foshan Expressway in the evenings, a myriad of thoughts keep occurring in my mind, at the sight of colorful neon lights passing quickly by my car windows. On several occasions, I feel the strong desire to get out of the car and rush into the deep night to embrace the land and look up into the starry sky.

I came to Guangzhou after I obtained my doctoral degree in economics from Peking University in the summer of 1991 and was the first doctoral degree holder in Guangdong Development Bank (now China Guangfa Bank). Professor Xiao Zhuoji, under whom I studied for my Ph.D. degree, is among the earliest scholars who have conducted researches in stock markets in China. My doctoral dissertation—*Comparative Studies in Securities Investment in China and Abroad*—makes a detailed comparative analysis of stock markets in America, Britain, Germany, and Japan and applies my findings to the construction and development of China's stock market. That dissertation is regarded as the first to have conducted comparative analyses of securities investment at home and abroad and to have filled the gap in relevant researches in China.

Thanks to my academic background, I was put in charge of preparatory work to set up the securities department of Guangdong Development Bank. We started up with a team of six people and a meager investment of a little over two million yuan. We began to ride bicycles through streets in Guangzhou and made frequent travels between Guangzhou and other cities in the Pearl River Delta. Through painstaking efforts, the securities department was set up, first affiliated to Guangdong Development Bank, later transformed into Guangdong Guangfa Securities Company, and now Guangfa Securities Co. Ltd (hereinafter shortened as Guangfa).

Guangfa, which started from a securities department of a local commercial bank and has developed into a large-scale national securities company, enjoys a "doctoral corps" in China's stock market circles, made up of 65 doctoral degree holders and 385 master degree holders. When I left, Guangfa had got a staff of over 1,900 and operated nearly 80 branches in major cities in China. Its total assets amounted to over 23 billion yuan, with net assets reaching 2.5 billion yuan.

At the beginning of 2003, I was appointed by Guangdong Provincial Committee of CPC as standing member of Foshan Municipal Committee of CPC and executive deputy mayor of Foshan City. I had to experience a shift from business to government and from microeconomic field to mesoeconomic field. Shifts from an academic to a business leader and from business to government have given me a lot of opportunities to train myself.

In 2004, I was appointed secretary of Shunde District Committee of CPC, Foshan, was elected mayor of Foshan in 2006, and started my office as secretary of Foshan Municipal Committee of CPC. It has been my great honor to have worked in Foshan, a frontier city of China's reform and opening up, and in Shunde, a pioneering district of Guangdong's reform. Immersed in the forefront of reform and innovation, I spent my spare time to conduct serious studies and think comprehensively about theoretical development and innovation in economics. Though I had stepped out of university, I did not stop thinking about theoretical economic issues, in particular issues arising from practical work. It is my firm commitment that only when you land on soil will you know the strength of the earth.

After I came to Foshan, I devoted most of my time and attention to issues concerning the relation of government to regional economic development. I think about them from economic perspectives. The past experience and the future development trends of such economically demonstrative regions as Foshan and Shunde can definitely provide excellent samples and mechanisms for theoretical economists.

My work experience in Shunde and theoretical reflections upon its industrial development make me deeply aware that China's development should have gone through the stage of "wading across the stream by feeling stones" and should enter into the stage of "foresighted leading". It is necessary to wade across the stream by feeling stones in the early stage of development, but government leading and planning are quite necessary when development reaches a new level.

This book is the crystallization of my thinking about economic issues in my post as a government leader. It is the accumulation of serious studies in my spare time and the reflection upon practical work. Now it is collected into a book, with a view to "casting bricks to attract jades", to use a Chinese idiom, and drawing more attention to the role and function of regional government and the foundation, approaches, and orientations of the scientific and sustainable development of regional economy.

As a government leader, I am fully engaged in government work, but I feel it is important to keep learning and conducting researches. As general secretary Hu Jintao remarked, government leaders of all levels must be aware that they will fall behind and will find it hard to shoulder great responsibilities if they do not learn, do not keep learning, and do not study hard, because our society is changing all the time, and the grassroots people are constantly creating innovations in their work. Government leaders must keep studying and enrich their mind with the knowledge the human society is constantly creating in order to be qualified leaders and administrators.

As is also stated by Wang Yang, member of the Political Bureau of CPC and secretary of Guangdong Provincial Committee of CPC, if one gives up studies, one stops making progress; if one chooses to study, one chooses his future; and if one keeps studying, one is sure to have a good command of his future. There ought to be more reading and thinking rather than hustles and bustles, more experience and knowledge rather than pleasure seeking, and more real ability and learning rather than personal gains and speculation. Our party leaders must keep learning, be good at learning, make progress, and apply what is acquired to practical work. Learning initiatives can be found in everyone, and thinking vitality can be seen everywhere. Thus, our society will be filled with cultural charms, and a nation or a region will achieve sustainable competitiveness in its development.

We are living in the age of knowledge economy, which has substantially reduced the dependence of economic development upon material resources consumption. Science and technology, knowledge and information, and innovative reforms have become the key driving force for economic development. It can be safely concluded that knowledge economy is, in the ultimate analysis, intelligence-dependent economy and innovative economy. Intelligence and innovation must be derived from human wisdom and must depend on human resources. One can never possess innovative capabilities without long-term constant learning.

Contents

Chapter 1
Introduction Foresighted Leading: Theoretical Innovations Based on the Economic Development in China

1.1 Exploring the Logic Track of the Economic Development in China

"The twenty-first century is supposed to be an era for Chinese economists to play more significant roles on the stage of world economy, and an era for them to emerge in the capacity of international master economists and lead the development of the discipline of world economics," reiterated Lin Yifu, professor of Peking University and a well-renowned economist in China, in the light of his observations on the development trend in the area of world economics years ago.

As is known to all, theory is seen as a set of logic systems for the interpretation of phenomena. According to Lin Yifu, it is no easy matter to determine whether one set of logic systems is of greater importance than the other if assessment is made merely of logic systems themselves. Then, what leads to the assumption that some theories are more important while others are less so? He believes that the essence of the matter resides in the importance of the phenomena the theory attempts to explain. If the phenomena a set of theories intends to decipher deserve world-wide attention, then the theories will be endowed with international importance and significance, and the theorists will accordingly be reckoned as world-rate masters.

What are the criteria for the evaluation of the status of economic phenomena? Lin Yifu argues that the significance of economic phenomena depends upon the importance of the country where those phenomena occur and the position it holds in world economy. The shift of world economic research centers and the locations that give birth to distinguished economists from one region to the other indicates the trend of transfer for world economic centers.

Lin's views are evidenced by the fact that the world's well-known economists, either in the school of Marxism and Leninism or in the school of capitalism, were active in the United Kingdom prior to the 1930s and have been active in the United States ever since. That shift of locations from the United Kingdom to the United States is accounted for by the transfer of world economic centers.

Y. Chen, *Foresighted Leading: Theoretical Thinking and Practice of China's Regional Economic Development*, DOI 10.1007/978-3-642-35368-0_1,

Let's come to China now. China attracts attention and gains respect world wide as a result of its remarkable accomplishments since the implementation of the open door policy in 1978 and its admirable performance in world financial crises. China's development and China's international image will be priority issues in the field of world economics. There is sufficient justification to argue that the findings and contributions from Chinese economic studies will be of primary significance and have abundant international implications.

No existing western economic theories can fully explain the unique phenomena of speedy and sustained economic growth in China over the past three decades. It is no surprise that economists in the west predict whoever can interpret such phenomena are to be awarded the Nobel Prize in economics.

As Georg Wilhelm Friedrich Hegel (1770–1831) remarked, "Only in the state does man have a rational existence". Economic miracles have appeared in China in the past 30 years and have gained strengthening momentum for another 30 years to come. This situation calls for systematic theoretical reviews on China's development and theoretical innovations upon traditional economics.

It is my privilege, as an economist in the forefront of economic practice, to be involved in the whole process of China's reform and development and witness its on-goings over the past decades.

Economics, as a science of benefiting people, is most intimately associated with practice. In terms of economic studies, I prefer to refine and intensify theories through analyzing phenomena in reality, apply them back to practice, test them against reality and amend them through practice. All this experience and observation enable an even more transparent panoramic view of China's present and future to unfold before me.

To put it in a nutshell, I use a four-character phrase: 超前引领 (*chaoqian yinling*, *chaoqian* meaning "foresighted", and *yinling* "leading").

It is my conviction that the concept of *chaoqian yinling* embodies a sound set of logic systems which reflect the interaction and coordination between the government and the economic sector in economic development.

1.2 From Adam Smith to John Maynard Keynes

The recognition of economics as an independent discipline is chiefly ascribable to *An Inquiry into the Nature and Causes of the Wealth of Nations* (also known as *The Wealth of Nations*) by Adam Smith (1723–1790), who argues that the seemingly disorderly free market is in fact regulated by an "invisible hand" and thus advocates liberal business activities, free competition and the laissez-faire economic system. He holds that the role of the government lies in maintaining security, stability and peace and investing in projects only for the good of general public.

Smith's theory of free economy quickly became popular and the concept of free market competition won wide recognition. The market economic system characterized by free competition accelerated the process of the Industrial Revolution in Britain and enhanced its prosperity. Some even think that Adam Smith's influence on Britain comes only next to Isaac Newton (1643–1727).

In spite of his increasing fame *The Wealth of Nations* brought him, Adam Smith remained in the position of customs officer in the 12 years following its publication. He was once invited to a Duke's residence where the nobility and business tycoons who manipulated the British economy met. Upon his arrival by coach and entry into the doorway, all the guests stood to greet him. At the sight, Smith promptly asked them to remain seated. However, William Pitt (1708–1778), the then British Prime Minister, responded with "No" and asked Smith to sit down first, stating that they were his students, which is proof enough that Smith was held in high esteem in Britain's social circles.

However, the world-wide economic depression between 1929 and 1933 radically transformed people's views on government roles in national economy and initiated disputes concerning its economic policies. Economists came to realize that market is not omnipotent and that it may sometimes malfunction. The free competition in market economy may result in severe inequality of wealth and income distribution, violent cyclic economic fluctuations and sharp social contradictions and conflicts.

While the West was still deeply engulfed in the economic depression and, to put it in a Chinese saying, "lived in deep water and hot fires" (an abyss of misery), the Soviet Union "enjoyed the landscape here beyond comparison", to quote another Chinese saying. The Soviet government created and executed a new mode of economic administration, called "planned economy". From 1928 to 1932, it implemented the first 5-year plan, which turned the country dramatically into a prosperous industrial power from an agricultural nation. The economic success of the Soviet Union became the highlight in the eyes of western politicians and economists. The Americans who wished for least government intervention and administration started to rethink about the relationship between government and the economic sector in economic development from different perspectives.

Now comes the turn for the great economist—John Maynard Keynes (1883–1946).

Keynes believes in the necessity of government involvement, i.e. the "visible hand", and the use of national power in driving national economy. He advocates the adoption of fiscal and monetary policies for national economic regulation and intervention so as to guarantee aggregate demand and economic growth. Keynes' theory helped western economies in their transition from laissez-faire to national interventionism, thus fundamentally transforming the public conceptualization of government role in national economy and its formulation of economic policies. His representative work—*The General Theory of Employment, Interest and Money* (1936) was popular with economic circles in western countries and represented one of the mainstream schools of economics.

Since the World War II, it has been the long-term national policy for western capitalist economies to follow Keynesianism and regulate economy via the "invisible hand" of market laws, coupled with government intervention. Keynesianism helped to lead capitalist economies into their prime period in their history of development so that that period is termed "the Keynesian Times" and Keynes is described as the saviour of capitalism and the father of post-war prosperity.

1.3 "Market Malfunction" and "Government Malfunction"

From Adam Smith to John Maynard Keynes, from the "invisible hand" to the "visible hand" and from market regulation to macro-level government supervision is derived the differentiation of economics into micro economics and macro economics.

Adam Smith argues that every individual merely wants to gain his own interests in economic activities and that self-interest, rather than sympathy or altruism, is their motivation. These so-called "economic beings" shall seek to maximize individual interests and gain the greatest benefits and values with minimum cost, which reflects how micro-economic activities are conducted. Individuals seem to be compelled to maximize their values and interests by the "invisible hand", and the maximization of individual interests in turn propels national economy.

It is clear that micro economy, which is considered an optimal mode of resources allocation characterized by equality, competitiveness, legality and openness, is operated under the influence of pricing and market and is self-regulated and balanced through competition. However, its limitations of spontaneity, blindness and hysteresis are obvious, and the involvement of people's consciousness and their psychological complexity are liable to cause market to malfunction.

It is found from the development of market economies in the world that market malfunction will chiefly result in the inequality of income and wealth distribution, competition failure, market monopoly, the incompatibility of regional economic development, the inadequacy of product supply, and economic fluctuations.

Certain forces will have to interfere and remedy whenever market malfunctions. Adam Smith was indeed aware of this and believed in the use of "internal force", i.e. human morals and virtues, rather than "external force". It may be assumed that in the eyes of Adam Smith, limitations in human ethics and morality and the resources available are the best means of restricting "economic beings".

Obviously, market malfunction will continue if only "individuals" and "internal force" intervene without recourse to government supervision and "external force". It has been proved that in case of market malfunction, the natural adjustment via market mechanism and individual ethics will be extremely time-consuming and costly, and the opportunity cost will be innumerable. In order to effectively remedy this malfunction, Keynes advocates the principle of government intervention in market by means of macro adjustment and control, i.e. by using administrative law, fiscal and monetary policies and other means to remedy market malfunction and counter-economic cycle with a view to maintaining economic stability.

In contemporary times, Keynesianism is well-known and widely practiced. In countries where market economy is established, their government will exercise certain degrees of supervision and regulation over their economy. It can be concluded that contemporary market economy is characterized by the integration of government and market and the combination of macro adjustment of regulation and control via the "visible hand" and the spontaneous market self-regulation via the "invisible hand".

Keynes' macro intervention and adjustment, however, have limitations, for they come into effect only in the course of market malfunction, or even after it occurs. Consequently, quite a few developed countries have sunk into stagflation since the 1970s.

Stagflation is described as inflation in economic stagnation, i.e. "stagnated" in economic growth and "inflation". In macroeconomic terms, it specifically refers to the economic phenomenon of the coexistence of economic stagnation and high inflation, and unemployment and depression. In familiar terms, it means that prices keep rising while economic growth comes to a halt. The objectives of government policies, according to Keynes, are high-speed economic growth, low unemployment rate and low inflation, and economic recession and inflation will not coexist. The hard reality is that many western capitalist countries experienced the co-existence of stagnation in economic growth, rising unemployment and inflation in the 1970s.

Two factors cause stagflation: unfavorable economic policies of government (including fiscal and taxation policies, monetary policies, trade policies and so on) and impacts of supply, which come from increasing production costs resulting in inadequate supply and inflation due to decreasing industrial output.

It is inferred from observations of stagflation that government is not omnipotent and that government intervention may also cause malfunction. Government malfunction may manifest itself in the following aspects: (1) faults in public decision-making are legion; (2) the expansion of government and their departments that result from the government and its officials taking themselves for assumed "brokers" and pursuing individual and organizational interests; (3) low efficiency of bureaucracies; (4) power peddling and corruption.

Government malfunction alerts people to the defects in the new economic theory. Joseph E. Stiglitz, the Nobel Prize winner in economics and professor of Columbia University, points out in his *Freefall: America, Free Markets, and the Sinking of the World Economy* (2010), that the new economic theory proposed by contemporary economists in the west has turned out to be imperfect and that traditional capitalist theories must be revised and innovated. He argues that market plays a leading role in all successful economies but that market is not vulnerable on all sides. Government should not stay away from economic activities and should have their role to play in saving the economy when problems arise in market, exercising market supervision and preventing the economy from falling into the same rut. In addition, the economy must enable itself to play a role in balancing the market and the government.

Li Yining, professor and economist of Peking University, China, commented in an interview by the press early in 2010 that China must take "pre-regulation" measures and establish early-alerting mechanisms instead of "post-regulation" measures if the vicious cycle of investment and its related assets bubble is to be broken.

1.4 Government Functions from the Perspective of Meso Economics

It is generally agreed that systems and regulations are more vital than technology and capital in economic development. Emphasis should be laid on innovation in systems and regulations for market economy in China. It is more important to note at present that more attention has been paid to technical innovation rather than system innovation.

A truly successful economic system implies that government must exercise foresighted leading by the aid of the foundations of market economy, its mechanisms and rules and employ the "visible hand" to overcome the defects and make up the margins caused by the "invisible hand".

The ideas of government's foresighted leading, namely employing its "visible hand" to fill gaps the "invisible hand" leaves behind, have converged in between macro-economics and micro-economics into an area called mezzo-economics. Thus, there appears a "region" between "enterprise" and "state". The studies on "enterprise" stand for micro-economics, those on "state" for macro-economics, and those on "region" certainly for mezzo-economics, all of which, to my mind, set up a complete and unified system for economics.

Explanations may also be given through analogy to natural phenomena. In natural terms, microeconomics may be referred to as streams, mezzo-economics as rivers, and macro-economics as seas and oceans. Streams flow into rivers, and rivers into seas. The ultimate goal of national economic administration is to achieve balance and coordination between streams, rivers and seas and oceans and keep them free from drought and flooding.

It is the same with China, where it will not work properly if merely macroeconomic policies are adopted to adjust and regulate micro economy, and meso economic policies must also be called into operation. Enterprises and individuals exercise microeconomic administration, while regional governments take responsibility for meso economic administration.

The government is an independent economic entity under market economy. Not only does it provide public administration and services, it also plays coordinating, promoting and leading roles in economic development, dealing with such public affairs as establishing economic regulations, maintaining market order, stabilizing macro economy, providing infrastructural services, fostering market systems, ensuring orderly market operation, making income redistribution and achieving social equality. Regional governments perform dual functions: representing enterprises and individuals in market economy and representing national government in playing leading roles in the coordination, regulation and facilitation of economic growth.

Some rules for regional development can be discerned and generalized from the perspective of meso economics. Our examination of the development rate and social welfare standards in different regional economies reveals that they vary from region to region and this variation is due to differences in regional natural resources and, more importantly, to the effectiveness and efficiency of regional government functions.

As far as newly emerging countries are concerned, their regional government is, more often than not, directly involved in regional economic development and act as a driving force. That accounts for the fact that those transitional economies develop faster.

In addition to enterprises, regional governments also play a major role in market competition in China. In other words, in China's development, competition exists not only between enterprises but also between governments. These two levels of competition are the "double forces" for China to have achieved speedy sustained economic development in the course of more than 30 years' reform, which possibly provides the key to the riddle of China's rapid economic growth over the past decades, and which has perplexed many in their search for answers.

With respect to China's economic development for the past decades, it is high time that theoretical generalizations be refined and heightened to a new horizon. For one thing, the findings will fill the gaps in economic studies and serve as guide for China's further economic system reform, and for the other, the absorption of regional government into economic theoretical systems will help to create multi-level market and enhance the stability of national economy.

Foresighted leading makes itself markedly different from Adam Smith's mechanism of market economy and Keynes's mechanism of regulation and supervision by government. It follows that the regulatory role of market economy mechanism forms the basis of economics as a discipline, and that the theory of regulation and supervision by government results in the division of economics into micro-economics and macro-economics, and that the theory of foresighted leading further differentiates economics into macroeconomics, mezzoeconomics and microeconomics.

As a theoretical system, "foresighted leading" can be defined as follows: *giving full play to government functions, particularly those of regional governments, in economic guidance, regulation and warning and taking the lead in promoting scientific and sustainable growth in regional economy with recourse to market rules and forces, by means of investing, pricing, taxation, legal and other measures and through innovation in organization, system and technology.*

1.5 Changing Roles from "Nanny" to "Guide"

There have been many successful cases in which government promotes regional economic development through foresighted leading.

A good case in point is Singapore, which, despite its serious shortage of resources, has completed its transformation from a small fishing village into a well-developed country within no less than 50 years. Its "foresighted leading" in national economic development attracted serious attention from the Chinese government and academic circles. Various levels of government in China have sent quite many delegations to Singapore to study its success experience since Deng Xiaoping delivered his famous speech in South China in 1992. In addition, many other countries, such as Russia, have shown continuing interest in Singaporean experience.

In the 1960s Singapore was undergoing a high rate of unemployment and population growth. In response to this situation, the Singaporean government spared no efforts developing labor-intensive manufacturing industry, which helped it to get out of employment predicament and paved its way to industrialization. By the 1970s, Singapore adopted opportunely strategies for industrial transfer and upgrading by transferring labor-intensive enterprises to neighboring countries and taking active measures to attract intellectual-intensive industries. Later on, the government continued its foresighted leading role in such areas as industrial guidance, human resources development, environment optimization, which eventually makes Singapore the center, for industry, trade and finance in Southeast Asia and wins the title of "Four Asian Tigers" with Taiwan, Hong Kong and South Korea. After entering the twenty-first century, the Singaporean government, confronted with globalization and the newly rising neighboring countries, began to rethink about their economic development strategies and implemented a series of foresighted leading programs, including the internationalization of its national enterprises, with intent to strengthen its leading position in regional economic development.

In China, it is worthwhile to study and appreciate Shunde's experience in achieving surprisingly outstanding economic success under foresighted leadership of the district government. Shunde District (formerly Shunde County), Foshan City, located in the hinterland of the Pearl River Delta region, does not boast geographic advantages or natural resources. However, in the course of over 30 years' reform and opening-up, Shunde has been leading the county-level economic development in China. Eventually, it has become China's first county with its GDP exceeding 100 billion yuan (15.748 billion US dollars), ranking first among the top 100 counties in China for several successive years.

Why is it possible for Shunde to have achieved such economic miracles? The key lies in the excellent performance in Shunde District government playing a foresighted leading role in its development. In the early 1980s, Shunde District government proposed a strategic "three-based" economic system, consisting of publicly-based economy, industry-based economy, and mainstay enterprises-based economy, with a view to promoting industrialization in rural areas. By the early 1990s, the output ratio of industry and agriculture amounted to 98:2, indicating that Shunde became basically industrialized within only 10 years. After 1992, Shunde District government pioneered system innovation in the area of property rights, which instantly emancipated the productive forces of enterprises and nurtured a large number of enterprise groups and famous brand products.

In 2005 another industrial development program was put forward, called the "Triple-Three Strategy", namely three categories of industry (the coordinated development of the primary industry, the secondary and the tertiary industry), three pillar lines (no less than three pillar lines to be supported within each category of industry) and three leading enterprises (within each pillar line of industry, no less than three locomotive enterprises to be nurtured). Meanwhile, strategic programs for industrialization, urbanization and internationalization were implemented in Shunde, with the hope of promoting its sound and rapid development. By 2006, Shunde's GDP exceeded 100 billion yuan. Shunde District government has become a good role model in its change of roles from "nanny" to "guide" in economic transition.

Similar examples are found in other parts of Guangdong and many more regions in Jiangsu and Zhejiang provinces, whose regional governments have played an active role in regional economic development, and the practice of foresighted leading has yielded the desired results.

Joseph Schumpeter, a great economist of the twentieth century, argued that innovation is to establish a new production function—the recombination of production factors, which means the integration of "new combinations" of new production factors and conditions into production systems for the purpose of achieving a "new reconstruction" of both production factors and production conditions. Schumpeter's argument reveals that innovation is the most fundamental motivation for economic growth. Likewise, innovation is the basic force for the development of economic theories. Only innovation can make theories flourish and maintain momentum for new developments.

Chapter 2
The "New Deal" in Shunde: Foresighted Leading Is Optimal Service

2.1 Removing the Difficulty in Industrial Upgrading in Economically Demonstrative Regions

Take the promotion of comprehensive competitiveness and the enhancement of overall economic well-being as the central task with a view to accelerating industrial upgrading and restructuring and achieving coordinated development of primary, secondary and tertiary industry through fine development of primary industry, upgraded development of secondary industry, and rapid growth of tertiary industry.

"Economically demonstrative regions" refers to those areas with prior economic development due to preferential policies and geographical advantages since China's reform and opening up in 1978. Geographically, they are mostly coastal areas in Southeast China, economically, they are the best developed, and in terms of systems, they are role models for other regions in China.

With the deepening of reform and opening up, those regions have gradually lost their previous advantages over the past decade. For one thing, international capital has begun to flow into Midwest China, as land, energy and other resources are becoming increasingly limited, and for another, they are confronted with problems in industrial upgrading for lack of scientific industrial planning over the previous two decades. It is high time that those regions should work out ways to crack the hard nuts.

"The scientific outlook on development" proposed at the Third Plenary Session of the Sixteenth National Congress of CPC in September 2003 regards "people first" as its core and balanced, comprehensive and sustainable development as its basic task, aiming at the integration of speed, structure, quality and efficiency through further transforming the mode of economic growth and optimizing economic structure, which serves as a beacon for economically demonstrative regions to speed up industrial restructuring and facilitate regional comprehensive competitiveness.

Over the recent years, the Shunde Government of Foshan City has performed extremely well in actively applying the scientific outlook on development to optimizing and upgrading its industrial structure.

Y. Chen, *Foresighted Leading: Theoretical Thinking and Practice of China's Regional Economic Development*, DOI 10.1007/978-3-642-35368-0_2,

2.1.1 Major Orientation in Industrial Upgrading: Coordinated Development of Three Categories of Industry

Located in the hinterland of the Pearl River Delta, Shunde is typically described as one of the economically demonstrative regions. Shunde has achieved miracles of rapid growth by taking full advantage of preferential policies and its superior geographical conditions since the 1980s, when Shunde attracted nationwide attention for its mode of township enterprise development and, together with Dongguan, Zhongshan, and Nanhai, was called "Four Little Tigers of Guangdong".

In the 1990s, Shunde again became a focus of attention for its leading role in the comprehensive reform, with the reform of property system as the starting point. It ranked first among top 100 Chinese counties (or cities) for four successive years from 2000.

Over the past two decades or so, by adhering to its strategic objective of building up through industrialization, Shunde basically completed its industrialization, established its major industrial structure comprising "two homes" (home appliances and home furniture) and "one flower" (floral plants and floriculture) and achieved its industrial transformation from agriculture to industry and its social transformation from rurality to township. However, problems also arose out of such transformation.

For several years, the secondary industry accounted for over 60% of Shunde's total industrial output, and its home appliances over 70% of the total output of the secondary industry. This single industrial structure explains why large taxpayers and enterprises have concentrated in home appliances manufacturing, with the majority of small and medium-sized enterprises (SMEs) surviving as their service providers. That put Shunde on a shaky economic foundation, as serious financial crises and social problems would arise once that industry met with risks and becomes destabilized.

"The scientific outlook on development" gives great prominence to the concept of "people-first", takes reform and development as its essence, and adopts "five overall considerations" as strategies for reform and development. The CPC central committee also called for the optimization of industrial structure and the enhancement of self-initiated innovation in 2004. In practicing "the scientific outlook on development", the Shunde government starts its industrial restructuring from the perspective of meso-economics and takes the coordinated development of three categories of industry as its major orientation for industrial upgrading.

Later on, investigations were conducted, full consideration was given to Shunde's existing advantages and the direction of industrial development at home and abroad, previous measures were incorporated and new thoughts absorbed. All these efforts are refined and elevated to the level of scientific strategies for regional economic development. And then, "the Triple-Three Strategy" for industrial development was put forward in the light of the experience from developed countries of "one enterprise nurturing one industry, one industry nurturing one industrial chain, and one industrial chain eventually pushing forward a region's and even a nation's economy".

The core of "the Triple-Three Strategy" lies in promoting a region's comprehensive competitiveness and its overall economic well-being and accelerating the upgrading and adjustment of industrial structures to keep three categories of industry under coordinated development, with the primary industry finely developed, the secondary upgraded, and the tertiary rapidly developed. No less than three pillar lines are supported within each category of industry, and within each pillar line at least three or more locomotive enterprises are provided with substantial support. Consequently, the traditional pillar industry, the newly emerging priority industry and the high-tech industry are to be under smooth development, and super large, large, medium-sized and small enterprises are to be under hierarchical development, gradually establishing a complementary pattern of key industries, key enterprises, and strong industrial townships. In this way, potentials of economic growth are to be strengthened, comprehensive industrial competitiveness will be enhanced, and risks in economic growth will be reduced and prevented.

2.1.2 Achieve Rapid and Healthy Economic Growth

Dramatic accomplishments have been achieved on the part of the Shunde government in cracking the hard nuts of industrial upgrading through years of industrial restructuring and effective implementation of "the Triple-Three Strategy". Shunde has enjoyed rapid and healthy economic growth for successive years thanks to the implementation of China's macro economic regulation policies. With respect to regional economy, Shunde has been leading China in balancing both domestic and international markets. Judging from its periodical growth, Shunde's economy has entered into a new round of rapid growth after some period of steady growth.

A close look at Shunde's industrial distribution shows that its pattern of the secondary industry holding the dominant position, with household electrical appliances manufacturing claiming the lion's share, has been radically transformed. A new pattern for its industrial distribution has been established, with three categories of industry under coordinated development, eight pillar lines under synchronous development, and large, small and medium-sized enterprises under hierarchical development. A fundamental transformation has also been under way for its mode of development to shift from resource-dependence to technology-dependence and from labor-intensiveness to capital-dependence. With respect to investment in fixed assets, the proportion of investment in technological innovation has been dramatically increased as a leading force, which gives strong impetus to industrial transformation and upgrading. Regarding the composition of GDP, small and medium-sized enterprises have been acting as the major driving force for economic growth, with increasing capacity to withstand financial risks.

(Originally carried in *Nanfang Daily* on October 8th, 2006, at which time the author was standing member of Foshan Municipal Committee of CPC, executive mayor of Foshan Municipal Government and secretary of Shunde District Committee of CPC, Foshan.)

2.2 The Triple-Three Strategy for Industrial Development

The Triple-Three Strategy targets the coordinated development of the primary, secondary and tertiary industry. In more specific terms, no less than three pillar lines are provided with substantial support within each category of industry, and no less than three locomotive enterprises are to be nurtured within each pillar line to strengthen and expand industrial chains.

I put forward "The Triple-Three Strategy" for industrial development after I started to work as secretary of Shunde District Committee of CPC in October, 2004. Shunde was then at a new turning point though its GDP was far ahead of other counties in China after 30 years' rapid growth since 1978. It can be assumed that the problems Shunde has encountered in its economic development are typical in the economically demonstrative areas in the Pearl River Delta region and will be what the relatively underdeveloped areas will have to deal with.

In the context of seemingly sound economic growth, the problem of the single economic structure lay behind the statistical analysis of the total economic output. Of Shunde District's GDP, the primary industry accounted for merely 3.8%, the tertiary industry 35.2%, while 61% came from the secondary industry. In other words, Shunde's economic output came mainly from the secondary industry, 70% derived from household appliances and electronic products. In addition, Shunde's development was unbalanced, with its eastern part, especially those areas bordering on Guangzhou, developing rapidly, and its western part relatively slowly.

In the current global context, international trade meets with increasing risks that result from intensifying frictions, more technical and environmental barriers and disputes concerning dumping and anti-dumping. That mode of "keeping all the eggs in one basket", characterized by single industrial economy, is apparently problematic and vulnerable to risks. What will happen to Shunde's economy if confronted with fluctuations in the price of raw materials or with frictions in international trade and similar issues? It is the government's duty to consider how to prevent and evade possible risks through nurturing more pillar lines and more industrial clusters and lead locomotive enterprises to expand and strengthen themselves.

Based on Shunde's reality, "The Triple-Three Strategy" was put forward for the purpose of securing its economic growth, establishing optimal industrial structure and guiding self-initiated innovation in core technology. "The Triple-Three Strategy" targets the coordinated development of the primary, secondary and tertiary industry. Namely, no less than three pillar lines will get substantial government support within each category of industry, and no less than three locomotive enterprises are nurtured within each pillar line to strengthen and expand the whole industrial chain.

"The Triple-Three Strategy", which is reckoned as a macro and overall system for industrial development, was adopted by the Shunde Government as a fundamental measure at the macroeconomic level. That system, which draws on economic theories and domestic and international experiences, aims at optimizing industrial structure and withstanding economic structural risks.

This strategy, according to some experts, is an innovation in concepts and systems through integration of economic principles and local practice and is leading China's industrial reform. It is reckoned by the media as a significant innovation on the level of meso-economics that connects national macroeconomic strategies and microeconomic growth. What underpin this strategy are the principles of macro, meso and micro economics, its special emphasis on regional development, and its effective integration of microcosmic tactics that put the strategy into real effect.

In reality, Shunde has taken the lead in economic growth among more than 2,800 counties in China for years. In its economic development, a variety of innovations chiefly made of private sector, such as those in policies, laws, regulations, organization, systems and technology, are supposed to be a directional indication of the economic development of China's counties in the future.

2.3 From "Wading Across the Stream by Feeling Stones" to Foresighted Leading

It will cost a great deal more of government resources and impair the government's capacity to provide public welfare to a greater extent if the government fails to prevent economic problems and must have them solved when they have already occurred. It is extremely impractical for the government to serve in a nanny-style in today's context of rapid economic expansion. It is no doubt that twice the result will be yielded with only half the efforts if foresighted leading and anticipatory service are introduced into the economic process rather than in the middle of the process (in-process service) or after the process (post-process service).

As is known to all, excessive investment of resources in economic development will result in shortage of public welfare supply, for resources held by the government are limited in certain periods. It has been proved that excessive government intervention in economy is liable to bring about bloated organizational structure and a series of negative impacts. The balance between economy growth and public welfare supply calls for the government's extraordinary ability to put economy under control.

Shunde has yielded the highest GDP with the smallest government size compared with other counties in China. In the formulation and implementation of "The Triple-Three Strategy", the Shunde government has brought in-process and post-process services one or two steps forward to turn them into foresighted leading and pre-process service, a shift which undoubtedly reflects the Shunde government's remarkable ability in economic regulation and its outstanding wisdom in governance.

2.3.1 Turning In-process and Post-process Services into Pre-process Service

If the government fails to prevent economic problems and must have them solved when they have already occurred, it will cost a great deal more of government resources and impair the government's capacity to provide public welfare to a greater extent. It is extremely impractical for the government to serve in a nanny-style in today's context of rapid economic expansion. It is no doubt that twice the result will be yielded with only half the efforts if foresighted leading and pre-process service are introduced into the economic process in advance rather than in the middle of or after the process.

Shortly after I assumed office in Shund, a journalist interviewed me and made comments that, according to quite a few experts, clear demarcations have been drawn between the central and the local government in finance and executive powers as a result of the 1994 national revenue sharing scheme, which leads in reality to "corporatism in local government" and causes the local government to put undue emphasis on maximizing economic interests and its leaders to work in the same way as board chairman.

My way of thinking and my work experience put me strongly against such comments. It is the ultimate goal for businesses to pursue profits, but the local government ought to spare no effort to serve the people and work for the all-round development of its region and society. It is true that the role the local government should play in regional economic development has been undergoing theoretical and practical changes. Early economists, such as Adam Smith—the originator of economics, argued that the government should not be involved in economic intervention and regulation and should promote economic development via "the invisible hand". For long, Smith's ideas were dominating economics.

After serious economic crises in the capitalist world, especially in the 1930s, the government in various countries came to realize the necessity of guiding, regulating and even intervening in economic development with a view to overcoming the disadvantages of economic liberalization and preventing similar economic depressions. The British economist John Maynard Keynes was the economist who advocated this theory.

"Mixed economics" and "integrated economics" were beginning to take shape in response to what sort of role the government should play in economy, but they followed the principles laid down by Smith and Keynes. By the 1990s, new ideas and theories kept emerging, arguing that the government can not only guide, regulate and intervene in economy by market means but also do so by means of executive powers and government resources and from a foresighted perspective. The concept of "foresighted intervention", a significant breakthrough in economic theorization, was put forward by some Chinese economists to prevent possible risks and dangers and put economic development on a steady and smooth track.

What originally sparked the concept of "foresighted intervention"? According to my observation, it was derived from a comparative summary of China's remarkable achievements in its reform of economic systems and the successes and failures in the economic development of developed countries in the western world. Shunde is a good case in point.

In the foresighted guiding, regulating and promoting of economic development in the light of market development, the Shunde government implemented a great variety of policies and measures that corresponded to those thoughts of "foresighted oversight" and "market-oriented government" advocated by economists. The Shunde government changed its ways of governance that used to be adopted under planned economy and played its part in "foresighted leading". Social harmony and progress were achieved through the establishment of market economic systems and the sustainable development of enterprises.

I am not in favor of the concept of "corporatism in local government", either, even from a theoretical point of view. The thought of "government for the people" advocated by the CPC Central Committee makes it clear that the ultimate goal for the government is to work for the people rather than pursuing economic benefits. Developing economy is merely a means of serving the people.

"To what extent does the board chairman differ from the secretary of a regional committee of CPC, as they are both experts in strategic management?" continued the journalist.

"In my opinion, the goal of a business is to pursue profits, which it depends on for development, while the local government seeks better welfare for the people, which relies on sound regional economic development". The similarities between these two roles reside in their common goal of promoting corporate or regional economic growth and their focus on such tasks as formulating and administrating strategies, recruiting and managing human resources, raising and allocating capital, and collecting and analyzing information.

Of course, business administration falls into the scope of micro-economics, whereas the promotion of regional economic development calls for macro-economic decision-making and government involvement. It is certainly advisable for those with working experience in enterprises and micro-level practices to make strategic policies from macro-level. However, it will be difficult for them to broaden their vision and open up their work situation on new horizons if they consider economic issues without broad visions and open mind.

2.3.2 Exploring the Interactive Relations Between Government, Business and Society

Spatially, "the Triple-Three Strategy" combines positive responses to national strategies and broad international visions, and temporally, it stands on the solid foundation of current regional conditions and the preservation and innovation of traditional strategy. "The Triple-Three Strategy" is formulated on the basis of the following considerations under domestic and international contexts:

First, it had its deep roots in Shunde's current situation. When I came to work as secretary of the Shunde Committee of CPC near the end of 2004, Shunde's GDP exceeded 60 billion yuan, 60% of which came from the secondary industry, and of the 60% household appliances and electronic products took up 70%. Considerable risks accumulated due to this single line of industrial structure. Shunde's economy was being boosted, but its urban construction and development fell behind, and Shunde's township economy was unbalanced, strong in the east and weak in the west. The question of which road for Shunde to take and how to respond to such a situation called for immediate attention and urgent explorations.

Second, it had deep roots in national strategies. The Economic Work Conference of the CPC Central Committee opened at the end of 2004 called for the optimization of industrial structure and the enhancement of self-initiated innovation. Faced with such requirements from the central government, Shunde, as a grass-roots region, had to work out ways of putting national strategies into operation.

Thirdly, it had deep roots in the advanced experience from developed countries. I had been thinking about how the United States and Japan become so strong economically? Japan had long been ranked among the top three world economies. I conducted serious investigations of Japan's industrial and regional economy on my visits to Japan for trade and investment promotion. It was found that, in Japan, an enterprise may nurture an industry, an industry may nurture an industrial chain, and their combined impacts exercise profound impacts upon Japanese economy. It was also found that each industry in Japan is supported by a complete industrial chain. Take automobile industry for example. The automobile industry in Japan is supported by the first-level, the second-level and the third-level supporting organizations. The Toyota Motor Corporation boosts more than 200 first-level supporting enterprises, and the number of the second- and third-level supporting enterprises exceeds 1,000, which means that one Toyota automobile requires the joint operations of over 1,000 enterprises.

In Japan, within each line of industry, at least three to five locomotive enterprises are formed to lead the industrial chain. Its automobile industry has such leaders as Toyota, Nissan, Honda and other locomotive enterprises. Its regional economic prosperity is accounted for by the existence of a variety of pillar industrial lines, such as automobiles and electronic appliances. I had conducted investigation tours in several developed countries, and Japan's economic and industrial modes of development left deep impressions on me.

Thus, "the Triple-Three Strategy" for industrial development was formulated in the light of Shunde's current development, implementation of national policies and successful experience from developed countries and regions.

Coincidentally, the strategy for Shunde's economic development had been associated with "Three", and the formulation of "the Triple-Three Strategy" had drawn on inspirations from the previous strategies advocated by the government.

In fact, it took us around half a year to comb through and rethink about the whole array of Shunde's economic policies carried out since the reform and open-up. Clearly, some policies were incompatible with the time, some still retained their core values, and some needed to be complemented and improved. Judging from the continuity of policies, "the Triple-Three Strategy" is marked by its inheriting and innovating of the previously existing policies.

It was the foresighted government policies that had been leading Shunde in its transformation from agricultural economy to industrial economy and from planned economy to market economy. It was also the foresighted government policies that put Shunde in conformity to international standards and led its participation in international competition. In leading its sustainable economic growth, the Shunde government worked conscientiously to probe into and improve the interactive relations between government, business, and society.

No specific conception was made initially for what might be used for the term "the Triple-Three Strategy". A series of discussions were conducted with Zhou Tianming, then head of the Shunde District Government, with Ou Guangyuan, the former head of the Shunde District Government and Chairman of Guangdong Provincial People's Congress, and with Chen Yongzhi, vice chairman of Guangdong Provincial People's Congress. Their appreciation and approval confirmed my rethinking and added new thinking, which enabled the Triple-Three Strategy to come out with a completely new look and content.

As *The Tao-te Ching* says, "One produces two; two produce three; three produce all things." It is our sincere hope that everything will be going well in Shunde.

2.3.3 The Fundamental Strategy and Direction for Coordinated Development of Regional Industry

"The Triple-Three Strategy" is specifically manifested as spurring further reform and innovation on the part of the Shunde government. "The Eleventh Five-Year Plan For Shunde's Social and Economic Development" aimed at building up an innovative, service-oriented, public-governance government. What measures should the local government take to encourage self-initiated innovations? In what aspects should the Shunde government make innovation in the future?

According to my observation, there are two categories of innovation in relation to government administration. The first category involves innovation via new measures, policies and directions beyond the bounds of the existing policies, laws and regulations, which is innovation to certain degree, but in practice, it does not work with the local government, as it may result in violation of regulations and laws from higher levels of government. The second category involves innovations in organization, system and technology within the limits of the existing policies, laws and regulations. Innovative awareness is another aspect and should come first. The above four aspects of innovation should be constantly promoted and strengthened in accordance to Shunde's actual conditions and the call of the central government for building innovation-oriented region.

Innovation, which is of primary significance, improves the efficiency of government, enterprises and society and finally facilitates economic growth and social harmony. What the Shunde government has striven to achieve through foresighted leading and innovation in private sector and in measures, policies and systems indicates a direction of regional economic development in China's counties.

Besides the perspective of innovation in government administration, "the Triple-Three Strategy" can also be assessed in economic terms.

It targeted at optimizing industrial structure, encouraging enterprise innovation and preventing risks in regional industry. To achieve this objective, the Shunde government issued a series of supporting and leading policies to upgrade and optimize industrial structure, strengthen market competitiveness and keep Shunde on the right road of scientific, balanced and sustainable development.

Theory comes from practice, but practice precedes theory. "The Triple-Three Strategy" is a result of generalization and sublimation of practice. Practice, in economic development, is a process of creation and can be termed as "wading across the stream through feeling stones". Practice calls for theory, which will be of great significance if it in turn offers guidance to practice. Economic theories are deemed to serve practical purpose, and application advocates simplicity and efficiency. The general principle is that the simplest is more often than not the best. In view of this principle, no complex economic term was coined to replace "the Triple-Three Strategy", which is easy to understand and embodies the essence of industrial economics and regional economics.

It should be mentioned that "the Triple-Three Strategy" differs fundamentally from the "Three Measures" or "Eight Steps" proposed by other regional governments, for it focuses on not only tactical and technical issues in economic growth but also on the fundamental strategy and direction for industrial development and coordinated development of regional economy. The fact that "the Triple-Three Strategy" is widely accepted by enterprises and the public shows its solid practical foundation and strong vitality in practice.

2.3.4 Be Expert Both in Strategic Planning and in Tactical Implementation

It is my belief that the local government should be expert both in strategic planning and in tactical implementation so that excellent strategies will not stop at empty talks. Tactical implementation requires strenuous efforts, innovative mind and great wisdom.

Then, what tactics and strategies were applied to the effective implementation of "the Triple-Three Strategy" in industrial development? Strategy and tactics must go together. For lack of tactics, strategies will certainly be empty talks. Thus, a series of policies and concrete measures were designed for the implementation of the strategy.

The Shunde government set its goal for the optimization of industrial structure: the proportion of the three categories of industries would be 1.7: 53.3: 45 by 2010. For the primary industry, considering the increasing scarcity of land resources, agribusinesses, such as "Guangdong-Taiwan Agricultural Development Base" through cooperation with Taiwan, were encouraged on the basis of its agricultural superiority and with support from the central and provincial government so that great undertakings would be possible at small places.

With respect to the secondary industry, considering national innovation strategies and Shunde's actual conditions, focus was laid on high-tech industry with potentials for development in optimizing its traditional industry. Besides, substantial measures, such as national standards for products made in Shunde, were introduced with intent to lead, expand and strengthen private enterprises.

As far as the tertiary industry is concerned, supporting industries, such as logistics, exhibition, trade and tourism, which are closely linked to the primary and the secondary industry, were vigorously promoted, rather than developing the tertiary industry for its own sake. For example, Shanghai Baosteel and South Korea's Pohang Iron and Steel set up their own logistics base in Shunde where huge amount of steel was needed for household appliances industry. To develop tourism, the Shunde government put forth a list of "Top Ten New Attractions", opened up tourist routes, such as "Guangzhou-Shunde Day Tour", "Hong Kong-Macao-Shunde Three-day Tour". All this helped to boost hotel, catering, shopping and other industries.

It is a common problem that national strategies serve only as slogans in quite a few regions. The central government put forward self-initiated innovation as a national strategy, which indicates a good direction and is favored by everyone. However, such strategies will be not implemented or achieved desired effects if no starting point is found in grass-roots units, or if no specific measures are taken, for their execution. Will similar difficulties arise in the implementation of "the Triple-Three Strategy"?

My work experience in Shunde tells me that the Shunde government possesses strong executive powers for the implementation of national strategies. In practicing the national strategy of "scientific and technological advancement versus self-initiated innovation", the Shunde government took as its starting point for evaluation and inspection the number of famous brand names and trademarks, the number of registered product patents, and the recognition of product specifications as national and international standards, through all of which advances in science and technology and in self-initiated innovation were promoted and ensured.

Therefore, full confidence was gained for "the Triple-Three Strategy" to be widely accepted and actively implemented by the grass-roots units like front-line government departments, townships and enterprises.

It must be emphasized that the implementation of "the Triple-Three Strategy" would be a dynamic process that would take time to achieve its desired effects. Its initial effects were beginning to show themselves in 2005, when the programs for trade and investment attraction, product standardization, the United Nations procurement center were put into execution. Household appliances and electronic products accounted for around 70% of the secondary industry in 2004, but less than 50% by the end of 2005. Other lines, such as machinery and equipment manufacturing, mould manufacturing, fine chemicals and coating chemicals began to take up a larger proportion of the percentage.

2.4 The Implementation of the Triple-Three Strategy Assisted by Five Sets of Supporting Mechanism

Five sets of supporting mechanism were devised and introduced in the form of joint consultation conferences, special funding supervision, entry and exit of locomotive enterprises with special government support, follow-up services for locomotive enterprises and publicity and guidance of "the Triple-Three Strategy" to jointly promote industrial agglomeration and intensify brand name effects.

"The Triple-Three Strategy" was the result of strategic rethinking on the part of the Shunde government about local industrial development and regional economic coordination. Tactics must go together with strategies. A series of policies and concrete measures, namely five sets of supporting mechanism, were created to guarantee the effective implementation of the strategy and deepen the reform.

First, the mechanism of joint consultation conference was set up for the effective integration and coordination of policies concerning various industries, lines and enterprises. Special task forces from various industries and lines, relevant government authorities and members from pillar-line industrial associations, together with invited experts, were called together on a regular basis to coordinate and solve crucial problems in the implementation of the strategy. The district government official was authorized to act as convener of joint consultation conferences, and a working office was set up to handle daily operations and prepare for the conference.

The joint consultation conference drew up a list of locomotive enterprises with special government support and formulated specific plans for enhancing optimal development of pillar lines in accordance with the attributes of industries and lines, integrating preferential policies and measures proposed by various government departments and putting them into timely operation in key pillar lines or locomotive enterprises. The joint consultation conference also helped businesses to make market analyses and create favorable conditions for the construction of human capital, financial capital and technology transfer platforms. Public-service institutions were encouraged to facilitate exchange and cooperation with enterprises through a variety of government activities.

Second, the supervisory mechanism for special funds was established to integrate and coordinate the existing special funds for industrial development, ensuring their being utilized scientifically, rationally and efficiently. The original special funds remained in the charge of former government authorities, with the list of supported enterprises and supporting measures submitted to the joint consultation conference for file.

The joint consultation conference took responsibility for the supervision of special funds utilization and the scientific assessment of its effects. It also made suggestions for better effects and better regional industrial development and submitted special reports to the district government. All the special funds were raised and allocated through the district government so that they could be used scientifically, rationally, and with maximized efficiency towards the goal of "the Triple-Three Strategy".

Third, an innovative mechanism of entry and exit of locomotive enterprises with special government support was established. Within the framework of "the Triple-Three Strategy", locomotive enterprises played significant roles in pushing forward and elevating the regional industry. A list of locomotive enterprises to be given government support was drawn up and decided by the joint consultation conference on the basis of recommendation by their townships and in accordance with selective criteria and procedures and the characteristics of industrial lines.

The selection of locomotive enterprises was contingent not only upon their output value (or turnover), tax revenues, technical levels, R & D investment, and self-initiated innovation capability and range (such as operating area, number of employees, etc.) but also upon the output density (output value per operating area), brand name, energy consumption and environmental factors.

The time limit for locomotive enterprises to be supported was temporarily defined within 3 years, followed by the addition to and exclusion from the list of locomotive enterprises based on the enterprise development and the effects achieved through government support. In order to stimulate enterprises to rapidly develop, expand and get strengthened through competition, the joint consultation conference drew up a list of locomotive enterprises to be added into the framework of "the Triple-Three Strategy" and given special support if enterprises outside the framework had made extraordinary achievements and reached the level for government support in terms of their capacity, scale and leading impacts in the industry. The addition of those enterprises would have to gain recommendation from their affiliated townships, and the added enterprises would be entitled to relevant preferential policies upon their entry into the framework. The previous preferential policies for continuing locomotive enterprises remained unchanged until the list was updated and readjusted. The joint consultation conference was entitled to readjust the list in accordance with formalities if locomotive enterprises failed to play an exemplary role.

The competitive entry and exit mechanisms devised for locomotive enterprises were intended to add to enterprise initiatives and reinforce the vitality and momentum for enterprise development.

Fourth, the mechanism of follow-up services for locomotive enterprises was established to timely solve problems in enterprise development. In addition to the continuing enforcement of "one enterprise, one policy", it established enterprise databases and made tables of preferential policies for locomotive enterprises in various lines to display the rights and obligations for enterprises to implement relevant policies and the accomplishments through implementation of "the Triple-Three Strategy".

The locomotive enterprises that were listed within the framework were followed up by relevant government authorities, and a written report on the effectiveness and problems existing in the implementation was submitted to the joint consultation conference for discussion and examination every 6 months. Exchange meetings between locomotive enterprises were held on an irregular basis in the light of the development of industrial lines and locomotive enterprises to spread advanced experience, study the effects of government support and propose new supportive measures and policies.

Fifth, the mechanism for the publicity and guidance of "the Triple-Three Strategy" was established for the purpose of enhancing industrial agglomeration and strengthening brand name effects. Forums on the development of key pillar lines were held irregularly by relevant government authorities and business associations, with invited foreign and domestic experts, line leaders and business representatives from Shunde District, to discuss the situations of industrial development, forecast the trend of industrial development, and help enterprises to broaden their horizons and keep abreast of the trend of industrial development, macro-level policies and the direction for corporate development.

Such channels as networks, media, promotions, seminars, and exhibitions were employed to publicize the strategic industry and locomotive enterprises that gained key government support. Those enterprises were encouraged to undergo industrial agglomeration, develop towards the downstream and upstream ends of the industrial chain, and forge links between and within industrial chains, with intent to create high-quality brand names and further heighten the image of "Shunde's Product, China's Pride".

2.5 Coordinated Development Signifies Real Development

In natural sciences, "triangular stability" is a universally recognized principle. In a sense, the implication of "not keeping all eggs in one basket" is typically reflected in the coordinated development of the three categories of industry in the economic field.

The implementation of "the Triple-Three Strategy" for industrial development is a process of optimizing industrial structure, leading self-initiated innovation on the part of enterprises and reducing risks of regional industries. In response to this process, a series of policies and measures for supporting and leading enterprises were advocated by the Shunde government to optimize industrial structure, enhance enterprise competitiveness on domestic and overseas markets, thereby ensuring Shunde to develop on a scientific, coordinated and sustainable path.

In China, people used to believe that the coordinated development of the primary, secondary and tertiary industry does not apply in the case of administrative regions below the provincial level, to which I would say "no".

In natural sciences, "triangular stability" is a universally recognized principle. In a sense, the implication of "not keeping all eggs in one basket" is typically reflected in the coordinated development of the three categories of industry in the economic field. It must be pointed out that the coordinated development of the three categories of industries does not mean equal proportion for each category. Reasonable distribution should be defined among the three categories of industry based on actual regional conditions, which is in fact the essence of the scientific outlook on development.

Take Shunde for example. Science and technology was utilized to develop agri-businesses specializing in agricultural extensions so that the primary industry would be transformed into a high-quality competitive industry. The tertiary industry was supported through developing its interfaces linked to the secondary industry, with focus laid on logistics industry related to the circulation of local products and on trade industry related to local product transactions. By so doing, the three categories of industry would be under coordinated development, with agriculture finely developed, the secondary industry upgraded and the tertiary industry rapidly developed.

To achieve the coordinated development of the three categories of industry, no less than three pillar lines must be provided with special support within each industry and no less than three locomotive enterprises must be provided with special support within each line so that risks are avoided, industrial clusters are formed, and the stable, coordinated and scientific development will be achieved.

With regard to the delimitation of pillar lines, some pillar lines may fall into the traditional industry, and some may be new in Shunde. It may not necessarily be scientific for the status of pillar lines to be completely determined by their output value. The regional industrial complementarity and upgrading should be taken into account when the government plans to foster pillar lines to avoid possible overlapping in the same region.

Respecting standards for defining pillar lines, the main consideration on the part of the Shunde government was the direction of national, provincial and municipal development as well as the complementarity to industries in the surrounding regions. The Shunde government strove to develop and lead the development of non-traditional industry or marginal industry, which represented the direction for this region's industrial development.

In agricultural areas, agribusinesses were advocated owing to Shune's increasing scarcity of land resources and its priority and superiority in agricultural development. Support from national and provincial government was obtained to promote agribusinesses and establish "Guangdong-Taiwan Agricultural Development Base" through cooperation with Taiwan so that great undertakings would be possible at small places like Shunde.

In order to promote the upgrading of the secondary industry in Shunde, the strategy for implementation of standardization was initiatively enacted to encourage enterprises to stipulate national and even international standards with intent to take the predominant position in competition. The first step was to foster centers of the United Nations procurement. Enterprises that become suppliers for the UN procurement centers will be in a better position to comply with international accounting standards and technical standards in world competition and to expand into international markets.

Second, enterprises were spurred to become listed on the stock market. That will not only enable enterprises to raise funds but also to operate and expand in accordance with modern enterprise systems. In addition, the strategy of "one enterprise, one policy" was implemented for locomotive enterprises in the light of their characteristics.

As to the tertiary industry, priority is given to the logistics industry. The construction of supporting infrastructure is accelerated so that better transportation links are built between Shunde and its neighboring areas. Full play is given to its location superiority, i.e. its proximity to the new Baiyun Airport, the Panyu railway station, and new Nansha deepwater port, and other transport links for logistics. Supporting facilities are also established, and leading logistics enterprises, such as Guotong Bonded Logistics for Agricultural Produce in Chencun, Whirlpool Logistics in Beijiao and P. G. Logistics in Ronggui, are fostered or introduced.

The exhibition industry is one of Shunde's industrial highlights. The exhibition of household appliances, furniture, machinery and equipment, and flowers and plants enjoys great reputation and superiority, though it needs further strengthening. Those well-known retail tycoons, such as Wal-Mart, Jusco, Tesco, Lotus, have successively made their way into Shunde with huge procurement potentials, and 70–80% of their procurement come from local enterprises in Shunde. Once the products made in Shunde are introduced into the global procurement system via those channels, they will move on the fast track to various parts of the world. Their procurements are low-priced but their volume is quite considerable, and for enterprises in Shunde, small profits at quick turnover can be achieved.

In the category of the tertiary industry, tourism also received special government support. Tourism in Shunde is backed with its profound cultural background. The *Zhuang Yuan* (Number One Scholar, or the top student in college entrance examinations) traditions, fish-pond mulberry trees, waterside villages and Shunde cuisine are all valuable resources for tourism development. In order to advance and enrich local culture, a new list of "top-ten attractions" has been issued to attract and lead social investment in tourism.

It is a significant part of implementing industrial restructuring to substantially raise the proportion of the tertiary industry in GDP, in addition to making agribusinesses specialized and strengthening and expanding the secondary industry.

There exists not only rational proportion but also coordination between the three categories of industry. The tertiary industry is classified into productive service and non-productive service. Within a given region, the tertiary industry will appear hollow if the secondary industry develops at a low level in a region. In the case of Shunde, productive service associated with the secondary industry should be foremost developed in the tertiary industry. Therefore, priority should be given to the development of productive service, such as logistics, exhibition, and industry-related trade. Such areas as technology and software research and development that are linked to the secondary industry remain relatively weak, so that supportive measures for newly emerging industry and high-tech industry must be contingent upon the development of the tertiary industry.

2.6 Upgrading Industrial Pillar Lines and Locomotive Enterprises

The industrial pillar line will lose all its vitality if no locomotive enterprises are fostered to lead the pillar line and create brand names on domestic and international markets, and if they are short of core technology.

Speaking from my years' working experience in the financial sector, a business in an industrial line must rank top five or even top three domestically if it desires to stand firm in its industry and stay competitive on the world market. The industrial pillar line will lose all its vitality if no locomotive enterprises are fostered to lead the pillar line and create brand names on domestic and international markets, and if they are short of core technology. Undoubtedly, it is of equal significance for the regional government to promote both pillar lines and locomotive enterprises.

In order to support locomotive enterprises, the Shunde government took the initiative to implement the standardization strategy. Just as the two popular sayings go,

"Third-rate enterprises manufacture products, second-rate enterprises trade technology, first-rate enterprises create brand names, and super-rate enterprises formulate standards"; "A patent influences an enterprise, and a standard an industrial line." In the global context of large-scale production, for lack of R & D, brand names, core technology and technical standards, the manufacturing industry in Shunde is positioned at the low-end or the middle-part of the value chain, demonstrating that our products lack international competitiveness and that our industry remains at a slow pace of internationalization.

In the 2005 list of China's famous brand names, eight new brand names came from Shunde, amounting to a total of 18 and ranking first among regions of the same level in China. In the post-brand name phase, the golden brand of "Made in Shunde" needed to be "polished". Thus, the Shunde government could not stop at merely implementing the "brand-name strategy" but aiming higher at the "standardization strategy" with intent to push enterprises ahead toward a higher level for their products to conform to international standards.

Implementing the strategy for standardization is of great significance for enterprises to strengthen their comprehensive competitiveness, to take commanding heights in terms of technology and management, and to follow market rules in conformity to international practices in competition. It is also an effective measure for expanding and elevating locomotive enterprises, for strengthening the competitiveness of "Shunde's Products, China's Pride" on international markets, and for more rapid and healthy development of national industry.

At that time, more than 100 product standards formulated by Shunde were adopted as national standards, and more than 800 standards were absorbed into the record library of national standards, which contributes to the formulation of national standards. To this end, the Shunde government issued the directive for implementing standardization strategy to encourage locomotive enterprises through incentives to actively play their role in drafting and formulating national standards and standards for industrial lines, with their products and service reaching or exceeding national standards, international standards and advanced foreign standards. As a result, the pattern of industry and agriculture was gradually transforming from "Made in Shunde" to "Created in Shunde", with locomotive industrial and agricultural enterprises undergoing transition from product manufacturing to standard formulation.

Effective measures were taken to push the tertiary industry to fully implement national standards and the locomotive enterprises to conform to international practices so that they gradually follow international standards and practices.

Incentive measures were taken to turn Shunde into a key procurement base for the United Nations and to lead its enterprises to become suppliers for the base through application. So far, 102 enterprises in Shunde were selected by the United Nations as official suppliers for the procurement base, accounting for nearly half of such enterprises in China.

To become a procurement base for the United Nations, businesses must rigorously comply with international practices in their operations and must meet the standards for product quality and technological application. The fact that so many enterprises in Shunde have become suppliers for the UN procurement base is a good confirmation of the quality of "Made in Shunde" and the best publicity for its products.

Meanwhile, great efforts were made to encourage locomotive enterprises to get listed on the stock market, which helped private enterprises to raise funds, own more core technology and establish modern enterprise management systems. State-owned enterprises were required to restructure themselves, and it was the same case with private enterprises. Going public is a sort of transformation for private enterprises from family-owned and father-son owned models to a modern business model that puts businesses under public oversight and ensures transparency of information. A series of policies were issued, and an office for listed business administration was set up to handle relevant affairs. In so doing, more enterprises benefited from capital markets and quickly got strengthened and expanded at low costs.

The development of pillar lines was accelerated while locomotive enterprises were led to be upgraded in accordance with supporting policies. Pillar lines, such as household appliances and electronic products, machinery and equipment, mould manufacturing, fine chemicals, and furniture, were provided special support. The construction of key projects, such as the industrial incubation base for new and high technology, special industrial base, the South China Research Institute for Household Appliances and the public platform for technology innovation, was speeded up, thanks to national and provincial tax preferential policies and financial support policies for the development of new and high technology industries.

Special support was also provided to such pillar lines as logistics, trade, exhibition and tourism. In the process of industrialization and urbanization, the planning and policy guidance for the tertiary industry were strengthened for its optimal industrial layout and structure, drawing on the integration of resources, the deepening of reforms and opening-up, with a view to improving its quality and effectiveness. The industrial marketization and internationalization were accelerated through continuously planning and tapping potential operative resources and through diversified and socialized investment in operative projects. Eventually, a modern system for the tertiary industry would be established to meet with requirements for regional economic and social development and people's living demands.

"The Triple-Three Strategy" is a strategic option for industrial development in Shunde. Thanks to its implementation, Shunde has formed a more solid industrial foundation, set up a more scientific and rational industrial structure, and more stable and healthy business development. Its overall capacity against economic risks has been intensified, with all its social and economic development moving on a sound and rapid track.

2.7 The "Five Phases" Regional Businesses Must Go Through

There are "five phases" regional businesses must go through in their development, represented respectively by five core tasks, namely, foundation consolidation, brand name creation, patent registration, standard speculation, OEM (original equipment manufacturer) operation.

The five phases portray the general route of development for small and medium enterprises (SMEs), summarizing the major tasks in the growth of both domestic and international SMEs. It is of universal implications to corporate development at different stages.

The implementation of the "five-phases" strategy in regional business development is based on the following considerations. First, it meets the requirement for practicing the "scientific outlook on development" and achieving sound and rapid economic growth. The strategy of "five-phase" corporate development, which embodies the essential elements of foresighted leading, maps out a broad road to a bright future for SMEs through improving corporate development.

Second, it meets the requirement for changing the situation of regional corporate development. The "five phases" represents an ascending progression for corporate development from lower to higher level, bringing about the expansion of corporate scale, the elevation of development quality, and the transformation from entrepreneurship to innovation.

Third, it meets the requirement for foresighted leading on the part of the government and serving enterprises from a foresighted perspective. The government provides foresighted policies and measures to guide enterprises on the road to standardization and enable them to follow international market and economic practices.

The "five-phase" strategy for corporate development involves five steps:

In the first phase, solid foundation is laid for corporate development. Strategic leading and policy guidance must be provided for enterprise development in accordance with its features in each of the five phases. "SME Growth Project" was implemented, social service systems for SMEs were set up and improved, service-aided mechanisms were established for business start-ups, and the social credit system was created within the Shunde District.

Second, enterprises are encouraged to forge brand names. The brand name-driven strategy and the supportive and incentive measures were intended to spur enterprises to foster brand-name products and become famous brand-name enterprises. Industrial parks, specialized towns, industrial clusters and special industrial bases were supported to develop regional brand names. Those enterprises with brand-name products were entitled to more preferential policies and support in such areas as product development, market expansion and resource allocation.

Third, enterprises are encouraged to register their patents as the third step. In this phase, the government needs to provide guidelines for patent registration. The working mechanism and data bases were set up to help enterprises transfer technical innovations into intellectual property. Within the primary, secondary and tertiary industry, and their pillar lines and locomotive enterprises, effective measures were taken to push ahead patent registration in accordance with their classifications, encourage strong enterprises to expand markets via independent intellectual property rights, and support other enterprises to intensify their capacity of intellectual property creation, administration, protection and utilization. By the above means, enterprises are expected to turn technical innovation into intellectual property rights and vice versa.

The fourth step involves formulating product standards. Standardization contributes to pushing product management, quality and level to new heights. Enterprises were encouraged and supported to get involved in the formulation of industrial standards, national standards and international standards. Incentive measures were taken to establish and improve corporate standardization systems and help line associations and technical service organizations to improve their service quality. Among pillar lines and industrial clusters, "union standards" were carried out for unifying technical standards and constructing fair technical platforms.

Meanwhile, more channels were opened up for enterprises to involve themselves in standardization so that more industrial standards, national standards and even international standards could be formulated in Shunde. Early warning and rapid response systems for trade barriers were established with intent to guard enterprises against possible risks and crises.

As the final step, enterprises are encouraged to conduct OEM operation. OEM operation requires enterprises to quicken the internationalization of brand names through taking advantage of regional brand names. Brand name operation was encouraged and supported in famous brand enterprises that conducted OEM operations by means of their own technology, patents and standards. Consequently, designing and innovation industry has been vigorously developed, promoting the transfer from "manufacturing" to "creation" so as to reach the advanced domestic level in terms of modern innovation, electronics, software, precision machinery, auto parts and other aspects.

2.8 Industrialization: Shunde Manufacturing Leads the Development of National Industry in China

Shunde enterprises have undergone the transfer from copying to reformation, then to creation, in which process entrepreneurs in Shunde shifted their emphasis from product quality and quantity to patents and intellectual property rights and eventually strove toward product standardization. Shunde's manufacturing and industrial development have lead and demonstrated the trend for China's national industry.

Shunde has made a history of changes. Over a hundred years' industrial development has confirmed its commitment that national development and prosperity is dependent upon industry and commerce. At every critical moment in history, Shunde people have been apt to capture market opportunities and undertake the most valuable industry to accomplish themselves. Thereby, Shunde manufacturing is not merely a sort of product making but more of culture and spirit. It is natural that this culture and spirit is widely identified and deeply rooted in the hearts of Shunde people.

2.8.1 Shunde Deserves Accomplishments

The year 2005 witnessed the wide spread of the promotion slogan of "Shunde's Product, China's Pride". As is known to all, the publicity of a region means its image and brand name promotion. Apparently, the promotion slogan is intended to highlight brand names created in Shunde, and the promotion of brand names may focus on comprehensive characteristics of brand names or their unique individual features. Of these two, the most representative economic and social culture, standing for Shunde manufacturing, was selected as a driving force for its industrialization, urbanization and internationalization.

The selection of Shunde manufacturing for promotion reveals the preservation and extension of its history and the achievement of its private enterprises and national industrial development. It indicates the orientation for the development of Shunde's industry in the future.

Modernization is generally described as a process of human society's undergoing revolutionary transitions from the traditional agricultural society to the modern industrial society through industrialization. It is evident that manufacturing exerts far-reaching impacts on social advancement.

Let's look back at Shunde. Shunde makes and deserves accomplishments. Shunde's accomplishments in each phrase of its history are closely associated with its brilliant glories in manufacturing.

Serious studies show that Shunde was the wealthiest county of Guangdong Province 100 years ago, thanks to its flourishing of filature industry. In the late nineteenth century, the number of filature factories exceeded 100, with more than 60,000 workers, totaling over those in Shanghai and Tianjin, which is considered by some economic historians "a phenomenon worthy of considerable attention" in the history of China's national industrial development. Around the First World War, the soaring price of silk on international markets pushed Shunde's silk industry into its heyday, with the number of large-scale filature factories reaching over 200, accounting for 80% of the total in Guangdong Province, and with the number of workers exceeding 200,000. Consequently, Shunde was known far and wide as "the metropolis of Southern Silk".

Since China's reform and opening-up, one of the primary objectives Shunde has been targeting at is industrialization. Generations of Shunde District leaderships have been working assiduously toward this objective by taking over from the past and setting and carrying out a new course for the future without going stray. Manufacturing and industrialization earned Shunde the title of "Four Tigers of Guangdong" and "the first of China's top one hundred economically strong counties". Internationalization, Shunde's next objective, needs to be backed up by "Made in Shunde" and a gradual heightening of manufacturing capacities and levels.

2.8.2 Shunde Spirit Is the Most Valuable Resource for Shunde

What lies behind Shunde manufacturing is the spirit of Shunde, its essence being the courage to be the first to venture and pioneer, and prosper through industry and commerce. When I assumed office in Shunde, what impressed me most is the power of Shunde spirit, the most precious resource for Shunde. The power of Shunde spirit goes beyond all other forces. The overall victory over the catastrophic floods in 2005 is a good case in point.

Several aspects of Shunde spirit that underpins Shunde manufacturing deserve attention. First, it is the enterprising spirit of being the first as pioneers. Owing to the market with unpredictable changes and fierce competition, it is hard to be among the first to capture opportunities for development without such enterprising spirit to seek development. Second, it is the down-to-earth spirit for practical undertakings. It is apparent that, for decades, the Shunde people have been engaged in industry, seeking practical effects by consciously turning ideas into practical undertakings. Third, it is the innovative spirit of pursuing excellence. The Shunde people have been striven for excellence and perfection in industrial transfer and upgrading and in product development and innovation. Finally, it upholds sincere and harmonious integrity, creating the image of "being honest inwardly, sincere outwardly". Shunde's integrity demonstrates a united and harmonious atmosphere from within and a reliable and credible image before the world.

2.8.3 "China's Pride" Is the Philosophy of "Made in Shunde"

What is the philosophy of "China's Pride" as part of Shunde's promotion slogan? It has a twofold implication. It is the appreciation of the fact that Shunde's product is the pride of China. It also signifies the pursuit of the core value of continuously improving and elevating Shunde manufacturing to make it a long-lasting mark of China's pride.

As mentioned above, Shunde manufacturing has long been the pride of China. So far, a complete industrial system has been established, so many well-known trademarks and brands have been nurtured and recognized, and many products have taken up a considerable proportion of both domestic and international markets.

However, it is undesirable to indulge in the past achievements and stop at the current situation. "China's pride" should be taken as a strong motivation for higher demands on Shunde manufacturing. It is my conviction that "China's pride" should be the philosophy of Shunde manufacturing so that products made in Shunde are the best in the world and are geared to the global market. Today, with the global economic integration and fierce regional competition, it means courage and is a natural option for Shunde manufacturing to take the pride of China as its objective.

Then, how should it be understood that this is a natural option for Shunde?

It is my belief that this option points to the direction for national industrial development in China. Shunde enterprises have undergone the transfer from copying to reformation, then to creation, in which process entrepreneurs in Shunde shifted their emphasis from product quality and quantity to patents and intellectual property rights and eventually strove toward product standardization. By 2005, more than 100 product specifications from Shunde had been adopted as national standards, and another more than 180 product specifications had been registered as alternate national standards. A few product specifications had filled in the gaps in national standards and become the international standard.

In this way, enterprises in Shunde have got strengthened and expanded through capital market, on the one hand, and their products have come to closer conformity with international practices by means of constructing the procurement base for the United Nations. The development strategy for standardization proposed by the Shunde government has made products "made in Shunde" follow national and international standards. Industry and manufacturing in Shunde are indeed leading the development of China's national industry.

2.8.4 Products "Made in Shunde" Enhance Competitiveness Through Independent Innovation

At present and in the future, Shunde must continue its road of new-type industrialization and improve its capability for independent innovation to make its manufacturing deserve "China's pride" and lead the development of China's national industry. During his inspection tour to Midea, Hu Jintao, General Secretary of CPC stresses that priority in industrial restructuring must be given to enhancing the capability for independent innovation and that proprietary core technology and key technology should be developed particularly through integration of introduction, digestion, absorption and innovation of advanced technology, aiming to intensify core competitiveness of enterprises.

Not long ago, Zhang Dejiang, the then secretary of Guangdong Provincial Committee of CPC, pointed out during a special investigation tour to Foshan that competitiveness is determined by the capability in independent innovation. Therefore, in the fierce international competition, the crucial issue Shunde manufacturing is confronted with is how to heighten the capability in independent innovation.

The American economist Paul R. Krugman argues that the rapid development of Asian economy is attributed to the sweat rather than the intelligence. That reminds us that, to stay firm and strong in international competition, Shunde manufacturing faces both opportunities and challenges.

From the international perspective, the competitiveness of China's enterprises is undermined for lack of proprietary technology and brand names, and their future competitiveness is further impeded due to low profit margins that cause investment inadequacy in research and development. China's enterprises, no matter whether it is "made in China" or "made in Shunde", are experiencing a variety of challenges. It is high time for transition to take place, a breakthrough from the mode of foreign technology-dependent, i.e. from manufacturing merely to creation and then to independent innovation. Only in this way will Shunde manufacturing be endowed with more values and stronger competitiveness.

The prospect of a region or a city is dependent upon its economic development. Shunde is in a critical stage of development. Within 5 years, the goal of creating another economic Sunde is bound to be achieved as long as the strategy for industrialization, urbanization and internationalization is implemented and promoted smoothly. Shunde will be rising up as a core city on the western bank of the Pearl River.

(Written in August 2005, then acting as standing member of Foshan Municipal Committee of CPC, executive mayor of Foshan Municipal Government and secretary of Shunde District Committee of CPC, Foshan)

2.9 Urbanization: Shunde Aims Higher

The value of a city is determined not only by its strong economy but, more importantly, by its capability of continuously improving the quality of people's life and providing more employment and development opportunities.

Urbanization is a trend for development under the global context. For China, the twenty-first century is supposed to be the century for urban development. It is predicted that more than half of the population in China will become city dwellers in the next 10–30 years.

Great opportunities, along with challenges, have been brought about in this transition that transforms market competition between enterprises into that between cities and in turn, localized competitive edges into urbanized competitive edges.

In line with this trend, the strategy for industrialization is taken as one of the three winning strategies for Shunde's future success. Under this general context, Shunde aims higher for its future development.

2.9.1 Urbanization Is a Breakthrough for Shunde in Its New Round of Development

Urbanization of Shunde is a natural outcome of its industrialization. The concentration in population and factors of production caused by industrial agglomeration thereby results in the construction of towns and cities. Owing to the long and strenuous efforts on the part of its generations of leaderships and its people, great achievements have been made in Shunde's urbanization and have laid a solid foundation for its development.

With China's entry into the World Trade Organization and the implementation of the scientific outlook on development proposed by the Central Committee of CPC, Shunde has been confronted with a series of newly emerging opportunities and challenges. On the one hand, its industrial structure needs adjustment and upgrading so as to meet new competition on the market, and on the other hand, further opening-up is needed and opening-up levels need to be heightened in order for its economic development to be geared to the future and international demands, to improve its international competitiveness and to satisfy urban service and developing needs as an international metropolis requires.

The breakthrough for solving these problems and contradictions is the implementation of the urbanization strategy. A city is characterized by the effect of agglomeration and scale. It plays an irreplaceable role in the spatial expansion of industrial development, in the attraction of talents from home and abroad, in the acceptance of the transfer of foreign industry, in the cultivation of such market elements as finance, insurance, technology, personnel, and real estate, and in the development of intermediary service organizations, such as law, accounting, auditing, evaluation, and consultancy.

It is clear that without Shunde's urbanization, there will be no carrier for Shunde's industrialization and no underpinning for its internationalization.

2.9.2 Shunde Positions Itself as a Core City on the Western Bank of the Pearl River

What confronts people in and out of Shunde now is the question of how Shunde marches on its road to urbanization.

First of all, Shunde must be clear about how it is positioned within the city system in Guangdong. Viewed from the urban planning of the Pearl River Delta, Shunde has been built as the core city on the western bank of the Pearl River, and as a central city with a million's population from Foshan's urban planning. Starting from these plans, Shunde should be constructed in accordance with the metropolitan standards. Three key points will help to clarify how to build such a metropolis as Shunde.

First, the downtown district must be well planned. A metropolis has its core area called "downtown". Viewed from its administrative division, Shunde's downtown district consists of the three townships of Daliang, Ronggui and Lunjiao. Geographically, it is reduced to "one hill, two roads, three rivers", namely the Shunfeng Hill, NO. 105 State Road and Bigui Road, the Daliang River, the Guipan River and the Desheng River. They are all unique landscape to function as the natural axes of the city of Shunde. Through these axes, the urban highlights are interconnected, forming unique scenic spots within the downtown area. Currently, the No.105 State Road and the Bigui Road are under construction in accordance with the standards for downtown scenic spots. The Shunfeng Hill Park is already under construction and is expected to exercise good leading effects. The urban landscape is being shifted from the former "Daliang-Guipan River" to the current "Desheng River".

Second, the intra-city transportation network must be constructed. A transportation network covering all parts of Shunde needs to be constructed to turn Shunde into a metropolis. The construction of the Pearl River Delta into a world-class urban group as the strategic goal of Guangdong has provided Shunde with an unprecedented opportunity to construct a traffic hub on the western bank of the Pearl River. Following the construction of New Guangzhou Railway Station, Western Guangzhou Expressway, No. 2 Belt Expressway of Economic Zone of the Pearl River Delta, Guangzhou Intercity Rail and Foshan No 1 Ring Highway, and Nansha Harbor in Guangzhou, the Shunde government is strongly urged to construct its intra-city transportation network and its connections, upgrade its traffic network and accumulate its competitive edge.

So far, all strength is exerted in the construction of three vertical roads such as No.105 Road, Bigui Road, No. 325 Road, and three horizontal roads such as Sanle Road, Longzou Road, Nanguo Road, and three bridges of Ganzhutan Bridge, Gaozhan Bridge, Xinyong New Bridge.

Third, traffic network of roads and bridges has to be upgraded in townships. With downtown and the traffic skeleton constructed, the interconnection between townships becomes essential. If transportation network can connect to Shunde and meet requirements for its one-million population size, the entire traffic network will display a general framework of a metropolis. It definitely requires joint efforts on the part of all relevant parties to build it up.

2.9.3 The Improvement of the Overall Quality of the City and Its People Comes Above that of Shunde's Landscape

It is clear that urbanization brings people great benefits. The city brings opportunities, profits and market to enterprises and employment, convenience and comfort to individuals. However, as a process of social and economic development, urbanization results in population concentration and exterior changes. More importantly, it brings about changes in values and culture.

Speaking of Shunde's urbanization, special attention should be devoted to urban awareness, urban behavior and urban management. In the process of urbanization, the Shunde government should work hard to improve the outward appearance of the city, and more importantly, the overall quality of the city and its people.

The quality of a city is manifested by its values, which are determined by not only its economic strength but, more importantly, its capability to heighten the life quality of its residents and provide them with employment and development opportunities. Advancing urban quality requires intensification of urban management, which is a big issue covering such specific aspects as city regulations and supervision, cultural construction, institutional innovation and the construction of technical platforms.

Enhancing the quality of urban population resides in intensifying urban awareness and standardizing urban conduct. The development of Shunde into a metropolis requires appropriate codes of concepts, words, deeds and the way of life for its residents.

As Top Phil, director of the United Nations Environment Programme, once explained, the success of a city contributes to the success of the nation. Likewise, Shunde has succeeded owing to the overall achievements in its urbanization.

(Written on October 2005, when acting as standing member of Foshan Municipal Committee of CPC, executive mayor of Foshan Municipal Government and party secretary of Shunde District Committee of Foshan)

2.10 Internationalization: The New Engine for Advancing Development in Shunde

The essence of Shunde's internationalization resides in its corporate internationalization. Enterprises in Shunde, especially local and private enterprises, will have to undergo internationalization if Shunde expects to achieve higher goals.

China has gradually integrated itself into the world economy since its entry into WTO. The internationalizing characteristics became increasingly highlighted in world cooperation and competition, especially within the initial transition stage of its entry into WTO. Under this unique context, Shunde was among the first to carry out its internationalization strategy in early 2005 and elevated it to an unprecedented height.

2.10.1 Shunde Seizes the Opportunity to Integrate Itself into the World

Two problems had to be cleared away for Shunde's internationalization. China was faced with more complex and changeable international markets in the transitional stage subsequent to its entry into WTO. Under those circumstances, it was urgent for Shunde to solve the problem of how to continue to accelerate its development, to take the lead in development, and maintain scientific and sustainable development. Another problem was how to integrate itself into the world economy and participate in international competition, a problem Shunde faced in its third transformation from domestic to international involvement after its first transformation from agricultural economy to industrial economy and its second transformation from planned economy to socialist market economy. The Shunde government must take advantage of the opportunity to expand and strengthen itself both domestically and internationally.

What makes a country or a region backward is not its economy but its thinking. In the course of internationalization, what Shunde encountered first was the conflicts in thinking, visions and perspectives. Therefore, the Shunde government decided to start from the internationalization of visions and perspectives. Take "international practice" for example. Generally speaking, it is a code commonly accepted as a sort of idea or rule complied with by people of all countries. Apparently, international practices and international rules are not formulated merely by foreign countries. People in China, including people in Shunde, in Shunde's enterprises and the Shunde government, can also do it.

As long as our culture, urban construction, economic construction and development level are examined against the global background and the development of Shunde's economy, culture and city is to be led from an international perspective, some of our ideas and rules will be standing at the forefront of international development and will be accepted by international communities, enterprises and governments. They will eventually lead to the formation of international practices and international rules.

Shunde's internationalization also requires its code of conduct and tactics to be internationalized. The problem Shunde encounters in internationalization is not strategic planning but operational tactics. The "two engines" Shunde relies on for its future development are the adjustment, optimization and upgrading of industrial structure and the enhancement of enterprise capabilities in independent innovation. To achieve this end, the Shunde government started in 2006 to implement a series of innovative policies and measures for the development of industrial clusters, modern city construction, industrial development, and the enhancement of cultural quality to lead Shunde to conform to international practices in global competition. Those policies and measures are best summarized in the "Triple-Three Strategy" discussed above.

2.10.2 "Two Engines" Push Shunde's Internationalization Forward

The essence of Shunde's internationalization resides in its corporate internationalization. Enterprises in Shunde, especially local and private ones, will have to undergo internationalization if Shunde expects to achieve higher goals. In the course of internationalization, Shunde has been moving forward on "two engines". The horizontally-integrated joint ventures were creatively established in the light of its own long-term endogenous development mode to absorb foreign capital and technology and accelerate the internationalization of its private enterprises. Meanwhile, measures were taken to embed them in global supply chains and guide enterprises to go public so as to accelerate the upgrading of enterprises and the internationalization of private enterprises. Substantial progress has been made in the strategy of "invited to come in" (foreign enterprises are invited to be set up in Shunde) and that of "encouraged to go out" (Shunde's enterprises are encouraged to be engaged in internationalization).

Panasonic Corporation was "invited to come in" in the 1990s, and it produced household appliances and electronics, which remains Shunde's strongest industrial line. Private enterprises in Shunde did not possess the capacity that Panasonic Corporation boosted in manufacturing household appliances and electronics with energy conservation and environment friendliness. That meant challenges and a direction for leading Shunde's industry as well. If Shunde's enterprises had possessed the capacity and technology, they would have been able to penetrate into global markets. Numerous similar cases can be cited in the process of Shunde's reform and opening up. The strategy of "invited to come in" impels enterprises in Shunde to intensify self-initiated innovation.

In the initial stage of the implementation of "encouraged to go out", enterprises in Shunde mostly did OEM. OEM and ODM (Original Design Manufacturer) can be are of help in increasing the international market share in certain periods. However, when the market share reaches a certain level, it will be difficult for enterprises to stand firm, strengthen and expand without their own brands, patents or product standards. Therefore, enterprises should ultimately rely on independent brands and patents and products with autonomous national standards or international standards. Shunde should facilitate its scientific and technological advances and independent innovation through the establishment of more famous brand names and well-known trademarks, effective registration of patents and the convergence of national and international standards.

2.10.3 Internationalization Should Be Implemented on Multi-levels and from Multi-dimensions

The internationalization of a city should take place at multi-levels and from multi-dimensions. It should be all-inclusive, covering industrial, municipal and cultural development and a lot of other aspects. Over the past three decades, Shunde has played an active part in global industrial competition and cooperation and has made continuous efforts to promote industrial internationalization.

Serious attention was paid to three interactive relations: to be capable of learning from others and to be courageous to challenge others; to actively strengthen oneself by learning foreign management and technology and to actively encourage independent innovation to lead one's high-tech development and to be engaged in global competition and development; and to strive to dominate domestic markets and to endeavor to expand into international markets.

Shunde will continue to lead China's internationalization and achieve admirable success in its economy, urban construction, cultural promotion and development through taking active measures to broaden its visions and horizons, act in conformity to international norms and practices and integrate itself into the international community on multi-levels and from multi-dimensions.

(Written in January 2006, when acting as standing member of Foshan Municipal Committee of CPC, executive mayor of Foshan Municipal Government and party secretary of Shunde District Committee of Foshan)

Chapter 3
Intelligent Foshan: The Road to Amalgamation of Industrialization, Urbanization and Internationalization via Informationalization

3.1 Intelligent Foshan: The Amalgamation of Industrialization, Urbanization and Internationalization via Informationalization

In response to the new setup following the 2008 international financial crisis and the trend of transformation from industrial society to information society, the new goal of "Intelligent Foshan via Fourization" (short for "Intelligent Foshan: the amalgamation of industrialization, urbanization and internationalization via infomationalization") is not only a strategic choice for enhancing cultural soft power but also a social need for transforming the mode of economic development and contributing to the people's wellbeing.

Standing at the new starting point and drawing on historical legacies and future innovation, the development of Foshan must take advantage of new opportunities and be guided by the new strategy and goal, namely, "Intelligent Foshan via Fourizaton". Shouldering this new task and goal, Foshan must forge ahead to promote its industrialization, accelerate its urbanization and upgrade its internationalization so as to achieve new breakthroughs in transforming the mode of economic development.

3.1.1 Culture Is a Strong Driving Force for Development

The Outline Plan for Building Guangdong into a Powerful Cultural Province (2011–2020) has recently been issued by Guangdong Provincial Government that provides the guidelines for the construction of a powerful cultural province, reflecting firm commitment in building Guangdong into a culturally strong province.

The construction of "Intelligent Foshan" requires cultural undertakings to be given priority. The competitiveness and charm of a region or a city is ultimately determined by its cultural soft power and its spirit of humanity. Cultural soft power

Y. Chen, *Foresighted Leading: Theoretical Thinking and Practice of China's Regional Economic Development*, DOI 10.1007/978-3-642-35368-0_3,

has become an increasingly significant manifestation of regional comprehensive competitiveness, especially with the rapid development of internet and information technology, the further convergence of culture and economy, the economic function of culture markedly enhanced, and the cultural content in economy increasingly intensified. Cultural development can not only satisfy the people's increasingly diverse, multi-level, multi-faceted spiritual demands but also open up new channels and space for economic growth, as cultural industry has become a strategic leading industry. Culture has become a key factor for Foshan to promote economic and social development and a key driving force for its industrial restructuring, urban transformation and environmental recycling.

In response to the new setup following the 2008 international financial crisis and the trend of transformation from industrial society to information society, the new goal of "Intelligent Foshan via Fourization" (short for "Intelligent Foshan: the amalgamation of industrialization, urbanization and internationalization via infomationalization") is not only a strategic choice for enhancing cultural soft power but also a social need for transforming the mode of economic development and contributing to the people's wellbeing.

The strategy of constructing "Intelligent Foshan via Fourization" targets not only intelligentization of physical entities but, more importantly, enhancement of human wisdom and cultural penetration. The concept of "Intelligent Foshan" is implied and highlighted through the elevation of social and cultural wellbeing of the whole society and the spiritual leading of modern humanity. Foshan, as a well-renowned Lingnan (Guangdong Province and Guangxi Zhuan Nationality Autonomous Region) cultural city, will wield more extensive influence and radiant force and glorify Lingnan culture with more extraordinary splendor in its future development.

Foshan is one of the important sources of Lingnan culture with enormous historical legacies. In incorporating Lingnan culture into the construction of "Intelligent Foshan", Foshan is in a better position to take the lead and plays a greater role in building Guangdong into a culturally powerful province.

At present and henceforth, Foshan will try every means to facilitate the construction of Lingnan cultural city and implement the development program for cultural industry. The focus will be laid on the strategic goal of "Intelligent Foshan via Fourization", following the main thread of "promulgating cultural heritage, strengthening cultural industry and improving cultural wellbeing". Continuous efforts will be made to advance cultural innovation, cultural soft power and cultural progression and prosperity so as to develop Foshan into "the center of Lingnan culture, the cluster highland for creative economy, a modern industrial service center, and an attraction for recreation and entertainment". The elevation of human wisdom and cultural quality will pump considerable vitality and driving force into the construction of "Intelligent Foshan".

As an essential part of "Intelligent Foshan via Fourization", cultural construction should center on building a Lingnan city of cultural fame, with a rich and diverse metropolitan culture, promoting cultural integration into industrial development and city life, and seeking new paths for cultural innovation.

3.1.2 Quickly Adapting to the New Context of Development

The world economy has now entered into the stage of post-2008 international financial crisis. All the countries in the world have been taking initiatives to adjust economic policies, with their economic structure undergoing in-depth adjustment and innovation in science and technology seeking new breakthroughs. Areas, like the Internet of things, green economy, low carbon technology and its industrialization, have become the strategic highlands that all countries strive to reach in the future.

In the present stage, only through economic restructuring can China maintain its economic growth. China can no longer rely on the extensive mode of resource-dependent investment and extension development, due to the increasing scarcity of energy, land and other resources and the limited environmental capacity. Rigorous measures must be taken to propel economic restructuring and transformation in achieving steady and rapid economic growth. Foshan, as well as other cities in Guangdong Province, is confronted with the arduous task of profound restructuring and transformation. It will fall far behind, under keen domestic competition from the leading transformation of the Yangtze River Delta, the rapid upgrading of the Bohai Sea economic belt, and the quick rise of the Midwest. Foshan will stay firm and ahead in the new round of development unless it accelerates economic restructuring, industrial upgrading and institutional innovation and takes the lead in the emerging industry.

Over the past 30 years' reform and opening up, Foshan has undergone three stages of transformation from agricultural economy to industrial economy, from domestic investment- driven economy to foreign investment-driven economy, and from low-end industry to high-end industry. In this early stage of post-industrialization, Foshan has been working conscientiously to conduct further reforms and facilitate economic growth to improve people's wellbeing through accelerating the transformation of the mode of economic development, constructing modern industrial system, promoting the integration of Foshan into Guangzhou and the Pearl River Delta, speeding up rural and urban integration via the income doubling program for farmer residents, and participating in international competition on a higher footing and in conformity with international standards. All this has furnished an important foundation on which to build up Foshan and pointed out the right direction for Foshan to develop.

The implementation of the strategy of "three great efforts and one promotion" is the key task of and the major approach to the "two transformations and one reconstruction" in Foshan in the 3 years to come and a primary measure for changing the mode of economic development and for shoring up the foundation of "Intelligent Foshan via Fourization". "Three great efforts" should be laid on transforming the mode of economic development to accelerate the construction of modern industrial system, implementing the income doubling program for farmer residents to accelerate urban and rural integration and striving to improve the people's wellbeing and social undertakings to accelerate the construction of a harmonious Foshan. "One promotion" refers to the promotion of reforms to facilitate economic growth in Foshan.

3.1.3 The New Strategic Trend in the Transitional Phase

A new starting point will have to go with new strategies and new goals. The Foshan municipal government shoulders the historical mission of planning for the future and leading social and economic development. The new strategy of "Intelligent Foshan via Fourization" geared to its future is deeply rooted in its excess of 10,000 US dollars' per capita GDP, the industrial transition from low-end to high-end in the early stage of post-industrialization, the advancement of industrial restructuring, the speed-up of urbanization, and the elevation of internationalization.

Foshan has been striving to keep abreast of the global IT revolution and the domestic and international trend for intelligent urban development, construct the modern industrial system, and take up the strategic highland for the newly emerging industry. All this, along with the strategies for integrating the Pearl River Delta, integrating Guangzhou and Foshan and integrating rural and urban areas, and for fully promoting the people's wellbeing and speeding up the construction of a harmonious society, has formed a general strategic innovation for its current and future development. All this has deepened and extended the implications of and approaches to an intelligent city on the basis of Foshan's developmental characteristics and industrial advantages. All this has been considered the major tasks and strategic breakthroughs in "two transformations and one reconstruction" throughout Foshan's "Twelfth Five-Year Plan" as well as the new round of transforming the mode of economic development.

"Intelligent Foshan via Fourization" will be taking shape through 3–5 years' endeavors to achieve industrialization, urbanization and internationalization via informationalization and to turn it into an intelligent city suitable for living, commerce and development and a pleasant homeland for its people to enjoy life and prosperity.

First, informationalization is to be utilized to drive forward industrialization and heighten comprehensive industrial competitiveness. Two approaches are to be adopted for the further integration of informationalization and industrialization. On the one hand, strenuous efforts are to be made to cultivate and develop new industries relating to informationalization, pull up resources to prioritize the development of such high-tech industries as photoelectric industry, modern service industry and electricity-driven vehicles, foster radio frequency identification (RFID), the Internet of things, cloud computing, service outsourcing and other leading industries, as well as new industries resulting from the integration of informationalization and industrialization. In addition, IT manufacturing bases are to be set up, and the clustering of emerging industries is to be accelerated.

On the other hand, informationalization is to be used to promote the transformation and upgrading of traditional industry, applying such information technology as integrated management software, 3D design, e-commerce, and the Internet of things to traditional industry for the purpose of transforming the mode and pattern of production and service, improving the intelligentization in products and the efficiency and effectiveness in resource allocation, and eventually realizing advanced manufacturing and modern services for traditional industry.

Second, informationalization will facilitate urbanization and urban competitiveness. Breakthroughs are to be made in the integration of telecommunication networks, cable television networks and the Internet to construct a ubiquitous "U" Foshan and provide network and facilities support for intensifying urban functions and modifying people's lifestyle.

What's more, the penetration and integration of information technology are to be strengthened in urban administration and social development, with intent to incorporate such advanced technology as the Internet of things into urban operation management. Effective measures must be taken to vigorously implement intelligentization in every industry and trade, such as transportation, environmental protection, land monitoring, public security, urban management, education, medical treatment, culture, commerce, government administration, and integrate them so as to achieve a higher level of intelligentization, more comprehensive interoperability, more effective exchange media and more collaboratively linked application, so that urban operation and governance is secure, efficient, convenient, green and harmonious.

Third, internationalization is to be accelerated via informationalization to enhance Foshan's international competitiveness. Service and support are provided for the participation of enterprises in international competition and the heightening of Foshan's internationalization through micro-level and macro-level integration of informationalization and internationalization. At the micro level, enterprises are guided to actively conform to international practices via widespread application of modern business management, such as ERP (enterprise resource planning), PDM (product data management), CRM (customer relationship management). Support is provided to establish an international system of research and development, production, marketing and service on the basis of the Internet of things, the Internet, RFID and other information technology, with a view to enhancing the capacity in exploring international market. In addition, the third-party electronically trading platform is to be vigorously developed to better facilitate enterprises in "going global" for further internationalization.

At the macro-level, the construction of the cross-sector, cross-line and inter-region information platform of "electronic port" is to be accelerated to enhance its competitiveness and provide import and export enterprises with "one-stop" customs clearance services in electronic payment, logistics and distribution, electronic declaration, electronic inspection and so on. In the light of the information technology-based analysis of the current status of the industry and the line concerning domestic and international markets, enterprises are supported to formulate developmental strategies for initiatively implementing the strategy for internationalization. Moreover, cooperation with Hong Kong and Macao is to be strengthened in areas like service outsourcing, information network, tourism, logistics, exhibition, customs clearance to jointly create a new favorable environment for regional development.

3.1.4 Development Transformation Is Driven via Knowledge Transformation

The strategy for "Intelligent Foshan via Fourizaton" must be implemented by starting with the most fundamental and strategic work.

First, right selection of approaches and projects must be made. *The Program for Building "Intelligent Foshan* via *Fourization"* must be implemented with greater vigor so as to lead the whole of Foshan's social and economic development. Priority must be given to such leading industries as the Internet of things and RFID, with focus laid on the selection of "seed" projects and the introduction of "umbrella enterprises" so that large projects will bring about the quick formation of industrial chains and new industrial clusters.

Second, clarification must be made of the tasks and responsibility. "Intelligent Foshan via Fourization" involves every aspect of social and economic wellbeing and requires all relevant parties to make joint efforts to actively carry out *The Program for Building "Intelligent Foshan* via *Fourization"*. The implementation plans must be formulated in accordance with *The Outline of Reform and Development Plan for the Pearl River Delta Regions 2008–2020* (hereinafter referred to as *the Outline*) to clarify the responsibility and tasks for leaderships and relevant departments so that preliminary work will be started as soon as possible, and all tasks will be accomplished as scheduled under full guarantee of time, capital, manpower, resources, policies, and the like. Breakthroughs must be achieved in due course to turn plans into tangible outcomes.

Third, resources have been integrated to establish workable systems. The current closed system within separate departments of information resources, networking, technology must be broken so that the construction of information facilities, information networks and integrated and standardized application platforms will be promoted and the integration of information resources and information services between various sectors of districts, departments, industries and trades will be accelerated. A unified public information platform should be built to form a city-scale information service system with longitudinal integration and lateral connectivity between districts, and relevant services effectively connected. All this will contribute to make management more efficient, services more satisfactory, life more convenient.

In the implementation of "three great efforts and one promotion" and "Intelligent Foshan via Fourization", human resources are always the crucial factor. Knowledge transfer and the construction of "talent highland" must go ahead to lead industrial restructuring, to accelerate urbanization and upgrade internationalization. Economy needs transformation, so do the society and our leaderships. Human resources must take priority in the implementation of "Intelligent Foshan via Fourization". Great efforts must be made to foster an innovative talent pool that can meet the requirements for urban development and industrial restructuring and upgrading to build up Foshan into a center for industrial human resources, an international talent pool, and an incubation park for talents in science and technology, to create necessary conditions for talents to emerge in multitudes and give full play to their capabilities.

(Written on July 20th, 2010)

3.2 Restructuring Industrialization, Accelerating Urbanization, and Promoting Internationalization

The Foshan government should not only adapt itself to its social transformation and the transition of the mode of economic growth but also lead the trend of social restructuring and economic transition and take initiatives to propel the transition of the mode of economic growth. In this critical stage of industrial transition from low-end to high-end, it is a natural and inevitable option for Foshan to take the road of "Fourization" and build up "Intelligent Foshan", in response to the fierce competition at home and abroad.

Social and economic transformation requires leadership to be transformed first. It is an important guarantee for Foshan to advance towards success in social transformation and economic transition to form a leadership team who are excellent at study and work, expert in innovation and earnest in efficiency and effectiveness.

Foshan is now in the critical period of "restructuring industrialization, accelerating urbanization, and promoting internationalization". The Foshan government should not only adapt itself to its social transformation and the transition of the mode of economic growth but also lead the trend of social restructuring and economic transition and take initiatives to propel the transition of the mode of economic growth. In this critical stage of industrial transition from low-end to high-end, it is a natural and inevitable option for Foshan to take the road of "Fourization" and build up "Intelligent Foshan", in response to the fierce competition at home and abroad.

3.2.1 Leadership Calls for Knowledge Transformation and Capabilities Enhancement

The transformation of the mode of economic growth has become increasingly urgent with the rapid advances in informationalization, industrialization, urbanization and internationalization. Foshan will gradually be marginalized if no transformation is undertaken. It will lose its priority and initiatives in its integrating into the Pearl River Delta if slow transformation is undertaken. It will get lost on its way if transformation is undertaken at random. Consensus should be reached concerning "whether transformation is necessary". More importantly, greater attention must be devoted to "how to undertake transformation". Whether Foshan leadership can achieve excellent performance in the transformation of the mode of economic growth depends on our efforts to transform the knowledge structure of government officials from single-type to compound-type, from experience-oriented to innovation-oriented, from traditional mode to modern mode.

The first issue to be addressed is what to study. Studies should focus on related knowledge regarding industrial restructuring, urban transformation and environment recycling, centering around the goal of "Intelligent Foshan via Fourization" and its related strategic tasks like the setup of a modern industrial system, the coordinated and integrated development of urban and rural areas, the improvement of people's wellbeing and social undertakings and the necessitation of reform and innovation. Prominence should be given to strengthening related knowledge about new strategic industries and the integration of informationalization into industrialization, urbanization and internationalization so that all government officials get well acquainted with specific schemes and core tasks in the program of "Intelligent Foshan via Fourization" and stand in a better position to lead the transformation in the modes with respect to economic growth, urban administration and social lifestyle.

The second issue to be addressed is how to study. Innovation is needed in learning modes and channels, which can be organized government official training, selected government leadership domestic or overseas training programs, self-study and Internet learning. Leaderships should take initiatives to learn more profoundly and extensively so as not to be an outsider in practice. By so doing, they can seize every new opportunity under ever-changing global circumstances and better lead industrial development and advances in science and technology.

The final issue to be addressed is how to test the learning effects. Learning effects should be tested and justified through practice by evaluating whether study has broadened vision, improved ability, solved problems and facilitated government work. Government officials should be assessed upon their ability to apply what is learned to practice and should be selected and promoted on the basis of their actual performance in the transformation. Those who are good at learning, have the courage to innovate, work hard and display excellent performance should be appointed, those who refuse to change, lack desire for progress, blindly keep their position and always follow a routine should make way, and those who are ignorant and perfunctory with all talk but without any action should be laid off. The selection criteria for government official appointment and promotion must embody requirements for knowledge transformation and capability enhancement.

3.2.2 Reality Is the Starting Point for Innovative Thinking and Approach Selection

"State affairs to be accomplished begin with details, undertakings ancient and modern are eventually realized in practice." The crux of transforming the mode of economic growth lies in the innovating and seeking approaches to transformation in accordance with Foshan's reality. Transformation should be implemented not merely in economic development but in urban upgrading, cultural development, social administration and undertaking. Advantage should be taken of informationalization to push forward Foshan's industrialization so as to improve comprehensive competitiveness, to heighten its urbanization to enhance developmental competitiveness, to accelerate internationalization to improve international economic competitiveness and to eventually build up Foshan into a harmonious and intelligent city with new advanced industries, farsighted social administration, intelligent public life and beautiful environment. The full implementation of "three great efforts and one promotion" is currently the primary task to fulfill in order to achieve the goal of "Intelligent Foshan via Fourization" through steadfast and strenuous efforts.

Great efforts are exerted to transform the mode of economic development and accelerate the construction of modern industrial systems. Modern service industry, in particular manufacturing-related service and outsourcing industry need to be rapidly developed, with chains of service industry continuously extended. Advanced manufacturing, as a major industrial force, should be facilitated to lead traditional industries. Vigorous measures must be taken to foster new strategic industries, with focus laid on optoelectronics industry, new materials and modern service industry, so that their total output will exceed 100 billion yuan (around 15.7 billion US dollars) by 2012, and on developing new drugs, environmental preservation and motor car industry. Self-initiated innovation must be encouraged to necessitate the new development of private economy.

Great efforts are exerted to implement the income doubling program for rural residents and speed up the urban and rural integration through the implementation of the income doubling program, the coverage of urban public service in rural areas, and the extension of urban infrastructural facilities into rural areas. New breakthrough must be achieved in transforming outmoded villages, promoting high-tech agricultural products, heightening agricultural industrialization and implementing the income doubling program for rural residents. New breakthrough must be achieved in the equalization of public service in urban and rural areas through provision of basic public services, such as elementary education, public health services and social pensions. New breakthroughs must also be achieved in the extension of urban infrastructural facilities into rural areas by constructing more rural public facilities and ensuring better living and ecological environment.

Great efforts are exerted to improve people's wellbeing and social undertakings and speed up the construction of a harmonious Foshan. Governments at all levels should devote more funds to improving people's wellbeing, promoting social causes, and solving prominent problems relating to people's welfare. Law and order must be reinforced to ensure social security and peace in Foshan. Rigorous measures must be taken to promote the construction of national-level ecological civilization demonstrative city, such as the environmental reconstruction project with water, atmospheric and ecological environment greatly improved. The public transportation network must be improved to provide more efficient traffic service and more convenient travel service. Market oversight must be strengthened for foods and drugs to guarantee safe supplies. Active measures must be taken to enhance Guangzhou-Foshan integration at all levels to provide people with better living and development environments.

Social and economic development must be further promoted through more extensive and in-depth reforms to enable Foshan to take the lead in setting up new systems and mechanisms for the active transformation of the mode of economic development in Guangdong Province. The administrative restructuring is to be intensified to deepen economic and social reforms and supporting reforms in related fields, though cross-department administrative restructuring reforms in the five districts of Foshan were completed by the end of September 2010. Through deepening reforms, government functions have been transformed, resulting in a service-oriented government with improved executive capabilities.

3.2.3 The Ways of Thinking Determine the Development Path

Foshan's brilliant accomplishments over the past 32 years of reform and opening up are the result of the emancipation of mind, the audacity to take the lead and the courage to make innovations. The acceleration of the transformation of the mode of economic development is reckoned as a profound economic change, calling for Foshan's government officials to intensify the awareness of reform and always stand at the forefront of economic reform and development.

The ways of thinking determine the development path. As is the way of thinking, so is the development path and approach to follow. Conscientious efforts should be made to free our mind from the shackles of traditional mindset and traditional mode of economic development and to get accustomed to modern thinking.

First, the government must abide by the principles of the scientific outlook on development and take all the factors relating to economic restructuring and development into consideration to achieve coordinated development.

Second, the government must abide by the laws of market economy and give full play to the fundamental role of the market in the allocation of resources.

Third, the government must have global visions and strategic thinking to plan for the future, to lead the new round of development by implementing the concepts of strategic emerging industry, modern service industry and advanced manufacturing, to dominate the highland of industrial development, and to build a new talent pool for emerging industry so as for them to be leaders in the transformation of the mode of economic development and in the construction of modern industrial system.

Fourth, the government must advocate the pioneering spirit of reform to make courageous explorations and innovations and play a leading and exploratory role in transforming the mode of economic development. Finally, the government must amass experience and learn lessons from the past so that Foshan can smooth and successful transformation of the mode of economic development and continue to lead economic restructuring and development in the Pearl River Delta region as well as in Guangdong province.

3.2.4 Enhancing Government Capability to Co-ordinate, Execute and Supervise

The implementation of the scientific outlook on development calls essentially for overall planning and coordination. Government officials of all levels have to familiarize themselves with the complicated situation subsequent to the international financial crisis and the dramatic development in informationalization, industrialization, urbanization and internationalization. They ought to make timely changes in leading styles and enhance their capability in overall planning and coordination. The mechanisms of collective decision-making on major issues, public notifications and hearings, decision-making consultation and evaluation ought to be improved so that all the executions and decisions thus implemented are consistent with the general development trend and all the measures work effectively. New innovations, new breakthroughs and new accomplishments should be achieved in promoting the balanced and integrated development between urban and rural regions, between economy and society, between districts, and between man and nature.

The right approach taken, people will be the decisive factor in implementation. Government officials are required not only to be able to discover problems but also to solve them and perform better in work. Executive power is determined by individual ability and work attitude. Individual ability is fundamental, and work attitude is essential. The enhancement of executive power requires the elevation of one's quality and work competence through intensive learning and training and the intensification of responsibility and the improvement of government services through developing good work styles and attitudes, so that each goal or task can be fulfilled with collective wisdom, team spirit and rigorous discipline.

Necessary countermeasures must be taken in establishing the operating mechanism for mutual restraint and coordination of decision-making, executive and overseeing powers. Supervision is needed to facilitate scientific decision-making and appropriate execution. Therefore, the supervisory mechanism for "three general efforts and one promotion" has to be established and put into execution. A task force for disciplinary inspection and supervision must be set up for leadership accountability and all-round inspection and supervision of major decision-makings, key projects and important issues in the construction of modern industrial systems, the balanced and coordinated development of urban and rural regions, the improvement of people's wellbeing, and other social undertakings. Departments and related officials are to be held accountable for slack in work, thus ensuring that decision-makings are scientific, execution is effective, and service is efficient.

(First published in *Foshan Daily*, June 9, 2010)

3.3 Cultural Antecedence in Constructing Intelligent Foshan

Cultural values shape cultural images, enhancing a city with cultural charms; cultural work motivates cultural creation, enhancing a city with cultural innovation; cultural service provides intelligence, enhancing a city with cultural wellbeing.

The real competitiveness of an enterprise, a region or even a state resides in its cultural competitiveness, and what an individual, an entrepreneur, a region or a state passes down to future generations is their spiritual and cultural products. Foshan's prosperity and intelligence call for both strong economic and cultural backup. Cultural antecedence and foresighted leading are especially needed in the new phase of implementing the scientific outlook on development, actively transforming the mode of economic development and promoting the construction of "Intelligent Foshan via Fourization". Big plans require broad horizons; large projects require great intelligence, and culture is advanced and enriched via major measures to promote economic growth, cultural prosperity and social harmony.

3.3.1 Culture Employed to "Civilize" People and Enhance Urban Cultural Intelligence

Culture is the driving force and soul for economic and social development. Cultural antecedence is required in response to culture-led economic and social transformation and cultural prosperity to meet the spiritual and cultural demands of the great masses.

Over three decades' reform and opening up, the Foshan people, led by the cultural spirit of the times, i.e. "emancipating the mind, seeking truth from the facts, and daring to be a forerunner", have taken the lead in reform and opening up and turned Foshan into one of the first demonstrative districts in China with its advanced experience and demonstrative role, for example, Nanhai's "five-wheel driving" ("five-wheel driving" refers to districts, townships, administrative regions, villages and individuals working together), Shunde's "three-orientation" (collective economy-oriented, industry-oriented and backbone enterprise-oriented), "constructing bridge on loans, charges for repaying loans" and "beauty gets married first"(good quality state-owned enterprises restructured first). Brilliant achievements have been made in Foshan's economic and social development, with new values and vitality poured into cultural development, bringing about Foshan's transformation from agriculture to industry, from domestic investment-driven economy to foreign investment-driven economy, and from low-end industry to high-end industry.

Currently, Foshan's per capita GDP has exceeded 10,000 US dollars. Foshan has entered the initial stage of post-industrialization, typically characterized by industrial restructuring, urbanization accelerating and internationalization upgrading, according to the theories concerning industrial development.

Simultaneous with economic and social transformation, cultural antecedence is more urgent than ever, demanding that the transformation of the mode of economic development be led by innovative thinking, the spirit of modern humanity and the scientific outlook on development. Moreover, with people's living standards constantly improved, cultural demands and cultural consumption tend to be diverse, multi-level, fast-growing.

It is apparent that the existing cultural system fails to respond to the current trend and satisfy the demands of building "Intelligent Foshan". The industrial workers who have transformed themselves from farm workers are mostly far from being qualified for industrial transformation and upgrading because of their lack of science and technology. The lack of cultural flavor and features in urban image creation is manifested in buildings being devoid of Lingnan Waterside characteristics and charms. Foshan must endeavor to improve urban cultural quality, produce high-quality cultural works and exercise more extensive cultural influence.

Public cultural facilities cannot meet the requirements for the construction of "Intelligent Foshan". There exists some distance between the scope and varieties of services and the public demands and a short supply of public cultural products. The development of cultural industry falls behind the construction of "Intelligent Foshan". Foshan's cultural industry accounts for around 5% of its GDP. Industrial clusters have not emerged, high quality personnel are needed for cultural creation. Cultural penetration, service and support capabilities in other industries lag far behind the demands of industrial transformation and upgrading. Culture advancement in Foshan will remain an empty talk if the problems in overall planning, foresighted leading and strategic mapping can not be resolved.

Culture antecedence means full play being given to the role in enlightening people's mind via cultural education so as to satisfy the demands of strengthening urban cultural intelligence. The core of culture is to lead the values and the ways of thinking, cultivate social values and improve people's all-round quality via its educational function and guidance. It helps change the ways of thinking for development, enhance social creativity, and prepare for and win the future via intelligence rather than merely via sweat to gain only wealth.

It must be pointed out that the twenty-first century is no longer led by traditional thinking, with attention paid only to tangible facilities. It is important to realize the more significant role the intangible aspects play in social and economic development. Otherwise, it would be hard to ascend to a higher level. In the current stage of Foshan's development, invisible and intangible productive factors, such as capital, standards, patents, software and thinking, have gradually become the decisive propeller for the advancement of productive forces. All this would be impossible without culture antecedence.

3.3.2 Culture Is a Key Force for Building "Intelligent Foshan"

A city's image and brand are composed of and contingent upon its environment, resources, culture, history, economy, and its humanity.

Foshan is known as one of the origins of Lingnan culture. It was founded in the Jin Dynasty (618–907), and got its current name in the Tang Dynasty (316–420) and was crowned as one of the *Four Well-known Towns and Four Commercial Centers* between the Ming Dynasty (1368–1644) and the Qing Dynasty (1636–1911). Foshan is famous as hometown of pottery, Canton opera and martial arts, with a long history, profound humanity, strong commercial and cultural backgrounds, and excellent natural environment and corporate brands. Foshan has become better-known to the outside world through Hong Kong movie characters like Huang Feihong and Ye Wen.

Prior to the founding of the People's Republic of China, waves after waves of immigration population departed for Southeast Asia to seek fortune. Over 1.8 million people became settled overseas and achieved considerable success in their pioneering undertakings, thanks to their immense wisdom and courage. Likewise, in the course of reform and opening up, Foshan embraces old traditions of Lingnan culture and has created social and economic miracles with their brave innovation and pioneering spirit, which has poured modern vitality and vigor into the ancient city and has fully displayed Foshan's cultural traditions and immense wisdom. All this not only shows Foshan's past and present but also represents Foshan's cultural charms and unique characteristics, leading its future development.

A questionnaire was conducted regarding Foshan's notability in the middle of 2010, when departments of publicity and culture in Foshan invited a research team from Tsinghua University to draft "The Program for Foshan City Image and Publicity", only to find that less than 50% of the subjects in the questionnaire chose "high notability" and "comparatively high notability". That shows that the promotion of Foshan city image is far from satisfactory and that there is a great deal of room for advancement. For instance, it is generally agreed that Foshan Kung Fu is well-known, but how can use be made of this city card? Martial arts masters Ye Wen, Bruce Lee and Huang Feihong are household names both at home and abroad, but the reality is that their names become popular through overseas channels rather than domestic publicity.

At present, Foshan's publicity is still in a natural state rather than being conducted under strategic planning. Stories and legends have become widely known about people from Shandong "venturing into Northeast" and about people from Shanxi "venturing beyond West Pass". There is no justification that no stories have been written about people from Foshan "venturing into Southeast Asia"? Books like *Guangdong: Nine Chapters* and *Classic Guangdong* have become popular, but no books like *Foshan: Nine Chapters* have appeared.

"Cognition speaks louder than facts". It is not sufficient to transmit and develop cultural heritage and traditions, which should be packaged, publicized and promoted in deliberate combination with modern culture so as to shape a city image that is more attractive and more readily accepted.

Culture forms the core of a city's soft power. With the increasing integration of culture and economy, the economic function of culture has apparently been enhanced, the cultural content of economy has constantly been consolidated, and culture has been playing a more and more prominent role in comprehensive competitiveness. The development of cultural undertakings and cultural industry have contributed considerably to opening up new ways and space for economic growth, promoting consumption, increasing employment opportunities, nurturing new cultural formations with a view to satisfying people's cultural demands and achieving sustainable development.

Full use should be made of Foshan's cultural advantage to further explore the connotation, essence and uniqueness of Foshan's culture in response to the development of the times so that cultural development becomes an important driving force in building "Intelligent Foshan" and in establishing modern industrial systems and heightening people's living standards.

3.3.3 *Building Foshan into a City of Cultural Charm, Creation and Wellbeing*

After a deliberate elaboration of the role of cultural antecedence in building "Intelligent Foshan", we now turn to the approaches to cultural antecedence. To put it in a nutshell, cultural values shape cultural images, enhancing a city with cultural charms; cultural work motivates cultural creation, enhancing a city with cultural innovation; cultural service provides intelligence, enhancing a city with cultural wellbeing.

It is expected that through 3–5 years' efforts, the pattern for cultural development will be basically established in accordance with the strategic requirements for "Intelligent Foshan via Fourization" so that Foshan turns into a city of cultural charm, creation and wellbeing, with its major indicators, such as cultural atmosphere, city image, and cultural development, ranking at the top in Guangdong Province with its advanced and comprehensive cultural strength, and a pacesetter in building Guangdong into a powerful cultural province.

Cultural antecedence in Foshan has been emphasized mainly in the following five areas.

Efforts should be exerted to heighten the city's humanity, enhance cultural intelligence and quality and promote people's all-round development so that people truly benefit from culture. In addition, mainstream values are to be actively led, humanity of the new era is to be nurtured and carried forward in Foshan, with cultural wellbeing guiding cultural development. It follows that the core values of the city, society and nation should be embodied in social life to internalize the sense of a social community.

Foshan was founded in the Jin Dynasty (316–420) and was so named in the Tang Dynasty (618–907). Many denominations have ever coexisted in the Xiqiao Hill, Nanhai District, Foshan, which is unique in China and is obviously the result of Foshan's social and economic development, related closely to its culture of convergence and harmony. Therefore, it is advocated that a harmonious social and cultural atmosphere be created, with an active, healthy, and magnanimous social psychology and humanistic environment, to promote the harmonious development of the society and economy.

Foshan's cultural wellbeing should be manifested in educational intelligence, like primary and secondary education, in cultural intelligence, like intelligent library service, and in medical intelligence, like intelligent medical treatment in hospitals, and in some other fields. The conceptualization of cultural wellbeing leading cultural undertakings is the process of cultivating the awareness on the part of government officials on all levels.

The creation of city image, cultural brand and existence constitutes the core of the city image and its quality. Cultural construction should be given full play in enhancing city image, building up city brands, and promoting Foshan in its cultural dissemination.

Great importance should be attached to shaping and publicizing Foshan's image by means of cultural antecedence. The implementation of Foshan image promotion project is to be intensified to highlight its unique characteristics and to constantly increase Foshan's notability and influence at home and abroad.

More elements of Lingnan culture are to be incorporated into urban planning and construction. Regarding urban planning, cultural formations and values featuring the metropolis are to be intensively cultivated. More elements of Lingnan culture are to be integrated into the architectural styles and the constructing of cultural landscapes on a higher footing. Emphasis is given to the integration of urban cultural image with urban functions and environments, with urban buildings, sculptures, squares, tourist attractions, together with advertisings, names of streets and stores, highlighting the charm of Lingnan culture, manifesting profound humanistic traditions and artistic flavor embraced in this historical and cultural city.

Special cultural brands are to be created by integrating the cultural resources of the city. Through carrying forward and enriching Foshan historical heritage and excellent traditions that embrace abundant cultural resources, such as ceramics, folk customs, Cantonese opera, martial arts, lion dance, dragon boating and great names in history, modern cultural products and outstanding movies and television programs featuring both China and Foshan are to be produced, for example, a TV series depicting "Venturing to Southeast Asia", which may be as influential as "Venturing beyond West Pass" and "Venturing into Northeast China".

The pace of "going global" has to be quickened to promote cultural exchanges and cooperation between Lingnan culture and world cultures and to constantly extend the international influence of Lingnan culture, so that Foshan, the historical and cultural city, regains more vitality in carrying forward cultural traditions and in the integration of modern civilization.

More work should be done to integrate urban and rural culture. In accordance with the coordinated urban and rural development, reasonable allotment of public cultural resources should be made to narrow down the gap between rural and urban regions in cultural development to upgrade intelligent cultural services and advance the integration of urban and rural cultures.

The coverage of cultural facilities at the primary level is targeted to build an urban-rural "cultural ring". The coverage and content of public cultural services are to be expanded via digitalization and networking, so that the equality of basic public cultural services can be achieved, and the "10-min cultural ring" in the urban area and the "5-km cultural ring" in the rural area can be set up.

Public cultural services should be encouraged to gear to the demands of the great masses, particularly the grass-roots, enabling them to share the fruits of cultural development.

The innovative capability of culture is to be enhanced via IT to create intelligent culture. The integration of culture with IT and Internet has to be speeded up, with new modes of cultural production and cultural industry being cultivated. Digital cultural resources featuring local traditions will be developed through intelligent projects, such as digital libraries, the digital Temple, digital museums and "intelligent stations", together with the construction of intelligent service platforms for public cultural information the sharing of cultural information resources. Intelligent culture should be nurtured via informationalization to innovate the mode of cultural production and develop more new products of "Intelligent Foshan".

Industrial upgrading and restructuring requires culture to be integrated into industry, into social progress and into popular forms of entertainment targeting the general public so that vitality of the culture is reinforced and Foshan's cultural industry become strengthened and expanded.

Cultural businesses must be built into a pillar line in modern services industry, and the integration of cultural creation and the manufacturing sector must be promoted to add to the cultural values of traditional industry. Traditional products with advanced culture and technology can bring about more generous benefits and rewards. With the improvement of original creativity as a major target, efforts should be focused on facilitating capabilities in the research and design, production and marketing of creative industries, industrial design, arts and crafts, garment design, advertising design, and so on. Cultural creativity can provide cultural nourishment and intellectual support for the upgrading and restructuring of traditional manufacturing of ceramics, furniture, household appliances, printing and copying, textile and garments, and enhance cultural vitality and competitiveness in traditional products.

Take ceramic industry for example. Through cooperation with well-known ceramic masters, Dongpeng Ceramics develops and produces pottery murals by combining the essence of traditional art and modern ceramic technology to significantly increase the cultural value and contents. As a result, common ceramic tiles now cost 480 RMB (about 74 USD) each due to the addition of cultural elements like paper-cutting, with an 80-time price increase over its original price of 6 yuan (about 1 USD).

The interaction of cultural resources and cultural industry is to be accelerated to promote cultural industries. The problem Foshan is confronted with is how to work out solutions and tap its abundant cultural heritage, which will remain historical precipitation if they are left where they are. Foshan folk art will generate multi-faceted effects with new developing modes and will be filled with vitality if provided with scientific, technological, and financial support. The industrial value and market potential in folk customs of traditional culture and Lingnan-style buildings are to be fully exploited and integrated. Cultural tourist bases and cultural resources with unique Foshan characteristics are to be forged into well-known brands so as to further advance cultural industrialization. Efforts should also be exerted to actively necessitate and expand cultural consumption.

Cultural reform must be conducted to activate the creativity of the whole society. Social creativity stems from cultural reform and the advancement of cultural productive forces. In activating social creativity, the atmosphere for cultural reform, which is supposed to be dynamic, highly efficient, more open and conducive to scientific development, must be created to respond to the demands of the times.

Greater importance must be attached to deepening the reform of cultural system and mechanism to further stimulate vitality and sustainability in the development of cultural undertakings. Improvement must be made in the market system of modern culture and the environment for cultural industrial development. Strenuous efforts must be made to form highly competitive teams in cultural creation, administration and originality by a series of measures, like building cultural industrial pools, setting up incentive mechanisms for innovative personnel, providing openings for such positions as "special experts" and "management consultants" and establishing such institutions as celebrity studios, creation research centers, so that soft environment will be improved to attract high-caliber cultural personnel from home and abroad. Favorable environment must be created to cultivate cultural masters and build Foshan into a city for well-known scholars, cultural celebrities and elites to conduct cultural undertakings and create cultural prosperity.

(Written on October 14th, 2010)

3.4 The "Foshan Road" to Transformation of Economic Development Mode

Foshan's scientific and sustainable development has been propelled by the implementation of five major strategies for transforming the mode of economic development, namely, "double transfers" (industrial transfer and labor transfer, the policy of "emptying the cage for new birds", i.e. traditional industries relocated in late-developed regions for the development of emerging industries), the introduction of large projects targeting industrial upgrading, advancement of science and technology and self-initiated innovation, the construction of industrial highlands by financial means, and "Intelligent Foshan via Fourization".

Foshan covers a total area of 3,800 km^2 with nearly six-million population of registered residents. In 2009, Foshan's GDP reached nearly 500 billion yuan, and its per capita GDP surpassed $11,000, ranking eleventh among China's large and medium-sized cities. In the late stage of industrialization or the early stage of post-industrialization, it is becoming more urgent to accelerate the transformation of economic development mode, under the new context of industrial restructuring, accelerating urbanization and upgraded internationalization. After serious investigation, five major strategies have been implemented to transform the mode of economic development as practices of "first trial and first execution".

3.4.1 Strategy One: Double Transfers and "Emptying the Cage for New Birds"

First, a huge number of enterprises have been closed down or relocated. Over 1,200 enterprises with backward facilities have been renovated or shut down, covering ceramics, cement, dyeing, small aluminum casting, glass, and 649 enterprises have been closed down owing to high pollution and energy consumption. At the same time, labor-intensive enterprises have been guided for relocation in the late-developed regions, resulting in about 460 projects being relocated in the industrial parks in Qingyuan and Yunfu over the recent years, which saves enormous space for Foshan's industrial upgrading and injects strong momentum into the economic growth of late-developed regions.

Second, a good number of enterprises have been upgraded. Traditional industries have been transformed into heavy, high-tech and high-end types by integrating informationalization and industrialization and supporting manufacturing with matching services. Take ceramic manufacturing for instance. Only 50 enterprises have survived after 3 years' renovation and upgrading from among more than 400 manufacturers in 2007. They have fully achieved clean production and productive technology for reengineering. The original manufacturing locations have been transformed into the bases for headquarters, exhibition, research and development, logistics and information processing. Over the past 3 years, the ceramic production in Foshan has fallen by 40%, but with 33% increase of its output value and tax revenues, 25% decrease of energy consumption per unit of GDP, and 20% reduction in sulfur dioxide emissions.

Third, a number of enterprises have been nurtured through investment attraction and industrial selection so that focus has been laid on industries of optoelectronics, new materials and modern services, with industries of new pharmaceuticals, environment protection and electric vehicle being nurtured and emerging industries of LCD display, new electric light sources, solar energy and photovoltaic facilities being rapidly developed. All this has contributed decisively to the effective reduction of the proportion of traditional industries and has turned Foshan into the national demonstrative base for new industries and for optoelectronics industry. Besides, new cities, new communities and new emerging industries have been developed through the renovation of "three outmodes" (outmoded towns, outmoded factories, and outmoded inside-city villages), which not only increases the efficiency of land utilization but also facilitates industrial restructuring, urban transformation and environment reconstruction.

3.4.2 *Strategy Two: Launching Large Projects for Industrial Upgrading*

In promoting industrial restructuring and upgrading, Foshan has focused on investment attraction and industrial selection, with strategic emerging industries, advanced manufacturing, leading projects of modern service industry as its major targets, and has expedited the establishment of strategic highland of industrial development through the introduction of leading projects of international level and the cultivation of new industrial clusters.

For instance, the project of electronic display panel module of Nanhai Chimei Innolux Corporation has attracted investment from upstream supporting manufacturers of chips, panels, moulds, plastics and other lines and the downstream manufacturers of complete television sets so that a complete industrial chain for LCD has taken shape and industrial upgrading of household appliances has been facilitated in Foshan. The project of Xi'an Rainbow OLED (Organic Light-Emitting Diode) has pushed forward the third-generation display industry, and the FAW (China First Auto Work)-Volkswagen project has been a driving force for auto parts manufacturing and its industrial clusters and chains.

So far, 47 of Fortune Global 500 have been introduced to invest 87 projects in Foshan, and 99 of China's Top 500 have invested 167 projects. A number of locomotive enterprises have been set up in Foshan to lead their industrial development in technology, standards and brands and have helped to effectively heighten Foshan's industrial structure and level.

3.4.3 Strategy Three: Advancement of Science and Technology and Self-initiated Innovation

Foshan has more than 347,000 registered enterprises, of which over 100,000 are industrial enterprises. Over 2,200 enterprises have an output value of more than 100 million yuan, and over 98% of the enterprises are small and medium enterprises with their output value below 100 million yuan.

Considering Foshan's industrial structure, the guiding and incentive policies have been formulated to consolidate industrial foundation, create brands, register patents, specify standards and export brand names. Enterprises are encouraged and supported to formulate industrial standards, national and even international standards on the basis of their own product specifications and use their own core technology, patents and brand norms to conduct OEM operation.

Over the recent years, the municipal, district and town-level government of Foshan have all set aside an annual total of 1 billion yuan as incentive funds for enterprises to intensify scientific and technological renovation and self-initiated innovation, which has led more than 22 billion yuan from enterprises to serve the same purpose in 2008, with an increase of 47% over the same period of the previous year and more than 30.8 billion yuan in 2009, an increase of 39% even under the severe context of the international financial crisis.

The industrial restructuring and upgrading led by scientific and technological renovation and self-initiated innovation has won Foshan the titles of "Top Ten National Innovative City", "China's City of Brand Economy" and "Metropolis of Chinese Brands". Foshan is the only prefecture-level city that has been awarded the title of "National Demonstrative City of Well-known Trade Marks and Famous Brands" in Guangdong Province. Foshan ranks first among prefecture-level cities in terms of patent application and registration, with a total of more than 130,000 applications and 86,000 registrations, and ranks fourth among China's large and medium-sized cities, with 42 well-known trademarks of China and 65 brand products of China.

3.4.4 Strategy Four: Establishing Industrial Highlands by Financial Means

Advantage has been taken of capital strength and financial means in Foshan to effectively combine enterprises with capital market for further development and expansion. Three financial development plans have been put into operation.

First, the "463" program for enterprise listing (within 4 years ten enterprises to be transformed into limited liability companies; six enterprises to go public or pass IPO examination; 30 billion yuan collected through IPO) has increased the number of listed enterprises from 13 in 2007 to 26 by now, with 102 enterprises to get listed as IPO on echelon. Besides, merger and acquisition have also opened good channels and set up new platforms for industrial restructuring and upgrading.

Second, industry and commerce are effectively linked up with finance by nurturing equity investment funds, guarantee funds for SMEs, human resources attraction funds. Currently, 15 varieties of funds are set up in Foshan, with equity investment funds taking up 1.2 billion yuan, of which 126 million yuan is invested by the municipal and district government, which brings forth 1.1 billion yuan of private capital and quickens the steps of the enterprises to get listed on SME board and growth enterprise market. Five enterprises are now ready to apply for IPO, and more than 30 are assisted or proposed to be restructured.

Third, financial innovation, including the development of rural banks and small-loan companies, provides impetus to industrial transformation and development. In addition, Foshan has been designated by the UN Industrial Development Organization as China's only demonstrative city for industrial clustering and effective capital market operations, and active measures have been taken to introduce foreign banks into Guangdong High-tech Financial Service Center.

At present, agreements have been signed for 28 projects to be opened in the center, with a total investment of 6.579 billion yuan. Since the implementation of the Supplements of CEPA (*Closer Economic Partnership Arrangement, Mainland China-Hong Kong*) in October 2009, four Hong Kong banks have stationed in Foshan, which has effectively strengthened the close links between capital market and corporate restructuring and upgrading, assisted enterprises in establishing a management mechanism congruent with international norms, promoted the establishment of modern enterprise system and the revitalized transformation and development in private enterprises. Private enterprises have contributed considerably to Foshan's economic growth, accounting for 61.8% of its GDP.

3.4.5 *Strategy Five: Implementing "Intelligent Foshan via Fourization"*

Foshan, keeping abreast with the global revolution of information technology and the building of intelligent cities, has advocated the strategy for "Intelligent Foshan via Fourization" as a major breakthrough in leading Foshan's future development and in transforming economic development mode throughout the Twelfth Five-year Plan period.

First, Foshan has endeavored to integrate informationalization and industrialization to nurture and develop emerging industries, such as photoelectric display, RFID, the Internet of things, industrial design, service outsourcing and transform and upgrade traditional industries. For instance, more than 1,700 furniture enterprises are located in Longjiang, Shunde District, but only a few enterprises' output value exceeds 100 million yuan, while Wayes Group, which employs three-dimension technology, provides personalized services, changes its sales mode of "ready-made furniture waiting to be purchased" and turns buyers' market into sellers' market, has had its aggregate sales exceed 300 million yuan within just a couple of years. Traditional household appliances made by Midea Group are upgraded through the Internet of things into appliances with artificial intelligence, which will bring about a new revolution in household appliances industry.

Second, Foshan has endeavored to integrate informationalization and urbanization and incorporate telecommunications networks, cable television networks and the Internet into a unified system so that intelligence systems for services and operations can be developed for transportation, environment protection, public security, urban administration, education, medical care, culture, commerce, and government administration. By doing so, the U-(biquitous) Foshan will emerge to achieve the three leapfrog transformations from city administration to services, from governance to operations, and from partial application to integrated services, which makes Foshan the homeland of intelligence most suited for living, for commerce and for development.

Third, Foshan has endeavored to integrate informationalization and internationalization and guide enterprises, assisted by such technology as the Internet of things, the Internet and EFID, to establish internationalized systems for research and development, production, marketing and services and enhance their capabilities to open up new international markets, for instance, employing the Internet of things to turn Foshan into an international procurement center for ceramics and household appliances. At the macro-level, the construction of the cross-sector, cross-line and inter-region information platform of "electronic port" is to be accelerated to provide import and export enterprises with "one-stop" customs clearance services in electronic payment, logistics and distribution, electronic declaration, and electronic inspection on their "expressway" to global markets.

Foshan's GDP amounted to 265.1 billion yuan in the first half of 2010, an increase of 13.8% over the same period of the previous year. The proportion of advanced manufacturing, high-tech and modern service industries has been on the constant rise and has manifested structural soundness and healthy development in modern industrial system.

In short, the above five strategies for transforming economic development mode have been expediting Foshan's scientific and sustainable development.

(Written on September 2, 2010)

3.5 Selecting Approaches to Transformation According to Development Stages

The answer to the question of which route and mode to adopt for the transformation of economic development mode has to match the economic development trend as well as the status quo of the region so that strengths are intensified, characteristics highlighted, and weaknesses circumvented.

Accelerating transformation of economic development mode calls for strong awareness and thorough understanding of one region's economic status quo and its development trend. As implied in the old saying that "know yourself as well as the enemy, you can fight a hundred battles with no danger of defeat," firmness and initiatives must be maintained and constantly enhanced in transforming economic development mode.

3.5.1 Development Modes Should Match Development Stages

The impacts of the international financial crisis on China's economy are essentially made on China's economic development mode rather than on its economic growth rate. That crisis has highlighted the problem of China's transformation of the mode of economic development. Only when China's economic structure is adjusted can the transformation of economic development mode be achieved, which has become an extremely urgent task.

It is one of the most significant strategic decisions made by the central government to accelerate the transformation of the mode of economic development. Hu Jintao, general secretary of the CPC Central Committee, pointed out that China is in the stage of post-international financial crisis, which is characterized by in-depth restructuring and adjustment of world economy, new breakthroughs in innovations in science and technology, and the active occupation of the commanding highlands in the new round of industrial development and scientific and technological innovations by developed countries.

On the basis of the judgment concerning the major changes at home and abroad, Hu Jintao required Guangdong "to firmly implement the adjustment of economic structure and promote economic transformation in a down-to-earth way" during his inspection to Guangdong in 2009. He urged Guangdong to take the lead in speeding up economic transformation, industrial upgrading and innovation in systems and mechanisms, take the strategic highland of emerging industries, and give priority to the development of new high-tech, advanced manufacturing and modern service industries so as to achieve new competitive edges. What Hu Jintao required applies to Foshan and Guangdong as well.

Wang Yang, secretary of Guangdong provincial committee of CPC, asserted that it is more urgent and important for Guangdong to transform the mode of economic development. Guangdong's social and economic development has entered a period that is characterized by features of a new stage and must undergo in-depth transformation, without which it will be difficult to achieve sustainable development merely on the basis of traditional development modes that have been brought into full play. When confronted with the enormous pressures brought about by the profound changes in the international situation, Guangdong has to implement transformation at all levels through overall enhancement of innovative capabilities, industrial quality and the occupation of the commanding highlands for competition in the post-crisis period. Only by doing so can the initiatives be firmly held in hands in the new round of international economic competition and greater strides be achieved on the road to scientific development.

The history of world economy reveals that the choice of economic development mode for a certain region is mainly contingent upon its stage of development. Different modes are selected to match different stages, and the differences in development modes are also manifested in different modes of economic development. A look back at the past 30 years of reform and opening up in Foshan shows that it has undergone three important social and economic transformations in three stages of development and has adopted three different modes of economic development.

The first stage, which started as a turning point in the 1980s, was marked by transformation from agricultural economy to industrial economy. Before China's reform and opening up, Foshan was mainly agriculture-oriented, and its primary industry accounted for 80–90% of its GDP. Its mode of development was self-contained production typical of an agricultural society. Since 1978, the transformation has been completed from agricultural economy to industrial economy, with the proportion of the primary industry falling sharply in its GDP and that of the secondary industry rising drastically.

The second stage, which started around the 1990s, especially after Deng Xiaoping's southern tour speech and China's entry into WTO, was marked by transformation from domestically-oriented economy to the gradual integration of domestically- and foreign-oriented economy. In the process of Foshan's economy transforming from domestic to both domestic and exogenous development, domestic enterprises ventured to go global for participation in international competition, and overseas enterprises were introduced to get involved in Foshan's development. More than 40 corporations of Fortune 500 were invited with more than 80 projects being in operation in Foshan, and private enterprises in Foshan tried to expand into global markets. Midea Group, the most successful example, set up overseas branch offices, made overseas investment and expanded into international markets.

Up to now, Foshan ranks fourth in Guangdong Province in terms of the total volume of import and export trade, with its general trade accounting for over 53%. The second stage is characterized by the rapid industrialized development, the quick expansion of foreign-oriented economy, and correspondently, the extensive growth pattern. In this stage, Foshan achieved economic growth mainly through resources investment.

The third stage, which has started just now, is marked by industrial restructuring from low-end to high-end. With the constant increase of economic aggregate and per capita GDP, industrial development is speeding up its paces from the low-end to the high-end of the industrial chain. In the beginning of the twenty-first century, Foshan's per capita GDP reached 3,000 US dollars. According to the theory of industrialization, this stage is to be highlighted by both good opportunities and sharp contradictions. The economic development will require that full use be made of the golden opportunities and that solutions be worked out to remove contradictions. By the end of 2009, Foshan's per capita GDP exceeded 11,000 US dollars. This achievement would have been impossible with the traditional development mode and without higher platforms and larger bases for development. Foshan is now in the transition from the late stage of industrialization to the early stage of post-industrialization, which, most importantly, calls for the transformation of economic development mode and scientific and sustainable development.

3.5.2 Transformation Must Follow Development Trend

Foshan has gone through three stages of transformation from agricultural economy to industrial economy, from domestically-oriented economy to the integration of domestically- and foreign-oriented economy, and from low-end to high-end. Foshan's current development characteristics and trends are congruent with those of the late stage of industrialization or the early stage of post-industrialization, which can be summarized as follows:

First, the transformation of the mode of economic development and the setup of a modern industrial system are well under way, a pattern that is expected to be gradually formed in the third stage of development. The central theme of this trend is the structural adjustment and self-initiated innovation. More space is gained through close-down of some outmoded enterprises and industries to cultivate and enhance enterprises of advanced manufacturing, emerging industries and modern service industries. Meanwhile, in building a modern industrial system, the integration of informationalization with industrialization, urbanization and internationalization is achieved at an accelerating pace to build an industrial city with intelligence and internationalization and to ultimately achieve the goal of building "Intelligent Foshan via Fourization".

Second, the unification of Guangzhou-Foshan and the integration of the Pearl River Delta regions are well under way. The formulation and implementation of *the Outline* signifies that the Pearl River Delta integration has been elevated to be a national strategy, and the Pearl River Delta will be developed into a world-class urban agglomeration in the future, in which process the Guangzhou-Foshan unification will be a good example of "first trial" to expedite the integration of the Pearl River Delta regions. In 2009, 52 projects were jointly launched by Foshan and Guangzhou, and 69 in 2010. Substantial breakthroughs are to be achieved, as the scope of cooperation has extended from traffic networks and industries to financial and communications areas. The Pearl River Delta integration, especially the integration of traffic networks, has brought about time reduction and space shrinkage, which demands new thinking about future development.

For instance, the Hong Kong-Zhuhai-Macao Bridge and the inter-city light rail of the Pearl River Delta, which are still under construction, will definitely exert influence upon Foshan's development of modern industry. Once the bridge and the light rail are completed, it is a little over half an hour's drive from Hong Kong to Shunde, and around 1 h to Foshan, and a 1-h economic ring will be a reality within the Pearl River Delta regions. These great changes in time and space are congruent with the leading unification of Guangzhou-Foshan.

Third, the urban-rural integration is well under way and has been accelerated by the income doubling program for rural residents. Foshan's GDP amounted to 481.45 billion yuan in 2009, of which the primary industry accounted for only 2%. However, rural residents account for 50% of Foshan's registered population, and the land resources in rural areas 54% of Foshan's total 3,848 km^2. It is obvious that it is high time to solve the problems relating to agriculture, rural areas and agricultural farmers, for the problems have become bottlenecks for Foshan's scientific development. It is high time take effective measures to implement the income doubling program for rural residents, to extend public urban services and urban infrastructural facilities to rural areas. Any delay in urban-rural integration will become major obstacles in the next round of development. It is a must-take option for Foshan to narrow down the gap in the dual structure between urban and rural areas and speed up urban-rural integration.

Fourth, internationalization is well under way and has been enhanced through further integration of international standards and further participation in international divisions of labor. By encouraging enterprises to go global and attracting foreign involvement in domestic industries, Foshan's industrial advantages are constantly strengthened, and industrial internationalization greatly intensified. The fortifying strategic expansion of international markets has increased Foshan's global market share and enhanced its international competitiveness. The pace of internationalization has been speeded up thanks to efforts on the part of government at all levels to create an environment most suited for living, commerce and development.

Fifth, the promotion of reform and social and economic development has always been the main theme so as to contribute more to people's wellbeing. Special emphasis on reform is a highlight of Foshan that makes it distinct from other cities. Foshan is well known for its experience in reform and as a leader and example in scientific development, "first trial and first execution" and its new matching systems and mechanisms. The five districts of Foshan carried out simultaneous cross-department administrative restructuring of government functions, the administrative streamlining reform of "stronger township with more authority delegation" was conducted extensively throughout its 33 towns through actively delegating power from municipal-level to district-level, and from district-level to townships, which covered the reforms in different types of institutions, financing systems, public financial systems, social administration systems, and other areas, which have injected new impetus and vitality into Foshan's future development.

More resources are converged through effective reform and development to improve people's wellbeing and to facilitate social undertakings so that the great masses can fully enjoy the fruits of reform and development.

The evaluative judgment respecting Foshan's current development and its development trend can make us more aware of Foshan's status quo and give us a clear understanding of the dramatic changes in its development. By tendency is meant the overall situation, the trend and the future. We should adapt ourselves to this tendency, and more importantly, should possess the wisdom and capability to control and work for it, so that our policies and decision-makings are congruent with the general trend and all the measures work toward the desired objective. Through all these efforts, Foshan will take the lead in working out ways to development modes for different development stages.

3.5.3 Foshan's Uniqueness: The Foundation for Transforming the Mode of Economic Development

The question of which route and mode to adopt for the transformation of the mode of economic development is well worthy of serious consideration. The starting point or the prerequisite for such thinking to match with it the economic development trend as well as the status quo of the region so that strengths are intensified, characteristics highlighted, and weaknesses circumvented.

Foshan is highly noted as a frontier area of reform and an economic demonstrative region in China. Over 30 years' rapid development has made Foshan highly distinct from other regions. The Foshan people are open-minded, lenient and tolerant, with the spirit and courage needed for mind emancipation and reforms. Its prosperous market economy, well-developed private economy, comprehensive strength and competitiveness, adjacency to Hong Kong and Macao, and higher-level internationalization have endowed Foshan, undoubtedly, with the foundation and advantages to seize opportunities and take the lead in future reforms and development.

Foshan is listed among China's top 24 cities with the greatest potentials in the next 10 years in *2010 Blue Book on Chinese Urban Competitiveness: China City Competitiveness Report* released by The Chinese Academy of Social Sciences, which is an indication of the acknowledgement of its advantages and manifests that "Foshan is able to stimulate the spirit of innovation in private sectors and open up new space for future development, with its super geographical location and huge potentials for economic development. Its private enterprises are great in economic strength and outstanding in innovative capabilities; under the guidance of the government and thanks to its adherence to industrial and commercial development, industrial restructuring and transformation are bound to succeed in the near future." The characteristics and advantages Foshan has obtained in economic development display great potentials for the transformation of the mode of economic development, which can be summarized as follows:

First, Foshan is a city mainly of industrial, typically manufacturing, economy with great potentials. Its GDP amounted to 481.45 billion yuan in 2009, of which the primary industry took up only 2%, the secondary industry 62.9%, and the tertiary industry 35.1%, with its gross industrial output value exceeding 1,200 billion yuan, approximately equating to that of Guangzhou or Shenzhen. Foshan has become a national demonstrative city for new industries, thanks to its complete modern industrial system. Manufacturing, as the major part of Foshan's economy, has formed its unique industrial characteristics that distinguish it from other cities in the transformation of economic development mode, and that is the advantage for Foshan to undertake the transformation with its own characteristics.

Second, Foshan enjoys great potentials for economic development, with private sector as its main body and driven by the "two wheels" of domestically-oriented economy and foreign-oriented economy. Of the 1,200 billion yuan of its industrial output, Foshan's private sector contributes more than 58%, foreign trade nearly 36%, and the public sector around 6%. That is why Foshan is considered a city mainly of private economy, which is also the uniqueness of Foshan's economy. Similar cases can only be found in Wuxi, Jiangsu Province in terms of economic structure.

In 2009, Foshan was designated as a demonstrative city with effective integration of industrial clusters and capital market by the United Nations after nation-wide investigations that brought forth the final candidate cities of Wuxi and Foshan. Excellent substantial results were achieved after 1 year's trial. It has proved that the advantages of integrating private economy and foreign economy in internationalization serve as the driving force for the transformation of economic development mode in Foshan.

Third, Foshan's economic scale has been constantly expanding through nurturing and strengthening enterprises, and there remain huge potentials for future development. By the end of 2009, more than 347,000 enterprises have registered with the Industrial and Commercial Bureau of Foshan, of which over 100,000 are industrial enterprises. More than 2,200 enterprises have the output value of over 100 million yuan, over 250 enterprises 1–10 billion yuan, six enterprises up to 10–100 billion yuan. There have formed in their respective industries a number of leading enterprises in technology, standard formation and brand creation, and industrial clusters in the form of industrial bases, industrial parks and specialized industrial towns, and economies of scale become bigger and stronger with more competitiveness through the extension of industrial chains.

Fourth, there remain huge potentials for leading private enterprises through the advancement of science and technology and self-initiated innovation. The majority of enterprises in Foshan are small and medium-sized ones and account for 98% of its total number of industrial enterprises, with the output value under 100 million yuan. Enterprises are led to enhance their innovativeness through example learning, joint development and independent research and development. Large-scale enterprises are encouraged through five stages of development to create their own brands, register their own patents, develop their own product specifications into industrial line standards and even international standards, and eventually possess their own core technology, standards, patents and brands to conduct OEM operation in Foshan.

Over the recent years, the municipal and district government of Foshan have invested over 1 billion yuan annually in advancing science and technology and promoting independent innovation, which amounted to over 22 billion yuan with the addition of enterprise investment driven by the government endeavors in 2008, up by 47% or more, and totaled over 30.8 billion yuan in 2009, up by 39% or more. Foshan has become well-known for its famous national brands as a result of innovative development.

Fifth, there remain huge potentials for creating new institutional advantages through constant reform and innovation. As far as financial reform and innovation are concerned, the three plans proposed by the Foshan government for financial development have yielded good results. Up to now, 23 financial enterprises have stationed at Guangdong High-tech Financial Service Center, Nanhai, Foshan, with a total investment of more than 6.5 billion yuan, with the result that financial industrial clusters and chains have gradually formed for providing services in banking securities, insurance, funds, futures, settlement, and data collection and processing via high technology.

In the case of land resources, Foshan is the first in Guangdong Province and even in China to implement the renovation programs for "three outmodes" and has completed the renovation projects covering an area of over 5,300 acres over the past few years, which has achieved the integrated effects of land utilization, urban renovation and corporate development.

With respect to the implementation of CEPA, Foshan, as a pilot city, goes ahead of others in linking up with Hong Kong and has jointly launched 23 projects with Hong Kong. They have all borne fruit.

Sixth, there remain huge potentials for the introduction of large projects of nation-level and ministry/province-level to lead Foshan's economic development.

At the national level, Foshan has been working hard in at least four areas. First, the renovation of "three modes" has been elevated to the national level. Thanks to Foshan's efforts in this regard, the pilot project of renovating "three modes" has been extended to the whole of Guangdong Province with a 3-year limit to solve the remaining historical problems, ensure sustainable development for land resources and build a city.

Second, Foshan is awarded the title of *2010 National Environmental Protection Demonstrative City*, and Nanhai the title of *National Environmental Protection Demonstrative District*, which will provide great opportunities for Foshan's ecological protection and environment building.

Third, Foshan was awarded the title of *National Demonstrative Base for New Industries* in early 2010, covering optoelectronics, lighting and photovoltaic industry, which are designated as strategic emerging industry to be nurtured and supported.

Fourth, Foshan was ranked first (Shenzhen second) by Guangdong Province in its application to the State Administration for Industry and Commerce for the title of China's Demonstrative City of Famous Trademarks and Products. If successful, Foshan will be the first prefecture-level city in China to win the title, which will play a significant role in the implementation of the strategy for brand creation and standardization.

At the provincial level, the industries of LED, the optoelectronic display and the electric vehicle are officially defined as the three key emerging industries in Guangdong Province. The provincial-level FAW-Volkswagen project has been officially settled in Nanhai, Foshan, which will yield an output value of nearly 100 billion yuan and will form 200 billion yuan worth of industrial chains and clusters. The world-rate leading project for cloud computing and multi-functional computer chips has been located in Chancheng District of Foshan and will give new strong impetus to the adjustment of industrial structure in Foshan.

Fourth, agreements were signed for overall cooperation between the Foshan government and the Chinese Academy of Sciences in 2009 to build six incubation centers and industrial incubation bases and launch 63 cooperative projects. Surprisingly, more than 170 cooperative projects have been launched and put into operation in 2010. What distinguishes Foshan from other cities is that Foshan has forged direct links of the Chinese Academy of Sciences with its industries and enterprises, and this mechanism has given projects even greater and more endurable vitality, as it not only helps to solve funding problems but more importantly, provide a good platform for knowledge transfer. Significant changes will take place in Foshan's industrial development as a result of the introduction and implementation of those projects.

3.5.4 Remove Obstacles and Race with Time

Compared with other cities in the Pearl River Delta, Foshan has its strong and weak points. Its radiating power is weaker than that of Guangzhou, its high-tech industry is less developed than that of Shenzhen, its large-scale industry is inferior to that of Huizhou, its urban and rural integration is less advanced than that of Zhongshan, its urban environment is less beautiful than that of Zhuhai, its downtown building is less complete than that of Dongguan, its natural ecology is inferior to that of Zhaoqing, its land resources are less abundant than that of Jiangmen. With an early start of reform and opening up, the inertia of Foshan's traditional modes of development has evidently surfaced and affected its development. Foshan has been encumbered by fame and fancy titles, and people tend to be contented with their present situation and with minor achievements, with no desire to work toward greater objectives.

Many drawbacks resulting from the investment-dependent extensive growth mode have become the obstacles to the transformation of the economic development mode in Foshan.

First, there is still some distance in GDP between Foshan and Guangzhou. The per capita GDP of Foshan grew by 12.8% in 2009, which was high in Guangdong Province but still 0.7% lower than the 13.5% rate of Foshan's GDP growth. The provincial government required that the growth rate of per capita GDP in the Pearl River Delta catch up with and exceed that of GDP, and Foshan is expected to lead the breakthrough within 1 or 2 years. Foshan's GDP and its per capita GDP are ranked third in Guangdong Province, but its economic aggregate lags further behind that of Guangzhou and Shenzhen over the recent years, which was respectively 911.28 billion yuan and 820.12 billion yuan in 2009, each nearly doubling that of Foshan. In terms of per capita GDP, Foshan will be able to catch up with that of Guangzhou or Shenshen through further efforts, for their gap is not wide, with Shenzhen's per capita GDP being 925,000 yuan, Guangzhou's 882,000 yuan, and Foshan's 806,000 yuan.

Second, Foshan's industrial competitiveness is far from strong. On the whole, its industrial development is generally located in the middle or the low-end of value chains and industrial chains, with only a limited number of enterprises at the high-end, a large number of enterprises falling into the extensive-growth type and encumbered with high-energy consumption, high emission, high pollution and low efficiency. Strategic emerging industries relating to high-tech and new materials, new energy are in low proportion. In the light of the latest statistics concerning high-tech manufacturing in Guangdong's modern industrial system, Foshan's high-tech manufacturing deemed above the provincial standards accounted for only 5.5% of its total industrial output value in the first quarter of 2010.

Foshan's investment in R&D remains at a very low level. Its expenditure on R&D for the whole city accounted for only 1.3% of its GDP in 2008 and is a great distance from the requirement of 2.5% in 2012 stipulated in *the Outline*, which has obviously impaired the innovative capabilities and international competitiveness of its enterprises.

Foshan's service industries need stronger enhancement, and their proportion in GDP has long remained relatively low, with productive services lagging behind industrial production. In 2009, the tertiary industry grew by 16.1%, 3.7% higher than the secondary industry, but accounted for only 35.1% of GDP, far below that of Guangzhou or Shenzhen.

Third, there is a great deal of pressure on energy conservation, emissions reduction, and the sustainable development for resources and environment. Traditional industries, such as ceramics, textile printing and dyeing, aluminum and cement production, are highly energy-consumptive and heavily pollutant. The norms set by the provincial government in 2009 for sulfur dioxide and chemical oxygen emissions control have been fulfilled, but new pressures have come upon further energy conservation and emissions reduction as a result of the increasing proportion of heavy industries and the construction of key projects, though recent pressures have been released through recent efforts on the part of relevant parties. It is required that Foshan fulfill the targets of further reducing chemical oxygen discharges by 32,000 t and sulfur dioxide emissions by 54,000 t in 2010 than the norms set in Foshan's "Tenth Five-year Development Program", which means great pressure.

The contradiction between land supply and demand is prominent in Foshan, for the rate of land utilization is merely around 30%, though relatively high in the Pearl River Delta. Land resources available are extremely limited, with the scale of urban construction land far exceeding the norms set by the provincial government, and there is only 9% of land resources that remain undeveloped.

At the current speed of land utilization, there will be no land available in the near future, which will be difficult for Foshan to attract large projects. In addition, there may be shortage of oil, electricity, coal, gas and other energy supplies, coupled with problems of air and water pollution, acid rain, dust haze, deforestation, and low urban green coverage, which will all need serious treatment.

Fourth, the level of urban and rural planning and construction needs heightening. A large gap exists between Foshan and the cities of the Yangtze River Delta and other developed regions in China in urban and rural planning and construction. Foshan's public facilities and services, along with city image, are not commensurate with its economic development, and unique urban construction styles have not taken shape, owing to the improper allocation of some public resources and the prominent problems of "villages within the city" and the disorderly urban-rural bordering zones.

Fifth, more efforts are needed for the balanced development of urban and rural areas. The income gap between urban and rural residents remains relatively wide, with farmers' income difficult to keep a constant increase. Although for the first time, per capita income growth in rural areas of Foshan surpassed that of urban areas by 1.5% in 2009, but the per capita income of urban residents (24,578 yuan) more than doubled that of rural residents (10,699 yuan). The farmland output reached 15,000 yuan per mu (equal to one sixth of acre), ranking first in Guangdong Province, but with limited potentials, and agricultural industrialization and technological content stay at a low level, compared with that of Taiwan and other developed regions in China. Only a low level of social pensions is maintained for rural residents, especially land-requisitioned farmers. Education, culture, medical care and public health in rural areas vary from one region to the other and far from the required equal public services. Development gaps even exist between the northwest and southeast parts of Foshan.

Sixth, technological support is relatively inadequate for accelerating economic transformation for lack of specialized personnel in science and technology. The dominant factors restricting the development of emerging industries and modern services or the enhancement of capabilities in innovation are the relatively inadequacy of specialized human resources, the lack of most favorable environments for attracting high-caliber personnel, and the lack of mechanisms of fully tapping potentials for self-training personnel. For instance, master degree or above holders account for only 1.14% of Foshan's population, lower than the average rate of 1.5% in Guangdong Province. The number of foreign experts and overseas returned students introduced into Foshan in 2009 was 266, far from that of Suzhou (1,411) and Wuxi (1,000). All this combines to cause the lack of proprietary technology and core technology for Foshan's industrial development and the considerable reduction of industrial competitiveness.

It follows from these drawbacks that Foshan's comprehensive competitiveness is on the whole far from strong. The *Blue Book* released by the Chinese Academy of Social Sciences in April 2010 shows that among more than 294 prefecture-level cities, Foshan's comprehensive competitiveness ranks 24, down from 15 in 2009, following Shenzhen (second), Guangzhou (sixth) and Dongguan (fifteenth) among the nine cities in the Pearl River Delta. The *Blue Book's* findings are not necessarily consistent with the actual situation but may partly confirm the existing problems in Foshan.

According to the analysis in the *Blue Book*, economic growth and scale do not stand for the whole of a city's competitiveness. Foshan's ranking for competitiveness in industrial level, development cost and income level is not desirable in the *Blue Book*, with its industrial level ranking 90, development cost 77, income level 49, which, to some extent, reflects Foshan's status quo of development and from a different perspective, its huge potentials for the development of high-end industry, modern service industry, environmental protection and rational utilization of resources.

In 2010, the Policy Research Department of Foshan Municipal Committee of CPC issued *A Comparative Analysis of Key Economic Indicators between Foshan and Other Major Large and Medium-sized Cities in China—2009*. It conducts a comprehensive comparative analysis of 22 large and medium-sized cities (excluding Hong Kong, Macao and Taiwan) with 335 billion yuan or above of GDP. Guangzhou, Shenzhen, Dongguan and Foshan in Guangdong province come among China's "Top 22" in China. Based upon both horizontal and vertical comparison, their ranking has changed, especially as a result of the global financial crisis, and Foshan is located at the medium level with respect to its overall strengths, but half of its key economic indicators rank within 11, which also shows Foshan's strong competitiveness in terms of economic scale, per capita economic aggregate, manufacturing and residents' income.

Foshan has performed prominently well in its growth rate. Among the 12 key indicators, nine have risen to a considerable height, which highlights its leading momentum for breakthroughs out the international financial crisis in 2009. However, indicators with respect to the tertiary industry, fiscal revenues, investment in fixed assets and foreign investment in actual use are ranked rather low, falling behind all the other cities.

It is clear from the above analysis that Foshan is positioned in the transition from the middle to the late stage of industrialization or in the initial stage of post-industrialization and is undergoing the transformation from the low to high level of industrial development. The strong impacts of the international financial crisis upon Foshan have given us a better understanding of the importance of transforming the traditional mode of economic development and have made us more aware that it is hard to sustain the economic development mode that is highly dependent on the international market in the midst of complex and changeable world economy, hard to sustain the industrial development mode that lacks core competitiveness in the midst of fierce international competition, and hard to sustain the extensive development mode solely through resources investment and scale extension due to the increasing constraints of energy, land and other resources and the limited environmental capacity.

Therefore, it is an urgent strategic task that admits of no delay to expedite the transformation of Foshan's economic development mode, which is congruent with its development trend.

Consequently, it must be clearly understood that, confronted with the dramatically changing situation of industrialization, urbanization and internationalization, no transform in economic development modes will gradually make Foshan marginalized and lose its rightful place in urban integration, slow transformation will deprive it of the golden opportunities and the original advantages and priorities in the integration of the Pearl River Delta, and random transformation will make it get lost in its development and suffer from setbacks and failures in the new round of development and competition, which will eventually affect Foshan's overall situation and lose its future. Therefore, the Foshan people should enhance their sense of urgency, sense of mission and sense of responsibility, make early planning, act promptly in response to the significant changes of the patterns and trends of social and economic transformation in the post-international financial crisis, and race with time to lead the Pearl River Delta regions and Guangdong Province in the transformation of economic development mode with all their strengths.

(Written in May 2010)

3.6 Switching from Production Factor-Driven Mode to Innovation-Driven Mode

Arduous efforts must be made to vigorously accelerate industrial transformation, urban upgrading and environmental reconstruction, shift economic focus from the second industry to the coordinated development of the three industries, from the low-end to the high-end of industrial chains, and from the production factor-driven mode to the innovation-driven mode, and strive eventually to lead the transformation of the mode of economic development.

The key to speeding up the transformation of the mode of economic development lies in starting from the reality of Foshan, innovating development thinking, defining the transformation targets, and working out the right ways of transformation. Full thoughts should be given to all factors, which will help in breakthroughs in major targets and "first trial and first execution". Currently and henceforth, it will be the top priority in the Foshan government's economic work to undertake the transformation of the mode of economic development, and with the goal of building "Intelligent Foshan via Fourization" as its central point and "three great efforts and one promotion" as the major work line, to expedite industrial transformation, urban upgrading and environmental reconstruction for the purpose of shifting economic focus from the second industry to the coordinated development of the three industries, from the low-end to the high-end of industrial chains, and from the production factor-driven mode to the innovation-driven mode, and strive eventually to lead the transformation of the mode of economic development.

However, the transformation of the mode of economic development is not merely restricted in economic development but reflected in urban upgrading, cultural development, social administration and the promotion of public wellbeing and social undertakings as well. It must be regarded as systematic engineering that involves the transformation of government functions and boosting economic development through reform. The measures can be summarized into "three great efforts and one promotion".

3.6.1 Great Efforts Are Exerted to Transform Economic Development Modes to Accelerate the Construction of Modern Industrial System

The reality of Foshan's being positioned in the early stage of post-industrialization requires the transformation of the mode of economic development and the construction of modern industrial system. Advanced manufacturing acts as the major driving force to constantly lead industrial upgrading, with high-tech and emerging industries growing rapidly and service industries, especially modern service, being speedily upgraded. In response to the reality and the development trend, new ideas and measures are needed for the transformation of traditional industries, the development of advanced manufacturing, the cultivation of emerging industries, the nurturing of modern service sector, and the enhancement of innovative capabilities.

First, the development of modern service industries, especially modern services and outsourcing services associated with manufacturing, should be accelerated. Among the three industries in Foshan, the tertiary industry takes up a small share, which is an obvious weakness, and needs to be dramatically enhanced through accelerated development. The approach Foshan has adopted for its development of modern service industries differs from others. Foshan should develop not only consumptive services but more importantly, production services, and constantly extend its existing chains of service industry. For instance, sound logistics has developed to provide support for more than 1.2 trillion yuan of gross industrial output in Foshan. World-class logistics corporations, like POSCO from South Korea, and domestic top-ranking logistics corporations, like Baosteel from Shanghai, have established their branches and started operations in Foshan.

Based on the development of logistics industry, RFID is integrated through cooperation with Hong Kong with logistics and gets speedy development in the field of the Internet of things as an extension of modern service industry. For another example, manufacturing industry is Foshan's underpinning strength, with more than 100,000 enterprises in the whole city, but their matching service industries are relatively weak. As a result, modern service industries associated with manufacturing must be vigorously developed, particularly in industrial design, information processing, industrial examination and inspection and other related.

These modern services are not merely geared to the needs of Foshan, nor merely to the industries with a total output value of more than 1.2 trillion yuan in Foshan, but more importantly, to the development of industrial service outsourcing as well, which will turn Foshan into a city of both manufacturing and industrial services and provide industrial service outsourcing to surrounding cities, neighboring provinces, and even the entire Asia Pacific regions. This is an objective in extending industrial chains that Foshan is striving to achieve in the future.

The financial industry, which has developed completely from scratch in Foshan, is now under innovative development, supported by Guangdong High-tech Financial Service Center as a backstage service base, to gradually form financial industrial clusters, become the logistics base, the information processing center and a center for financial innovation, and finally provide financial service outsourcing at home and abroad.

These are the new ideas and new starting points for the extension of Foshan's modern service industrial chains.

Second, advanced manufacturing industry will act as the main driving force for the constant upgrading of traditional industries. Foshan has gradually formed industrial clusters, but most of its traditional and private enterprises still remain in the middle or the low-end of industrial chains. Over the recent years, a number of enterprises have been closed down, restructured, or upgraded, and a number of new enterprises have been nurtured and supported. The number of closed-down enterprises exceeded 1,200, covering ceramics, cement, bleaching and dyeing, casting and others with serious pollution and high energy consumption. Over 200 enterprises were transferred to less developed regions through the implementation of "double transfers".

At the same time, special efforts have been made to foster industrial clusters and develop the "3 + 9" industrial bases (three world-class industrial bases for household electric appliances, new display devices and modern ceramics, and nine nation-level industrial bases for professional mechanical equipment, metal material processing and products, textile and garments, food and beverage, furniture, medicine and health care, automobiles and spare parts, new materials, energy conservation and environmental protection) so as to transform and upgrade the traditional industries through example learning, joint development and independent innovation.

Third, strategic emerging industries have been fostered and developed. Foshan has clearly defined its strategic industrial layout for the development of strategic emerging industries, with focus laid on optoelectronics industry, new materials and modern service industry and their output value exceeding 100 billion yuan in 2012. In addition, stress is laid on the cultivation of those industries that are highly integrated with Foshan's existing industries, like new pharmaceuticals, environmental protection, and electric vehicle industries. For instance, Foshan is designated as a national industrial demonstrative base for new-type industries, mainly owing to its optoelectronics industry, including photoelectric display, lighting and photovoltaic products.

Policies have been made by the provincial government to foster industries relating to LED, photoelectric display and electric vehicles, with the LED project based in Foshan. China's total output value of LED in 2009 amounted to merely 82.7 billion yuan, and Guangdong Province took up 39 billion yuan, and Foshan 5 billion yuan. Foshan now has more than 230 LED manufacturers. Semileds Corporation of the United States, the world-class LED enterprise, which settled in Foshan and started its production in the second half of 2010, together with the existing enterprises such as Osram from Germany, FSL, Nationstar, Nanhai Real Faith Co. Ltd, has developed into an industrial cluster. Manufacturers of ceramics, building materials, and solid mercury as the supporting material for the production of LED, have established solid foundation for the development of new material industry in Foshan. As is known to all, mercury is liquid at normal temperature. Only eight enterprises in the world can make it solid as raw materials for LED, and two of them are in Foshan, one in Chancheng District and one in Gaoming District of Foshan.

It may be no exaggeration to say that Foshan has reached the world's leading level in the development of some new materials. Foshan has over 250 new materials manufacturers, including nano-technology and high-end chemical raw materials. Their total output value is expected to exceed 100 billion yuan by 2012 through further efforts to nurture and develop them.

As for new pharmaceutical industry, proprietary Chinese medicines in Foshan have an influential tradition and a sound foundation for cluster development, which has a highly promising prospect if their production is effectively associated with biopharmaceuticals, microbiology and gene. In the case of environment, the quantity of sewage treatment and the density of sewage treatment plants in Foshan rank first among prefecture-level cities in China and can bring forth, along with garbage classification and atmospheric administration, a large environmental protection industry. As far as the electric vehicle industry is concerned, automobile industry in Guangdong Province is mainly located in Guangzhou, but most of spare-part manufacturers are in Foshan. FSL, for example, provides the key parts for electric vehicles, and the introduction of the German Volkswagen in 2010 will mark a major breakthrough in Foshan's auto industry from spare parts manufacturing to the assembly of the whole vehicle.

Fourth, efforts have been made to facilitate innovation that leads the development of private sector. Only about 2% of the enterprises in Foshan have reached the production value of more than 100 million yuan, and 98% come under that. Most SMEs are still in the stage of example learning and joint development for lack of independent innovation and necessary facilities. Take for example Longjiang, Shunde District, where around 1,700 furniture manufacturing enterprises are located and the output value of only three exceeds 100 million yuan. For such areas, industrial clusters should be encouraged through joint development.

The government should help set up public platforms for research & development to support SMEs in technological development and encourage those leading enterprises and headquarters enterprises to undertake independent innovation and get strengthened and expanded through the following five-step development: shoring up solid foundations, creating brand names, registering patents, and formulating their own standards that are to be established and recognized as industrial, national or even international standards. During the final phase, brands, patents and standards are to be franchised for OEM by enterprises from home and abroad, which is the ultimate goal so that enterprises in Foshan will truly become large-scale international enterprises.

The ultimate goal of Foshan's development is to build "Intelligent Foshan via Fourization". Foshan is currently accelerating its industrialization, urbanization and internationalization. In addition to the integration of informationalization and industrialization, great efforts should also be made to incorporate informationalization into urbanization and internalization to realize "fourization". Speaking of internationalization, customs modernization can be gradually achieved by applying RFID to importing and exporting and customs inspection and quarantine and linking them to the Internet of things. Besides, informationalization is to be integrated with urbanization through connections of the Internet and the Internet of things to other terminal digital industries and digitalized cities to enhance the integration of internationalization with intelligent industrial cities and eventually build up "Intelligent Foshan".

Foshan's proposal of building "Intelligent Foshan via Fourization" is made in response to the rise of intelligence in the world, the development of smarter cities and the characteristics and rational reflections on Foshan's urban development. At the end of 2008, IBM raised the concept of "a smarter planet", which involves full application of the new-generation internet technology to all walks of life, namely sensors being implanted in the globalized systems of hospitals, power grids, railways, bridges, tunnels, highways, water supply, dams, and oil and gas pipes to construct "the internet of things" via global internet networks and enable human beings to live a more convenient life and manage production more dynamically by means of super computers and cloud computing. Consequently, the world will become "smarter" with the integrated formation of "the internet and the Internet of things" into "a smarter planet".

This concept has triggered off a new wave of informationalization around the world, so that Europe, America, Japan, South Korea, China and other countries elevate the development of the internet of things to the national strategic level and strive to seize the commanding heights of the world's economic territories.

The construction of smarter cities is well under way in Beijing, Shanghai, and Hangzhou and other cities in China to win competitive edges in the future. The proposal of building "Intelligent Foshan via Fourization" is based upon the understanding that the construction of modern industrial system should not be confined merely to industries. It also requires the effective matching integration of all other relevant aspects, which is the incorporation of informationalization into industrialization, urbanization and internationalization.

The Development Program for Intelligent Foshan via *Fourization* has specified the objectives, tasks and approaches, namely, using informationalization to expedite industrialization so as to promote overall industrial competitiveness, to upgrade urbanization so as to strengthen the competitiveness of urban development, and to accelerate internationalization so as to improve the international competitiveness of economic development. All this will combine to promote the transformation of economic development mode, urban operations management and social lifestyles.

3.6.2 Implementing the Income Doubling Program for Rural Residents to Accelerate Urban-Rural Integration

With years of efforts to solve the problems concerning agriculture, rural areas and rural residents through industrialization, urbanization and agricultural industrial enhancement, the urban-rural integration of Foshan has gradually assumed new characteristics. Its urbanization has been accelerated by renovating the "three modes". The government's public services have been extended to rural areas through streamlining township administration and delegation of power to lower levels. The city infrastructure and public facilities has been extended to rural areas through the implementation of the "double-hundred-percent and six-access project" (i.e. the 100% rate of hard-ground road and public transportation in administrative villages and the 100% access rate of power grids, television network, telephone network, information network and postal services in rural areas). For the first time, the rate of income growth for rural residents exceeded that for urban residents in 2009, showing that the income gap has been narrowing down between urban and rural residents.

In response to this trend, the urban-rural integration should be promoted with the income growth for rural residents as the starting point and the work goal. Thus, the coordinated and balanced development between urban and rural areas is to be achieved by implementing the income doubling program, the coverage of urban public services in rural areas, and the extension of urban infrastructural facilities to rural areas.

First, breakthroughs are to be achieved in the implementation of the income doubling program for rural residents. Three tasks are to be accomplished. The first task is to speed up the renovation of "old villages" into "new communities" so that the lifestyle of rural residents will be transformed and the countryside will assume an entirely new look. The second task is to establish demonstrative parks of agricultural science and technology and promote high-tech agricultural products, with more efforts made upon their introduction, experimentation, demonstration and promotion and upon knowledge transfer to help farmers to foster new varieties, open new markets and increase their income. The third task is to heighten the level of agricultural industrialization, apply the notions of industrial development to promoting modern agriculture, and set up modern agricultural bases to expedite agricultural industrialization and modernization. Measures must be taken to increase the utility of rural land resources and the contributory rate of agricultural economy so that rural residents living upon agriculture can benefit from industrial development through stable rental income and its sustainable growth.

Second, breakthroughs are to be made in promoting the equalization of urban and rural public services, which can be promoted and strengthened through vigorous development of primary education, public health, basic social pensions and other public services. Greatest efforts possible are to be made to cope with the sharp contradictions between the rapidly growing public demand in rural areas and the relatively insufficient supply of public service and to let rural residents enjoy substantial benefits from the balanced urban and rural development.

Third, breakthroughs are to be made in the extension of urban infrastructures to rural areas. The construction of rural public infrastructure, transportation networks and public traffic networks has to be accelerated and improved. Basic facilities, such as water and electricity supply, gas, telecommunications, and road lighting, are to be extended to rural areas, and public transportation services, hard roads, garbage and waste water treatment are to be completely improved. Meanwhile, the construction of living and ecological environments in rural areas and urban-rural greenway networks has to be speeded up so as to provide the best environment for living and production.

3.6.3 Improving Public Wellbeing and Social Undertakings and Building a Harmonious Foshan

With the gradually deepening transformation of economic development mode has come a new turning point in urban development, urban-rural integration and public wellbeing and social undertakings. One of the most important manifestations is that more financial recourses have been employed by the government at all levels to develop public welfares and social undertakings and more attention has been devoted to the issues concerning the people's wellbeing and the construction of a harmonious society. Over the past years, Foshan's governments at all levels have taken many measures to benefit the people, including the annual ten public welfare projects specified in the government work report, housing for fishermen to move ashore, farmland conservation subsidies and the living allowances for the elderly.

Four major tasks have been accomplished to deal with sensitive and thorny issues resented by the masses and the issues concerning the people's wellbeing. First, with respect to public security, three major campaigns were launched to guarantee the security for Guangzhou Asian Games by the end of June 2010 and to strengthen social security and harmony for Foshan. In order to expand the monitoring zones, Foshan deployed patrols on the main roads and the key areas, which will be retained as a long-term measure. Substantial measures will also be taken to exercise controls on motorcycles on the streets.

Second, strenuous efforts have been made concerning environmental protection. Advantage has been taken of the Asian Games in Guangzhou, Foshan's being awarded the title of the National Model City of Environmental Protection, and Foshan and Nanhai's being awarded the title of the National Environmental Protection Demonstrative Area to fully promote environmental reconstruction and to considerably improve water environment, atmospheric environment and ecological environment.

Third, the construction of transportation infrastructure has been further accelerated, including public transportation, underground transportation, light rail and other transportation connects, to secure fast and convenient travel for citizens and traffic safety for the Asian Games and for the public.

Fourth, great efforts have been made to strengthen market oversight in order to guarantee food and drugs safety for the good of people's life and health.

3.6.4 Institutional Breakthroughs to Enhance Development

The greatest difficulty in transforming the mode of economic development resides in institutions. The fundamental transformation of the mode of economic development would be hard to achieve without major breakthroughs in institutions and systems. Thanks to the pioneering spirit of mind emancipation, bold thinking and courageous reforms, Foshan took the lead in achieving admirable breakthroughs in institutional reforms. At the beginning stage of its development, with its pioneering spirit, bold explorations and first trials in marketization, Foshan adopted effective measures to solve the bottleneck problems of funds, technology and lack of specialized talents. Compared with other cities, the uniqueness of Foshan lies in its perseverance in constant innovation, piloting, and contribution of fresh experience.

For instance, the cross-department restructuring of government functions and the institutional reform in streamlining administration are commended as benchmarks and examples in Guangdong Province, and the experience in the renovation of "three-modes" has been widely promoted and followed. Now, the acceleration of the transformation of economic development mode calls for a new round of overall reform, which will again make Foshan a model in being the first in Guangdong to build institutional mechanisms conducive to the accelerated transformation of the mode of economic development.

The current focus of reform in Foshan is laid on deepening institutional reforms of administrative organizations to provide support for social and economic reform. Recent arrangements require that the cross-department restructuring of government functions be completed in all the five districts of Foshan by the end of June 2010, and that the reform of stronger townships via streamlining administration and more power delegation in 33 towns be completed by the end of September 2010, and that the institutional reforms by type be completed by the end of 2010. All these reforms intend to achieve the objectives of transforming government functions, building service-oriented government and improve adminstrative governance.

In terms of institutional arrangements, local governments and government departments have centered on the construction of a policy system conducive to the transformation of the mode of economic development through a comprehensive review of previous policies and regulations and clear up all those unsuitable for the transformation. Meanwhile, in accordance with their functions, the government at all levels and its departments have lost no time in conducting investigations and formulating new policies and regulations aiming to accelerate the transformation, particularly in areas of investment, taxation, land, finance, environment protection, technical standards, and intellectual property rights, and to establish a sound policy system for the facilitation of the mode of economic development.

There is no example to follow in reform. Reform allows of success as well as failure. Adhering to the principle of "being pioneers, encouraging creativity, achieving breakthroughs and tolerating failures" in reform, Foshan pays respect to the pioneering spirit of the grassroots masses, gives full play to the initiatives of the whole society, and makes regular sum-ups of experience and lessons, with a view to constructing a favorable atmosphere for joint participation of the whole society in the reforms and transformations.

(Written in May 2010)

3.7 Changing Ways of Thinking and Enhancing Knowledge Upgrading

The transformation of the mode of economic development is bound to make profound changes in thoughts and ideas and in the economic field. The traditional mode of economic development, which was formed under the guidance of the traditional ways of thinking, will not work any longer in today's context.

The key to the success in the transformation of the mode of economic development in Foshan is, to a large extent, determined by the kind of thinking, insights and perspectives of government officials at all levels and by the kind of knowledge structures that are required to satisfy the needs of the times and the needs for development. Consensus has been reached on the question of "whether transformation is necessary" among government officials of all levels, so efforts should be focused on the question of "how transformation should be conducted".

3.7.1 Full Play to Be Given to Foresighted Leading on the Basis of Modern Thinking

The ways of thinking determine the routes of development. As is the way of thinking, so is the development route and approach to follow. Modern thinking is the way one thinks about problems and works out solutions to them. The traditional ways of thinking tend to seek theories and solutions to problems from a priori knowledge and existing experience and are likely to result in conservatism in ideas and block ways of thinking. Quite a few government officials are still thinking in the traditional ways and stick to the old modes of economic development. When confronted with conflicts and problems in the market economy, they still resort to the government's administrative authorities rather than adopting economic, legal and market means to handle these problems.

In practice, they speak about the scientific development but follow the traditional way of thinking. The methods and measures taken are still those doctrines of a priori knowledge, represented by old experience and old methods, which are lacking in new thinking, new approaches and new measures.

It has become clear that the transformation of the mode of economic development is bound to make profound changes in thoughts and ideas and in the economic field and that the traditional mode of economic development, which was formed under the guidance of the traditional ways of thinking, will not work any longer in today's context. With economic transformation, corporate restructuring, social transition, and the gradual perfection of market economy, the government is undergoing functional transformation via streamlining administration and delegating powers to the lower levels.

As a result, the resources held by the government will be considerably reduced and limited. Under such circumstances, the government, rather than taking on everything, should adapt to the laws of market economy, shift its roles from previous direct leadership in economy and direct participant in market to the guide, coordinator and environmental creator for social and economic development and enhance its progress in accordance with the laws of market economy. Under today's particular context of economic globalization, plenty of new things, new knowledge and new problems may occur. They tend to be strange to us. As the old saying goes, "an experienced revolutionary encounters new problems". Obviously, old ways cannot solve new problems.

Therefore, the primary issue in the transformation of the mode of economic development is that the traditional ways of thinking with strong coloring of planned economy have to be abandoned and replaced by the spirit of self-revolution to change minds, ideas and thinking, upgrade knowledge and develop ability. New modes, new routes and new methods are to be explored through ceaseless efforts in order to adapt to the new demands for scientific development and the new modes for economic development and to better accomplish the mission of transforming the mode of economic development.

"Breaking" intends to achieve better "establishing". The shackles of the traditional mindset and development modes must be broken, and modern ways of thinking must be established.

First, in accordance with the requirements for scientific development, all the factors involved in transformation will have to be taken into consideration to integrated and coordinated development of urban and rural areas, social and economic undertakings, various regions, and mankind and nature.

Second, full play is to be given to the fundamental role of the market in resources allocation in conformity with the laws of market economy. Excessive government intervention and involvement in the market will restrict the development of market and diminish the vitality of the civil society. The government should concentrate on creating a fair development environment and an impartial social environment, adhere to the market orientation in adopting approaches to reform and follow the principle of the market as the guiding line for development, and uphold the market-based approach to the allocation of resources. Two sessions of education expo have been held successfully in Foshan, for instance, through the mechanism of civil leading, social investment and business operation, and without any government spending.

Third, the planning of Foshan's new-round development should be based on global visions and strategic thinking and led by the concepts of strategic emerging industries, modern service industry and advanced manufacturing. Efforts must be made to dominate the highland of industrial development and build new human resources pools for emerging industries so as to turn Foshan into a leader in the transformation of the mode of economic development and in the construction of modern industrial system.

Fourth, experience and lessons should be reflected upon and summed up adeptly and fully. No reform and development in the world are plain sailing, without meeting with setbacks and failures. As Deng Xiaoping said, "look-on is allowed, but we must try." Failure does not mean anything. What counts most is to draw lessons from failures and try to avoid detours and make as few mistakes as possible.

3.7.2 Innovation in Personnel Training Helps Accelerate Knowledge Upgrading

Once the right route is decided upon, cadres will be the decisive factor. Consensus has been reached among our cadres on the route of sustainable development after years of implementation of the outlook on scientific development. It is required that cadres should have the ability not only to discover problems but to solve problems as well. Those who can identify the situation should be performing better in work. It has turned out to be difficult for some cadres to fulfill new tasks of transforming the mode of economic development for lack of proper knowledge structure and required ability. Some cadres even feel nervous at new approaches in cases where old ones do not work.

Some cadres have only a single line of knowledge structure and know traditional industry well, and modern industries are rather new to them. Some cadres are still in the habit of giving orders for others to fulfill their duties rather than employing economic and legal means. Some cadres are narrow-minded and are unable to work out new ways of deal with the problems that occur in the course of scientific development. All this points to the fact that it is always of primary importance, in promoting the transformation of the mode of economic development, to train and cultivate cadre teams and leading personnel needed for scientific development and take effective measures to accelerate their knowledge upgrading.

First, it is well worthwhile to highlight and specify the core contents of leader training and its major objective, which is to enable all government officials to have a good command of the specific scheme and the core tasks outlined in the program of "Intelligent Foshan via Fourization." The focus of training should be laid on relevant knowledge respecting emerging industry, informationalization, the integration of informationalization with industrialization, urbanization, and internationalization, the construction of modern industrial system, the promotion of independent innovation, the balanced development between urban and rural areas, and the nurturing of strategic emerging industry, which should all be covered in the training curriculum. Lectures, seminars and special training programs should be conducted by authoritative experts and scholars in relation to the current situation of industrial transformation and upgrading in Foshan.

Government leaders should take the lead to do more profound and thorough learning so that they will not behave like an outsider or a layman in their work and will seize every new opportunity under such instantaneously changing circumstances and stand in the position to lead the development of industry, science and technology.

Second, training modes for cadres and leading personnel must be innovated. Training can take the following forms: special subject learning programs for municipal government leadership, extensive leader training, including heads of some key enterprises, short-term leader training in mainland universities and those in Hong Kong, Singapore and other places, and self-taught and internet learning. Plans should be made to recruit and develop specialized talents of high-caliber and with strong technical competence in response to the demands for diversified talents in industrial restructuring and transformation, advanced manufacturing, modern services and emerging industry and the transformation of existing personnel.

3.7.3 Focusing on Economic Transformation and Learning Reinforcement in Official Promotion

The learning effects are evaluated by whether cadres have broadened horizons, improved ability, solved problems and enhanced development. Surveys should be conducted respecting the effects of their application of what has been learned to practice, and the results should be used as back-up for their future appointment.

Cadres should be selected and appointed mainly in accordance with their ability and performance in the transformation of economic development mode.

Those who are hard working and capable, with modern ways of thinking and efficiently transforming the mode of economic development, should be placed in proper posts so as to guarantee the specialized personnel and cadres needed for the transformation of the mode of economic development. Those who are backward in ideas and ways of thinking and lacking in necessary abilities should have their posts changed. All these selective and promotional measures will strengthen the awareness of the importance of knowledge upgrading for government officials.

The transformation of the mode of economic development is a long-term strategic task and will be a tough and protracted battle, which calls for meticulous preparation and long-term planning and requires full consideration of both the current situation and the future development. In the course of transformation, it is difficult and even painful to abandon some existing things, break out of the existing interest pattern, and make self-denial of the ideas and experience that proved applicative in the past. It will be difficult to achieve breakthroughs and success if there is no determination and courage for self-revolution and the wisdom and ability for making pioneering endeavors. It is a trying moment for everyone.

(Written in May 2010)

3.8 Implementing Brand Strategies for Transformation of Development Modes

Brand strategy is central to corporate development and is also an important development strategy for a city and even for a country. On the basis of this strategic consideration, the state has established national demonstrative cities for the implementation of brand strategy. It is an inevitable option for Foshan to cope with keen competition from home and abroad to use the implementation of brand strategies as the starting point to make Foshan the first to achieve breakthroughs in the transformation of economic development mode and to lead Foshan in its economic development.

In 2010, Foshan was appointed by China's SAIC as one of the first demonstrative cities for the implementation of brand strategy. The establishment of a demonstrative city for the implementation of brand strategy will provide Foshan with new opportunities, new engines and new carriers for the transformation of economic development mode and is regarded as a significant starting point for building "Intelligent Foshan via Fourization". It will contribute considerably to the upgrading of Foshan's overall competitiveness, the fostering of international brands, expand industrial clusters and eventually expedite the transformation of economic development mode.

Foshan had only 16 nationally well-known brands in 2007, and that number increased to 42 by 2010, ranking second in Guangdong Province and covering as many as 15 industrial areas. Foshan was awarded the titles of "China's City of Brand

Economy" and "Metropolis of Chinese Brands". Another five products, such as black gourd produced in Sansui district and arrowroot in Heshui, Gaoming District, have been successfully registered as trademarks of geographic indication, making Foshan rank first in Guangdong Province.

In spite of all the achievements, there is still a long way to go in the construction of Foshan into a national demonstrative city for the implementation of brand strategy, and it is an extremely arduous task for Foshan to become prominent among the 53 demonstrative cities in China. The proportion of brands to nearly 350,000 market players in Foshan is low, with an average of only one well-known brand out of 10,000 players. Though Foshan is among the top cities in China in terms of the total number of famous trademarks, the number of brands with absolute competitiveness and influence at home and abroad is still rather limited, and products with high added value account for a small proportion, and their influence on economic development is not significant.

The importance of the implementation of brand strategies is not fully recognized in some districts and towns, which results in inadequate investment in public services to support enterprises in developing brand, inadequate attention to the creation of regional brands, and the significantly low indexes for brand development. Some enterprises have not attached great importance to brand creation, and some corporate CEOs have not considered and conducted brand operation and administration from a strategic perspective. The brand strategy has not been included in the development planning of some businesses with little spending on that.

All this indicates that there is still a great distance away from the construction of Foshan into a national demonstrative city for the implementation of brand strategy.

3.8.1 Brand Is the Most Powerful Economic Card of a City

Brand strategy is central to corporate development and is also an important development strategy for a city and even for a country. On the basis of this strategic consideration, the state has established national demonstrative cities for the implementation of brand strategy. Foshan is in the critical stage of transforming its industrial structures, accelerating its urbanization and heightening its internationalization. It is an inevitable option for Foshan to cope with keen competition from home and abroad to use the implementation of brand strategies as the starting point to make Foshan the first to achieve breakthroughs in the transformation of economic development mode and to lead Foshan in its economic development.

Advantage should be taken of building a national demonstrative city for implementing brand strategy as a powerful driving force for the transformation of economic development mode. Foshan's per capita GDP of over 10,000 US dollars indicates that it is in the late stage of industrialization and that it is becoming more urgent to speed up its economic transformation. The key to its transformation is to treat the reality of Foshan as a starting point for innovating ways of thinking about development and discovering the desirable route for transformation to achieve the goal.

The development of market economy generally goes through the three stages of product operations, capital economy and brand operations. Developed countries have long been in the stage of brand operations.

The awarding of the title of "National Demonstrative City for Implementation of Brand Strategy" to Foshan by SAIC will exert profound and far-reaching influence upon the ways of adjusting irrational economic structure and low value-added brands. Endeavors should be made to accelerate the implementation of brand strategy through fully employing supportive measures, expediting high-end, high-quality and high-tech industrial restructuring, and transforming the mode of economic development from scale-driven to structure-driven and shifting focuses of competition from quantity and earning foreign currencies to product reputation and independent brand development.

The establishment of Foshan as a demonstrative city for the implementation of brand strategy should be taken as a significant starting point for building "Intelligent Foshan via Fourization". "International competition is, in the ultimate analysis, competition in intellectual property rights," commented Chinese Premier Wen Jiabao. Today, it has become a popular trend for enterprises to go globalized with their resources allocated optimally worldwide and to participate in the internationally-integrated competition. As its economic internationalization is on the constant rise, it will be difficult for Foshan to stay firmly on in national and global competition without a considerable number of competitive brands with strong market influence.

In 2010, the program for building "Intelligent Foshan via Fourization" was put forward by the Foshan Municipal Government to use informatioalization to push forward industrialization and improve comprehensive industrial competitiveness, to use informatioalization to upgrade urbanization and enhance developmental competitiveness, and to use informatioalization to accelerate internationalization and enhance the international competitiveness of economic development. All this will consequently contribute to the transformation of the mode of economic development, urban administration and social lifestyles.

It will be a tough task to fulfill the objective of building "Intelligent Foshan via Fourization". The construction of Foshan as the national demonstrative city for the implementation of brand strategy should actively serve the strategy of building "Intelligent Foshan via Fourization". Through the implementation of brand strategy, a number of emerging enterprise groups and industrial clusters will be fostered and developed with well-known independent brands to promote industrial restructuring and upgrading and speed up industrialization, a number of high-end brands with national fame will be fostered and developed to contribute to the heightening of urban construction and accelerate urbanization, and a number of exporting enterprises with their own brands will be supported and developed to strengthen their capability in participating in international competition and elevate internationalization. Obviously, "Intelligent Foshan via Fourization" must go together with the implementation of brand strategy.

The construction of a national demonstrative city for the implementation of brand strategy should be taken as an effective carrier for the upgrading of Foshan's overall competitiveness. Brands, with trademarks as their core, is a typical representative of a region's economic image, a highly concentrated indication of a city's economic strength, and a most powerful economic card of a city. Such trademarks as Wuliangye Liquor of Yibin and Changhong Television of Mianyang have become exemplars of driving the rise of their cities. A mention of Qingdao will bring into mind the brand of Qingdao beer and Haier electronics, and a mention of Foshan will bring into mind Foshan ceramics and Shunde electronics.

Brand protection is another important index for a city's civilization, modernization and internationalization. The environment for economic development, including brand policy environment and law enforcement environment, tend to be the decisive factor for enterprises to expand and get strengthened and for local governments to attract investment. Prices can differ significantly once the products of the same material, the same style, and the same quality are tagged with different trade marks.

The real pain of China's manufacturing industry resides in its lack of the property right of core technology, its lack of rights to formulate standards, its lack of rights to fix prices, its lack of rights to collect added values, and most important of all, its lack of independent brands. In effect, trademarks are the gene of brands but do not necessarily go with good brands. However, good brands will certainly possess trademarks.

Foshan is one of the representative cities of China's manufacturing industry. The vigorous construction of Foshan as a national demonstrative city for the implementation of brand strategy enables enterprises to take the road of brand strategy and develop an overall mode with wide-ranging well-known brands and enterprise, rapid rises of certification trade marks and collective trade marks, with increasing numbers of national trade marks and famous trade marks, and with the quick emergence of highly notable competitive brands and top-notch international brands. All these efforts will give rise to a mode of economic development with independent innovation and brands as its core value and will constantly contribute to Foshan's administrative efficiency, overall competitiveness and popularity.

3.8.2 Brand Consumption Has Become an Increasingly Globalized Trend

Under the modern trade system of global economic integration, competitive global brands have flooded the markets around the world. Brand consumption has become an increasingly globalized trend. Among all general brands in the world, only 3% can be reckoned as world-class brands, but their total output value accounts for more than 40%, and their total sales reach approximately 50% of the total sales worldwide, and even up to 90% with a small number of enterprises. In the light of the characteristics of industrial development in Foshan, the major objective of the construction of Foshan as a demonstrative city for the implementation of brand strategy is to enable more market entities to have more of their own well-known brands, win over larger market shares, participate in more global competition, and let more rural residents reap greater benefits.

Great efforts have been made to nurture independent brands, propel Foshan to become the vanguard for international competition. During an inspection tour to Foshan, Wang Yang, secretary of Guangdong Provincial Committee of CPC remarked that Foshan should do its best to become the vanguard of Guangdong Province for participation of international competition, the main force for the Pearl River Delta integration and the leading pioneer in the exploration of the mode for scientific development. Over the past few years, Foshan has committed to promoting the "five-phase development" strategy for corporate growth. The ultimate target of Foshan's implementation of brand strategy is to encourage and support its enterprises to create their own brands, patents and standards and conduct OEM operations.

The construction of Foshan as a demonstrative city also calls for the all-round construction of supporting elements for creating brands, the establishment of the independent innovation system for invention patents, technical standards and other relevant components, and the nurturing of world-renowned brands for participation in international competition. Brands function as the "passport" for enterprises to go global and the "permit" for engagement in international integration and competition. The internationalization of brands is taken as the major strategy to spur enterprises in the implementation of brand strategy. A number of enterprises should be selected to set examples for others to follow. Active measures should be taken to provide guidance and services for enterprises to register international trademarks, focusing on international registration and protection of trademarks and internationalization of domestic brands, and for enterprises to actively react to overseas trademark disputes and make appropriate use of local laws and international rules to prevent trademarks from overseas infringement and counterfeiting.

Vigorous measures should be taken to develop agricultural brands and make the income doubling program for rural residents achieve real effects. One aspect of the strategy of "three great efforts and one promotion" advocated by the Foshan municipal government is the implementation of the income doubling program for rural residents, which aims to speed up urban and rural integration. In building the demonstrative city for the implementation of brand strategy, the project of "demonstrative agriculture, rural areas and farmers" should also be included, because they are the important foundation for urbanization and industrialization and a prominent weakness in urban-rural integration. Therefore, greater efforts should be exerted to vigorously develop modern agriculture and actively popularize the brand strategy of "one village one brand, one zone one trademark" so that brands of agricultural and sideline products flourish everywhere.

Agricultural resources within Foshan should be further tapped, and the trademarks of agricultural products and the registration of geographical marks should be vigorously publicized and guided by the policy. Farmers, rural agents, rural economic organizations and agriculture-related enterprises should be actively supported to carry out the registration of trademarks and geographical marks of agricultural products, increase the added value of agricultural products and enhance its market competitiveness. The industrial operational pattern of "company plus brand (geographical marks) plus farming households" should be promoted to a greater extent, and brands are to play a more significant role in modernization, industrialization, large-scale agriculture. In popular terms, make an egg worth a chicken, make a chicken worth a pig, and make a pig worth a cow, so that farmers can get substantial benefits and achieve the goal of income doubling.

Efforts should be exerted to create regional brands and constantly advance and expand industrial clusters. Over 30 years' reform and development, the number of specialized towns and industrial clusters is so great that they have become one of the most unique and dynamic characteristics of Foshan's economy. Specialized towns and industrial clusters have not only brought enormous scales of economic benefits but also played an inestimable role in enhancing industrial competitiveness and creating employment opportunities. However, no time can be lost in accelerating the transformation and upgrading of industrial clusters, as traditional industries have a small proportion of highly value-added products, and their brands have not produced desirable effects.

In April 2010, when the assessment team of *the Outline* delegated by the State Council made an inspection of Foshan, they fully affirmed the achievements made through the implementation of "*the Outline*", as well as pointing out the problems, among them the lack of large-scale corporate groups and industrial clusters, which demanded immediate attention and urgent settlement. To achieve this end, industrial adjustment has been undertaken through introducing new high-end industries and nurturing emerging industries, and the creation of regional brands has been substantially supported and developed for the purpose of fostering regional brands to facilitate the integration of industrial chains and enhance the "hematopoietic" function of industrial clusters. The establishment of regional brands will lead the transformation of development modes of the existing industrial clusters to turn the advantages of industrial clusters into geographical brand strengths.

A comprehensive review of the current situation of Foshan has been made with respect to industrial clusters regarding their scale, status quo and prospects, the composition of upstream and downstream industrial chains, their social influence and driving capacity for regional development. Those industrial clusters with significant influence upon Foshan's social and economic development have been carefully selected with an attempt to accelerate the creation of regional brands, whose competitiveness are enhanced through the administration, marketing, promotion and protection of certification trademarks and collective brands. Each district government should determine the pilot unit based upon its actual economic development and increase investment in the creation of regional brands to enhance the competitiveness of brands within industrial clusters. The selection of "Foshan ceramics" and "Yanbu underwear" as pilot regional brands should provide more experience for the creation of regional brands in the whole city.

Effective services are to be provided for emerging industries to promote new-type industries. Over the recent years, the development of strategic emerging industries has been advanced as the key strategy for the adjustment of industrial structure, the promotion of transformation, the sustainable growth and the construction of modern industrial system, and great progress has been made in emerging industries, such as new lighting industry and new energy. In 2009, the gross industrial output value amounted to about 140 billion yuan, and in 2010, Foshan was awarded the title of

"National Demonstrative Base for New-type Industries". Currently, strategic emerging industries in Foshan concentrate on "three-light" industries, i.e. photoelectric display, lighting, and photovoltaic products, biological pharmaceuticals and new materials. The lighting industries, mainly LED industry, have dramatically developed into competitive industrial clusters. Foshan has become one of the largest production bases for electric lighting products.

As indicated in *Foshan's Strategic Supportive Measures for Emerging Industries (Trial Version)*, priority and substantial support are to be given to the development of key industries. Relevant government departments should take into account capital guidance, tax revenue incentives, and financial innovation, with focus laid on the ways of intercalating brand services in the development of new strategic emerging industries and of implementing brand strategies by enterprises so that the implementation of brand strategies will achieve practical effects in facilitating new emerging industries through early involvement, early follow-up, early cultivation, early standardization and early accomplishments.

Foshan considers it an honor as well as pressure and responsibility to be designated as one of the first national demonstrative cities for the implementation of brand strategy. Foshan should seize the opportunity, and under the guidance of the outlook on scientific development and "first trial and first execution", strive to achieve substantial results with the wisdom of the Foshan people in expediting the transformation of its economic development mode through brand strategy.

(Written on July 5th, 2010)

Chapter 4
The Road and Direction of Economically Demonstrative Regions in China

4.1 Operating a City Means Managing It as Resources

Under the market economic system, the government should abide by the principles of economy and open operative projects to the market and society by means of capitalization and capital management so as to build and govern the city in a sound and beneficial way.

Cities will be the highlight of the twenty-first century. The advent of the twenty-first century will give cities a more prominent role in social and economic development. Since its entry into WTO, China's economic transformation and rapid accrual in social capital assets have demonstrated that city operation, that is managing a city as resources, should be put on the agenda for serious consideration by governments at all levels.

4.1.1 The City Is a Kind of Resources

A great deal of controversy remains regarding the concept of "city operation" as a mode of urban development, but that concept, dating back to the 1990s, follows an indisputable principle—that is, under the market economic system, the government should abide by the principles of economy and open operative projects to the market and society by means of capitalization and capital management so as to build and govern the city in a sound and beneficial way. That embodies the essence of operating a city. The most crucial point of this theory lies in that market, capitalization and internationalization will, on one hand, help governments at all levels to break the bottleneck of capital shortage in building big modern cities, and will, on the other hand, upgrade city management, give full play to city functions, and improve its environment and quality, which will in turn boost its capacity, radiating force, influence and competitiveness and ultimately push forward its social progress on a full scale. This idea of operating a city should run through the whole process of urban development.

Y. Chen, *Foresighted Leading: Theoretical Thinking and Practice of China's Regional Economic Development*, DOI 10.1007/978-3-642-35368-0_4,

The idea that the city is a kind of resources can be interpreted from the following dimensions.

First, the city as a kind of resources can be interpreted in the general sense, referring to its economy, history, culture, geography, environment, humanity, technology, image, spirit, policies, systems, ideals and needs of every field of social life.

Secondly, a city consists of a lot of infrastructural resources, like roads, bridges, subways, light rail, transportation, modern central building clusters, environment protection, stadiums, or even infrastructures for energy production, water conservancy and information technology. This kind of resources comprises tangible infrastructures and intangible technological network. Both exercise great influence on the image, attribute, quality and function of a city.

And finally, a city is a kind of industrial resources. The differences in economic, geographical and natural conditions of a city determine its choice of which category of industry as its major orientation for development. It is certain that in the development of economy, cases may occur where great strides in tertiary industrial areas, such as logistics, exhibition, finance, tourism, intermediary service, retail industry and so on, may accompany the development of primary industry or secondary industry.

It is of primary importance for the government to realize that urban resources can be classified into two categories: operative resources and non-operative resources. The former includes infrastructure, transportation, environment protection, water supply, power supply, gas supply, non-compulsory education, science and technology, culture, public health, sports, name rights of major objects, etc. The latter refers to public welfare projects, covering all other items with the exclusion of those mentioned in the first category, though part of them are also related to public welfare and may overlap. The categorization of urban resources delimits government functions in urban construction and development.

The government should do its best to open operative resources to the market, the society and the investor, whether at home and abroad, by means of capitalization and capital management.

In the case of non-operative resources, which cannot be manipulated via market mechanism, the government is duty-bound to assume a leading role in employing them for city construction, administration and development. That explains why public finance, which is collected from the people and used for the people, should weaken its function in constructive projects and strengthen its function in public welfare projects.

4.1.2 Managing a City as Resources

As is indicated above, operating a city as resources means managing all kinds of operative projects in urban development as resources, which requires us to think about two problems: what ownership forms to be used to operate those projects and how to raise capital for their construction and operation.

Operative projects can be organized in the form of sole proprietorship, joint ventures, cooperatives and joint-stock systems or even state-owned but private-run enterprises. This organizational model enables us to stay abreast of current trends of market demand and supply and international economic development so as to guarantee effective investment, optimize industrial structure and promote social and economic development. In addition, effective market prediction will help in effective regulation, evade risks and avoid losses.

Therefore, in city operation, particularly in reforming the mode of urban development, the government should transform the property ownership of deposited assets, originally operative projects, so that their operation will follow the natural laws and meet the requirements of market economy and take appropriate ownership forms suited to capital market, i.e. in the form of state-owned but privately-run enterprises, joint-stock systems, joint ventures, cooperatives, or sole proprietorship through auction off to foreign investors. The newly added operative projects should, from the outset, take the form of sole proprietorship, joint ventures, cooperatives or joint-stock systems so that their operation will conform to market rules and a firm foundation will be laid for urban development.

Those corporations, whose newly added operative projects are short of capital and lacking in investors and whose fiscal funds or public finance are employed as assurances for bank loans, should transform its ownership in a timely and effective way in the process of investment and construction. Measures should be taken to guard against newly added operative projects reverting to their former state-owned management system.

As to how to raise capital for those projects, financing in capital market will work in various ways: (1) issue bonds and convertible bonds; (2) issue stocks; (3) set up project funds or seek investment from home and abroad; (4) purchase listed shell companies; (5) securitize project assets; (6) acquire and merge projects and manage them in a tie-in manner; (7) leasing; (8) mortgage; (9) replacement; and (10) auction. Projects can also progress by means of project financing from domestic organizations, overseas companies, private enterprises or enterprise groups.

Franchising finance may also be practiced by granting rights to charge and price, by means of DBO (Design-Build-Operate), BOT (Build-Operate-Transfer), BOO (Build-Operate-Own), BOOT (Build-Operate-Own-Transfer), BLT (Build-Lease-Transfer), BTO (Build-Transfer-Operate), TOT (Transfer-Operate-Transfer), etc.

The government can adopt a variety of financing means or a combination of financing means in the light of characteristic and conditional differences in operative projects. The government should hold all or a great portion of shares for the construction, operation and management of such projects as environment protection and water supply, which have direct impacts upon or close relations to the interest and life of the people.

As for sewage projects, the government can adopt the "3P" mode, i.e. water supply companies as **p**ublic companies forming cooperative **p**artnership with one or more **p**rivate companies to build, operate and manage sewage enterprises and facilities in the franchising forms of BOT and TOT. Sole proprietorship is another possible form.

If the "3P" mode operates properly, maximum benefits will be achieved at minimum cost. When appropriate occasions arise, the sewage projects of the whole city can be operated as a listed company issuing urban sewage or public utilities stocks. By doing so, the government will be able to push the operation and management of public utilities projects to a higher national and even international level. At the same time, the stock issuance on the capital market will raise large sums of fund, which can be further invested in environment protection projects, thus snowballing the urban environment protection industry.

Following the demands of market mechanism and internationalization, the government should adopt multilevel and multi-channel means of direct financing, in combination with public finance, necessary indirect financing like bank loans and the role of government revenues of "achieving most by least efforts", to overcome the bottleneck of capital shortage and guarantee scientific and sustainable urban development. In this way, limited fiscal funds can be effectively used for public welfare so as to meet the growing demand of the people.

4.1.3 Operating a City Means Reforming Government Administration

It must be understood that the government at all levels should play different roles in urban construction and development in different stages of China's economic development.

Under planned economy, the government should play its role chiefly by giving executive orders and building ostentatious and non-commercial projects.

In the initial stage of socialist market economy, the government should function to facilitate urban construction and development through government initiatives, social involvement and market operation.

In the more advanced stage of socialist market economy, government leading and market operation should become the major form of government administration in urban construction and development.

China is now in the growing stage of socialist market economy, a transitional stage from its planned economy to the market, socialized and internationalized economy. At this stage, the government should not just provide free and shared services and welfares without considering benefits of investment and construction, should not just construct projects without considering their operation, and should not just emphasize their social functions and public interests without considering their economic benefits. In the long run, there will be great losses of urban resources and wasteful duplication of construction, and city administration will remain at a low level and in a disorderly and inefficient state.

Governments at all levels should realize that whatever cities they are in China, they boost huge amounts of "deposited assets" (assets accumulated through long-term investment) and "would-be assets" (assets to be invested to accelerate and upgrade urban development and administration). Cities should be reexamined and reevaluated according to the principles of socialist market economy, and the approaches conforming to socialist market economy should be adopted to reform and restructure "deposited assets" and operate and revitalize "would-be assets".

Operating a city means managing it as resources. In the current stage of China's economic development, governments at all levels should adopt "government initiatives, social involvement and market operation" as the major strategy for facilitating urban construction and development.

Government at all levels should regard city operation as a means of government administration reform. Resource allotment should be made on the basis of the principles of market economy and laws rather than executive directives, as is done under planned economy. The focus of city administration should shift from micro-level management of specific projects to macro-level strategic planning, development, utilization, operation and management of city resources as a whole so as to optimize and upgrade the living and working conditions of urban citizens and improve the ecological environment.

Government at all levels should treat the concept of city operation as a starting point for planning city construction, tapping urban resources and forging brand cities, work out ways to open up new channels of financing and create new platforms for investment, and try every means to revitalize urban assets and integrate urban resources. In so doing, the government is bound to build and develop their cities in a leading, coordinated, and sustainable way.

(Written in *March, 2004*)

4.2 Conventional Banking Tools and Modern Financial Regulation

Nowadays, China's financial market is based on the operations of commercial banks coexisting with some degree of capital market, which mainly have interest rate, exchange rate, spot goods and futures as its major factors. Modern financial theories, policies, tools and measures should be employed to promote, regulate and monitor the development of modern financial market.

Traditional banking theories mainly center around currency, focusing on its relation to price and interest rate. Modern financial theories have their foundation in the operation of commercial banks and the development of capital market and focus on assets pricing, especially the pricing of securities assets, including such factors as interest rate, exchange rate, stock and futures etc.

In 1983, the People's Bank of China was separated from its former body and began to solely function as the Central Bank of China. Prior to 1983, the Ministry of Finance in China took the responsibility of monitoring traditional banking services and issuing treasury bonds. Between 1983 and 1992, the People's Bank of China assumed the responsibility of monitoring traditional banking services and capital market that had treasury bonds as its mainstay and stock market still in embryo. In 1992, China Securities Regulatory Commission was founded, followed by the promulgation of

"The Commercial Bank Law of the People's Republic of China" in 1995. Several years of development brought into existence the framework of China's financial management system, with the People's Bank of China functioning as the Central Bank of China, China Banking Regulatory Commission monitoring commercial banking services, China Securities Regulatory Commission monitoring capital market transactions, and China Insurance Regulatory Commission monitoring insurance market dealings. That is known as the system of "One Bank and Three Commissions".

4.2.1 Modern Financial Market Is Taking Shape in China

Up to now, China's financial market has gradually shaped itself into a market-oriented capital system, comprising modern commercial banks constituting the currency market with strong liquidity and modern investment banks, which have bonds, stocks, funds and futures as their major factors and are still on their way to maturity.

Let us illustrate here with the 2007 data.

1. Bank savings: By the end of 2007, the savings deposits in Renminbi and foreign currencies of all financial institutions reached 40.11 trillion yuan, an increase of 15.24% over last year.
2. Interest rate: In 2003, the Sixteenth National Congress of CPC proposed a steady market-oriented reform of interest rate and optimized allocation of financial resources. The Third Plenary Session of the Sixteenth National Congress of CPC further pointed out that a sound mechanism shall be established for interest rate to be determined by the demand and supply of market and that the People's Bank of China shall apply monetary policies to regulate interest rate.
3. Exchange rate: Since July 21st, 2005, China started to implement the floating exchange rate system which uses the demand and supply of market as its basis and is subject to regulation and monitoring, with a package of currencies as its frame of reference. Before July 22nd, 2005, the exchange rate of US dollar to RMB is 1–8.2765, while by December 2007, the rate was 1–7.3676, indicating an increase of about 11% and a great tendency for further appreciation of RMB.
4. Market value of listed companies: By the end of 2007, 1,550 companies were listed on domestic market, and 148 on overseas market. The total value of Shanghai and Shenzhen Securities Market was 32.71 trillion yuan (about 4.44 trillion dollars), an increase of 265.91% over the previous year. The circulation market value was 9.31trillion yuan, an increase of 272.2% over the previous year. A-share market raised 772.8 billion yuan within that year, an increase of 217.8% over the previous year. The funds raised by companies listed overseas totaled 107.508 billion US dollars, among which 12.616 billion dollars were raised in 2007.
5. Bond market: By the end of 2007, the total transaction value of bond market totaled 62.91 trillion yuan, with a government bond balance of 5.34 trillion yuan. The par value of government bonds issued in 2007 reached 2.35 trillion yuan, a radical increase of 1.46 trillion yuan over last year. Financial bonds amounted to 1.11trillion yuan, and 37.65 billion yuan sub-prime debt was issued in 2007.

518.1 billion yuan was raised by issuing debenture, among which 334.91 billion yuan was short-term bonds, 171.986 billion yuan enterprise bonds, and 11.2 billion yuan debenture, 124.3 billion yuan more than last year, and an increase of 31.6%.
6. Funds: By the end of 2007, the net value of fund was 3.28 trillion yuan. Fifty-nine were financial institutions with QDII (Qualified Domestic Institutional Investor) qualifications, among which 23 were banks, 20 insurance companies, 12 fund companies and 4 securities companies, with their total investment quota amounting to 45.588 billion dollars. 49 institutions were accredited with QFII qualifications, with their investment quota amounting to 30 billion dollars and 9.995 billion dollars already in use. The total market value of social security funds amounted to 516.2 billion yuan.
7. Futures: The volume of commodity futures transaction reached 40.974 trillion yuan, and financial futures were already under consideration.

As indicated above, China's financial market is based on the operations of commercial banks coexisting with some degree of capital market, which mainly have interest rate, exchange rate, spot goods and futures as its major factors. Though lagging behind western developed countries, China's financial market is no longer what it was, with a complete set of factors, a clear frame of systems and a comprehensive range of functions.

Consequently, modern financial theories, policies, tools and measures should be employed to promote, regulate and monitor the development of modern financial market.

4.2.2 Understanding Finance from the Modern Perspective

As is known to all, the Great Depression from 1929 to 1933 forced many banks to go bankrupt and made countless depositors penniless. In 1933, the Federal Deposit Insurance Corporation (FDIC) was founded and the Glass Steagall Act of 1933 was enacted in the United States. Between 1934 and 1985, American financial industry, inclusive of commercial and investment banking, developed gradually through separate operations and management. Subsequent to 1985, there was a sharp increase in mergers of commercial banks in the US. In 1989, J.P. Morgan started to set foot in securities, insurance and real estate. The enforcement of the American Financial Services Modernization Act in 1999 in the United States brought forth the cross-services of banking, securities and insurance industries and the successive emergence of "financial supermarket".

Modern financial system in China comprises the following components:

1. Financial products: Besides commercial banking services, financial products on the capital market, such as bonds, stock, funds and futures, have come to the scene and have been developing into a more complete set, a greater array of varieties and an increasing volume of transactions.
2. Financial institutions: The framework of modern financial system has been taking shape, with banks, securities, funds, futures, settlements, insurances and exchange offices coexisting with overseas financial institutions.

3. Financial supervision: The monitoring framework of "one bank and three commissions" is typical of modern financial system characterized by the combination of currency market and capital market.

Since the 5-year transition period of China's entry into WTO, the development of domestic financial companies, together with the appearance of international financial institutions, have made Chinese financial industries more competitive and financial investment institutionalized. High technology is an effective means of winning advantages, and competition for talented personnel has become a focal point. Cross-sector, cross-region or even cross-border mergers have started to appear, and "financial supermarkets", which will provide all-round financial services, are already coming into shape. Financial industries have become a new round of areas for economic accrual, with some degree of potential risks.

All this demonstrates that a series of substantial changes have been taking place as a result of financial market transition from traditional banking services to modern financial market, which have pushed China's financial system into a brand-new era. This requires us to understand finance from the modern perspective and take precaution not to let our understanding stop at traditional theories, modes of transaction and supervising measures.

4.2.3 Money Supply Should Take Common Funds of Money Market into Consideration

In the early 1990s, with the gradual perfection of modern financial system, the United States incorporated common funds of institutional and non-institutional money markets respectively into M3 and M2, according to the relation between increased money supply and economic performance. It indicates that the Federal Reserve Board (FRB) of the USA, by analyzing the relation between American economic development and financial market and drawing on examples of financial innovation in actual operations, can formulate effective monetary regulatory policies and objectives for modern financial market.

For example, in 1971, FRB adopted M1, M2 and M3, but mainly M1, as the major regulatory indicators for money supply. After 1987, the emergence of financial innovation and the relaxing of financial control weakened M1's influence on economic performance, and common funds were incorporated into M2 and M3, and then M2 became the major indicator for financial regulation. After 1990, when M2 failed to reflect economic performance, FRB relinquished M1, M2, M3 as regulatory indicators. Instead they took federal interbank loan rate as the object of monetary policy regulation. Those flexible and effective policies and measures in relation to the regulation of money supply were conducive to America's economic growth.

China's financial market is not so well-developed as that in America. Common funds of institutional and non-institutional money markets are not included in M2, the broader indicator of money supply. The key starting point of China's present monetary policy is to prevent inflation, which has posed challenges to the current money supply as well as the previously close relations of credit plans and cash plans to economic performance. There has occurred deviation of the regulation of money supply from the mode of economic growth.

Under the present financial system, the assets structure has been under transformation, interest rate has exerted increasing influence upon stock market, and common funds in money market have also become variables of considerable significance. Although total money supply may not necessarily be adopted in China to regulate macro-economic performance, it is important, in the present stage of modern financial development, to realize the limitation of M1, M2 and M3 in economic regulation, incorporate common funds of institutional and non-institutional money markets into M2 and M3 and adjust and regulate monitoring objects so that money supply or monetary policies conform to the actual economic performance.

4.2.4 *Open Market Operation Is the Main Approach to Macro-financial Regulation*

The improvement of modern financial systems has integrated the regulators of both money market and capital market into monetary regulating instruments. In the United States, monetary regulating instruments include not only the well-known "three magic weapons"—open market operation, discount and rediscount, deposit reserves rate but also the overdrawn rate of securities investment, which is the regulator specially applied to monetary circulation in capital market. Those four instruments are the major regulatory measures of the Federal Reserve, which plays significant roles in promoting economic growth and curbing inflation by taking regulatory measures of money and credit supply.

The goals of monetary regulation are to promote economic growth, stabilize prices, create employment opportunities and guarantee the balance of money flow and credit flow necessary for maintaining the balance of international payments. This equilibrium is achieved by adjusting the reserves of financial institutions in the following ways:

1. Open market operation: Government bonds are bought and sold on the open market so as to influence monetary reserves as well as the total amount of money and credit supply.
2. Discount rate: The discount rate is used to influence savings institutions' investment costs, which will affect loans and investment, and that will ultimately affect m onetary reserves.
3. Deposit reserve rate: The change of deposit reserve rates will affect money multipliers.
4. Overdrawn rate of securities investment: The fluctuation of overdrawn rates of securities investment directly affects investment on securities market.

In the early stage, the discount rate was the major means for the regulation of money and credit flow in the United States, and other regulatory means were added in the later stage. However, it came to be understood that open market operation and deposit reserve rate have the same function to perform, and that open market operation has greater flexibility in actual practice. As the rigidity of deposit reserve rates is susceptible of reduction in money supply, economic depression and its concomitant unemployment, the Federal Reserve called off all the requirements for deposit reserves for all term deposits in December 1990. In addition, the deposit reserve rate for current deposits dropped in April 1992 from 12% to 10%. Countries like Canada, Switzerland, New Zealand and Australia relinquished all such requirements. Open market operation has ever since become the most significant monetary instrument in the modern financial system in developed countries.

China has more monetary instruments than other countries, namely open market operation, rediscount rate, deposit reserve rate, interest rate, credit (or window guidance), central bank loan, credit guidance plan and policy-based loan. China strived to reform monetary instruments and the transmission mechanism of monetary policies in the past. In particular, between 1998 and 2000, open market operation played an important role in helping China out of the Asian Financial Crisis. Other monetary instruments and the transmission mechanism of monetary policies also underwent a lot of transformation.

However, some problems remain to be solved:

1. When all monetary instruments are put into operation, they may conflict with each other and eventually lead to consequences contrary to expectation.
2. From September 21, 2003, when the deposit reserve rate was increased from 6% to 7%, to June 25, 2008, by which date the deposit reserve rate had been increased for 21 times, the rate had risen to 17.5%. All this leads to the wrong impression that China's macro-regulation is simple and limited and that it brings in side effects, such as the slowing down of assets capital growth and the recession of small and medium enterprises, resulting in the bankruptcy of certain enterprises and the increase of unemployment.
3. More importantly, in the shaping and development of modern financial systems, the selection and application of major monetary instruments should be in accordance with market principles rather than executive power. Open market operation, assisted by other monetary policies, is to be the orientation of macro regulation for Chinese modern financial systems.

The selection and application of monetary instruments, though seemingly simple, are actually complicated in China. On the one hand, both the shaping of modern financial systems and the interaction between money market and capital market are the subjects that remain to be explored; on the other hand, errors and deviations will be kept to the minimum in the market-oriented reform and internationalization, as long as explorations are made to improve and implement policies and measures that comply with the development of modern finance.

(First published in *Study Times*, July 28, 2008)

4.3 Foshan's Secrets of Successfully Breaking Out of the 2008 Financial Crisis

Foshan, as one of the first regions in Guangdong to have been struck by the 2008 Financial Crisis, is facing unprecedented challenges and pressures in economic development. However, the Foshan Municipal Committee of CPC and the Foshan Municipal Government are optimistic, affirming that the foundation of Foshan's economy remains sound and opportunities for economic growth still exist, thanks to its competitive basic industries, private enterprises, key enterprises, industrial clusters and brand products.

The 2008 Financial Crisis started in America and spread gradually to the other parts of the world. China's economy, especial that of the Pearl River Delta region, could not keep itself invulnerable to the financial turmoil, which lead some to doubt whether the "Made in Foshan" products could survive the crisis. As remarked by the great Chinese thinker and philosopher Lao Tzu (c. 571 BC-471 BC), "misfortune may be a blessing in disguise". The Chinese expression "危机" (weiji, crisis) actually combines "危" (danger) and "机" (opportunities). What should be done on the part of the government was to convert "danger" into "opportunities" so as to make even greater strides.

That is what Foshan was thinking about and trying hard to do. Foshan took the lead in the Pearl River Delta region to break out of the Financial Crisis. In 2009, Foshan's GDP reached 481.45 billion yuan, an increase of 13.5% over the same period of the previous year and with an excess of 2.5% compared with the expected target.

Two patterns for the development of the manufacturing industry in the Pearl River Delta region have emerged—the Eastern Pearl River pattern and the Western Pearl River pattern. The former, represented by Dongguan, focuses on the processing industry, is typically characterized by its international feature, i.e. raw materials being purchased from and products being sold to outside China rather than in China. The latter, represented by Foshan, Zhongshan and Zhuhai, has its own lines of industries, name brands as well as marketing networks. Most enterprises are privately owned and have grouped into industrial clusters. Their products are mainly sold on the domestic market. The private characteristic of its economy and self-initiated innovative capacities explain why Foshan can maintain a strong and steady momentum for economic development.

The two patterns resulted in variations in Foshan's economic performance during the 2008 Financial Crisis. The root causes for such variations are:

1. Industrial structure: In Foshan, for example, the secondary industry accounts for around 65% of its GDP, with industrial manufacturing forming the foundation of its economy.
2. Two-wheel driving: Foshan's economy is powered and driven by the two wheels of private enterprises and foreign-invested enterprises. Its private enterprises in the present stage perform as pillars of its industries and have strong capacities against financial risks and malaises.
3. Effect of large enterprises: Foshan boosts over 2,200 enterprises whose output value exceeds 100 million yuan, over 250 enterprises whose output value lies

between 1 billion and 10 billion yuan, and six enterprises whose output value exceeds 10 billion yuan. All those enterprises were not seriously affected in the crisis.
4. Excellent entrepreneurs: Entrepreneurs in Foshan have grown up through hardships and possess enough wisdom to cope with difficult situations.
5. Industrial upgrading and self-initiated innovation: Foshan proposes the strategy of five-stage development for enterprises. During the first stage, a solid foundation is to be laid, during the second name brands are to be developed, during the third patents are to be registered, during the fourth standards are to be established and recognized as industrial, national or even international standards, and during the fifth brands, patents and standards are to be franchised for OEM (Original Equipment Manufacture) by other enterprises.

Foshan, as one of the first regions in Guangdong to have been struck by the 2008 Financial Crisis, is facing unprecedented challenges and pressures. However, the Foshan Municipal Committee of CPC and the Foshan Municipal Government have faced the crisis with optimism and confidence, affirming that the foundation of Foshan's economy remains sound and opportunities for economic growth still exist, thanks to its competitive basic industries, private enterprises, key enterprises, industrial clusters and brand products. Therefore, Foshan must take firm steps, grasp opportunities and proceed with wisdom and initiatives to cope with the crisis.

America's sub-prime crisis led us to speculate that it would aggravate industrial economy and would eventually evolve into a world-wide financial crisis. In the light of this observation, The Foshan Municipal Committee of CPC and The Municipal Government of Foshan paid immediate and serious attention to the situation and sent delegations to the grass-roots units to hold about 20 discussions about the economic situation. Visits were paid to more than 100 enterprises. They predicted that the international economy would move in a U-curve in 2009, while China's economy would go in a V-curve.

To cope with the delicate situation, the municipal government put forth a timely document "*Decisions concerning the Promotion of Rapid and Steady Economic Growth in Foshan*", which put into operation 42 measures categorized into ten classes for the purpose of increasing investment, expanding domestic demand and facilitating the rapid and steady growth and upgrading of Foshan's economy. The document also planned for 102 key construction projects to be launched in order to absorb a total investment of about 180 billion yuan through government promotion, enterprise participation and market operation, and a total of 120 billion yuan was put into use between 2009 and 2010.

Government assistance and support were strengthened to encourage enterprises to "swim" in winter rather than "hibernate". A series of preferential policies were implemented to benefit enterprises, such as export tax rebate, the conversion of added value tax, the reduction and elimination of administrative charges, the implementation of national revival programs. New markets, both domestic and international, were opened to promote sales of household appliances, machinery equipments and textiles made in Foshan.

Enterprises were encouraged to exploit and expand domestic markets through a series of sales promotions, such as selling household appliances to the rural residents, subsidizing the purchasing of agricultural machines, and launching promotional sales of Made-in-Guangdong products. In order to stabilize exports, more financial assistance and support were provided to encourage enterprises to expand overseas markets by ways of exhibitions and trade talks.

The financing problem was solved in due course to ensure the granting of the 280 billion yuan line of credit approved by six commercial banks. The new additions of loans reached 227.3 billion yuan for the whole of 2009, with 131.2 billion yuan loaned to enterprises. The government set up platforms for small and medium-sized enterprises (SMEs) to raise capital. More than 3,000 enterprises participated in talks between the government, the bank, the guarantor and the enterprise. Financing guarantee mechanisms were established and improved, and guarantee institutions provided financing assurance of 8.3 billion yuan for 1,880 enterprises in 2009.

As the old saying goes, it is more opportune to overtake at a bend. Foshan took advantage of the financial crisis to enhance its optimization and upgrading of the industrial structure. It was assumed that the crisis signified both the risk of traditional modes of development and the opportunity for scientific modes of development. The central task was to ensure economic growth. However, measures must be taken not to revert to the former modes of low quality growth but to make use of the financial crisis to transform Foshan's economic growth from the traditional mode to the scientific mode.

Foshan is the base for traditional manufacturing, and its traditional industry accounts for a large portion of its economy. However, traditional industry does not necessarily stand for "backwardness" and can be reformed and converted into modern manufacturing by means of information technology and advanced applicable technology. In recent years, Foshan aimed at forging itself into an international city of ceramics, a center of household appliances, an industrial base of flat panel displays, and unique national industrial bases for professional machinery equipment, the processing and manufacturing of metallic materials, furniture, new materials, auto and auto components, food and beverage, textile products, energy-saving and environment protection products, and medical care. Foshan was determined to implement the strategy of "three groups of industries", that is to weed out a group of industries of low capacity and productivity, to upgrade a group of traditional industries, and to cultivate a group of newly emerging industries.

Self-developed brands and self-initiated innovation form the core of competitiveness and are the most effective way to resist financial risks. Foshan regarded it as a task of primary importance to promote capacities of self-initiated innovation so as to cope with financial crises and enhance competitiveness. In 2009, Foshan took advantage of being selected as the key demonstrative city for Guangdong's new-round cooperation with The Chinese Academy of Sciences to promote strategic cooperation under which the incubation center of industrial technology innovation was set up and 100 cooperative projects between enterprises and institutions were established. In addition, Foshan cooperated with the Ministry of Science and Technology and Guangdong Province to build the national torch high-tech business incubator and implement "The Ten Billion Program for One Thousand Projects of Technological Renovation and Innovation". Enterprises were organized to participate in 1,000 projects of technological renovation and innovation, drawing a total investment of 10 billion yuan.

By 2009, five cooperative innovation coalitions of Industry, University and Research Institutes at provincial or ministerial levels were formed in Foshan, with 33 demonstrative bases set up and 21 colleges and universities opening offices there. Among them, 18 were established by research institutes. Another 13 studios were set up for academicians. In addition, 493 engineering and technology development centers were founded for enterprises of different levels, 19 public platforms were created for technological services at the level of township, and nine incubators were set up for high-tech businesses to emerge.

Thanks to the municipal government's efforts to promote the registration of patents and name brands and the establishment of industrial standards, 1,853 inventions applied for patents and 646 of them were granted approval by the end of 2009, an increase of 17.7% and 76.5% respectively over the previous year. Nine brands were added to the list of well-known national trademarks. Foshan participated in establishing and issuing 105 national standards and eight industrial standards.

Reform is not only a driving force for development but also an important guarantee for scientific development. The financial crisis, which came all of a sudden and caused throbs of pain, intensified urgency for reforms, pushed reform forward at an accelerating pace and provided the historical opportunity for deepening reforms in systems and mechanisms. The debut of *the Outline* provided a good chance for Foshan to deepen its reform in major sectors under the guideline of "scientific development, first execution, first trial".

First, as the starting point, the most important, the most urgent and the more fundamental problems and the problems that the public complain about and resent must be tackled as early as possible. Thus, reforms in public welfare sectors, such as medical care and social pension systems, must be given prior prominence.

Secondly, the transformation of government functions was carried out to especially streamline their administrative structures and operations. The number of Foshan Municipal Government departments has been reduced from 33 to 31. Shunde District undertook the most intensive reform and reduced the number of its administrative departments from 41 to 16.

Thirdly, substantial support from the municipal government was provided for the Shunde District Government to practice as a pilot region of comprehensive reforms that entitled it to enforce the administrative power of a prefecture-level city in economic, social and cultural areas. The departments at the municipal level delegated the authorities of 616 administrative items to the Shunde government so that it could exercise operative powers in these items.

Fourth, reform was conducted in Shishan Town in Nanhai District and Ronggui Town in Shunde District as pilot towns with the principle of "administration simplified and township strengthened". Except for what must be coordinated and administered by the district government, the two pilot towns are entitled to county-level administrative powers in such areas as economic development, market supervision, public service, social administration and welfare undertakings.

Apart from all this, reforms in administrative formalities, public institutions, investment and financing, and financial systems were also speeding up.

The focus on welfare undertakings provides the social bedrock for coping with international financial crises, and the essence of scientific development resides in abiding by the principle of "people first". People are entitled to enjoy the fruits of social development so that they have enough money to spend and have no worries about their life expenses. Accordingly, domestic demands will be expanded and consumption increased. Thus, the economy will be driven by great domestic demands and develop in a sound way.

On the one hand, the structure of fiscal expenditure should be optimized, and more support should be given to the sectors of agriculture, employment, social pension, education and medical care. The government should give more assistance and subsidies to families of low income. To improve social pension systems, the government should invest more to raise the social security standard for people of low income and increase pension and veteran benefits. Public finance should be favorably inclined towards welfare undertakings. Between 2008 and 2009, Foshan expended 20.147 billion yuan and 23.698 billion yuan of the general fiscal budget on public services and for the improvement of people's living conditions, accounting for 82.5% and 88.76% of the general fiscal expenditure budget respectively.

The government made annual plans to undertake ten projects relating closely to people's life. In 2008, the housing project for homeless fishermen was carried out to help them live ashore, and their housing problem was eventually solved. The range of free compulsory education was expanded so that free compulsory education could cover the 13 categories of children who were not registered residents in Foshan. Primary out-patient medical treatment insurance for residents and employees was established for Foshan to become the first city in Guangdong or even in China to move into the era of "healthcare for all people". There was also an increase in the basic pension for enterprise retirees and subsistence allowances for impoverished residents.

In 2009, 2,440 affordable apartments were built to meet the basic housing requirements. Agricultural insurance for rice covered all rural areas. Hospitalization insurance for urban residents was planed by the city as a whole. The reimbursement range of primary medical treatment was broadened. Forty-five new community health service stations were set up and 205 community health service stations were equipped with information infrastructures. Special missions were launched to rectify the pig and meat market and guarantee food safety. One hundred and thirty two projects were carried out to reconstruct and renovate drinking water supply facilities in old revolutionary base areas. In the past 2 years, the government had fulfilled its annual promises to complete ten livelihood-related projects. The hot issues that people cared about most were solved. All this contributed considerably to the guarantee and improvement of the subsistence and welfare of the people and laid a solid foundation for coping with the international financial crisis.

The year 2010 was crucial for consolidating the achievements in coping with the international financial crisis and maintaining rapid and yet steady economic growth. The outlook on scientific development was put into effect, and measures were taken to make sure that *the Outline* would be fully implemented. The government focused on promoting economic growth, adjusting industrial structure, reforming and improving people's life. Measures were taken to transform the mode of economic development, expand domestic demands, and adjust industrial structure on a regular basis so as to establish a modern industrial system. Moreover, the municipal government quickened its steps of regional urban-rural integration, adhered unswervingly to the policy of reform and opening-up, promoted self-initiated innovation, guaranteed and improved the subsistence of the people so that social economy would gain speedy and healthy development. To be specific, the following objectives were to be emphasized and achieved:

1. The government unswervingly adjusted industrial structure and promoted the quality and efficiency of economic growth. Adjusting industrial structure was the number one economic project for Foshan in 2010.

   First, the structure of demand was optimized. All the national and provincial policies and measures of expanding domestic demands were put into effect. The government made more efforts to control the over-heated real estate market, invested more to improve the subsistence of the people, improved social pension systems, enhanced income and consumption capacities of the citizen, boosted the upturn of exports, guided and supported enterprises to expand into new international markets while maintaining traditional domestic markets.

   Second, effective measures were taken to promote urban-rural integration. The Central Economic Working Conference pointed out that industrial structure should be optimized so that urbanization would be steadily pushed ahead. Considering Foshan's situation, the municipal government made great efforts to quicken urban-rural integration. More fiscal budget was planned for the countryside, more public infrastructure was extended into the countryside, and more public services were provided to the countryside. Consequently, a new mode of urban-rural development was taking shape, which greatly improved and heightened the comprehensive capacities for industry, resources, talents and information.

   Third, the reconstruction of "three outmodes" got started and was making headway. The reconstruction, as part of structural adjustment, was to be conducted and pushed forward according to plans and by steps so that the "532 project" (i.e. an area of 50,000 μ to be renovated and reconstructed by 2010, another 30,000 μ by 2011, and another 20,000 μ by 2012), would be launched and completed through reconstruction. Within 3 years, the dream of "building up a new Foshan" will come true. Among the 100,000 μ under renovation and reconstruction, 69,800 μ, which were used for industrial and storage purpose, would be reallocated for innovative, high-tech and highly value-added enterprises, resulting in a gradual shift of the mode of economic growth in Foshan from "Made in Foshan" to "Created in Foshan".

   Fourth, modern service industry was to be developed to the greatest possible extent. Equal importance and attention were paid to both manufacturing service and daily-necessity service. Specific measures were taken to launch and carry out "the 314 program" for service industry, i.e. within 3 years, 100 key projects of modern service industry to be set up, and by 2012, the added value of tertiary industry taking up more than 40% of Foshan's GDP. Twelve modern service industry zones would be developed with distinct functions, extra-large scale and strong radiating forces. Commercial centers and key projects, such as Linnan World, Outlets and Yundonghai Tourist Resort, should be constructed at an accelerating rate.

Fifth, new-type strategic industry was developing fast. The municipal government made careful studies of industrial guiding policies and industrial revitalization programs issued by the central government, completed and implemented the development plan for the 15 key industries in Foshan, tried to set up funds for fostering the new-type industry, built 12 leading industrial bases with strong self-initiated innovative capacities and a wide range of radiating forces, and accelerated the development of such key projects as flat panel LCD (liquid crystal display), radio frequency, photovoltaic, film solar energy, and South China gene valley.

2. Full play was given to the strategic role of key projects that drove Foshan's economy onto a fast and steady track. The government played its role in planning, application and approval of the key projects. In 2010, Foshan approved 250 key construction projects on the municipal level, with a total investment of about 310.1 billion yuan. Fifty-nine projects were listed as key construction projects on the provincial level, with a total investment of about 227.4 billion yuan. And an array of reserved projects invested by the central government was under application. More importantly, the government highlighted the planning of key projects for investment and construction. The work plans for the projects, especially those whose funds had been granted, were worked out in details so that the projects could be launched in due course. Respecting the projects that were approved or already in operation, the government supplied a variety of services and monitored them to speed up their construction so that they would be completed as scheduled. As for those projects that had not been started, the government helped complete the formalities and solve the problems of location selection and capital collection so that they would be put into operation as soon as possible.
3. Continuous efforts were made to further implement *the Outline* and accelerate the integration of regional economy. *The Plan for Integrated Development of Guangzhou and Foshan* was put into effect to advance the integrated operation of Guangzhou and Foshan. Efforts were also made to construct key cooperative projects, such as road and bridge construction and environmental protection, which were to be completed before the opening of the Asian Games. Meanwhile, the integrated development of finance, communication and logistics were facilitated, and the cooperation in the sectors of culture, tourism and social utility were strengthened.

In order to merge into the integrated development of Pearl River Delta, Foshan carried out the five plans for specific projects aiming at the integration of the Pearl River Delta regions, especially the link-up plan for Foshan's involvement in the construction of the bridge which was to connect Hongkong, Zhuhai and Macau. Foshan incorporated itself into the transportation network of the Pearl River Delta, rendered assistance to the construction of railways (rail transit) and expressways, practiced the mutual recognition of annual transportation tickets, and opened inter-city bus lines.

The first 37 key cooperative projects, which were intended to enforce *the Guangzhou, Foshan and Zhaoqing Economic Cooperation Framework Agreement*, were pushed ahead with vigor. Foshan strengthened its all-round cooperation with Hongkong and Macau, and strove to be the pilot city for the cooperation of Guangdong, Hongkong and Macau. Meanwhile, communication with Hongkong was conducted to promote the 23 projects already signed in the areas of modern service industry, and policy support were obtained by implementing CEPA (Closer Economic Partnership Arrangement) and its complementary protocols and hosting forums on the demonstrative city under CEPA. Foshan also availed itself of the opportunity of joining the Guangdong-Singapore Cooperative Board to heighten its level of foreign economic cooperation and strengthen its ties with ASEAN (the Association of Southeast Asian Nations).

4. Reform and innovation were speeded up in key sectors so that systems and mechanisms conducive to scientific development were in place. To deepen reforms, those systems and mechanisms that impeded the scientific and harmonious development of the society were eliminated so that substantial progress was made in some key sectors at critical stages. Reforms were implemented and pushed to a higher level in administrative systems, the restructuring of government institutions at all levels, the streamlining of government operations. More support was provided to Shunde District to make it a pilot zone for overall reforms.

   Further reforms was conducted in administrative examination and approval systems. Administrative services of higher quality and efficiency not only reached the five districts of Foshan but also extended to the villages distant from city centers. The restructuring of administrative authorities was promoted under the principle of "administration simplified, township strengthened". It is worthwhile to summarize and popularize successful experience from Shishan and Ronggui's practice as pilot towns of restructuring administrative powers. The mode of rural community administration was brought into being to perform the functions of social administration and public services. Reforms in social administrative systems were accelerated. Social organizations, such as industrial associations, chambers of commerce, charitable institutions, were encouraged to be formed. Deeper reforms in fiscal and financial systems became urgent. More fiscal expenditure were used to support and guarantee the subsistence and welfare of the people. The three plans for financial development were put into effect to encourage active financial innovation and develop capital market so that more enterprises would go public and more capital would be raised for further development. Eventually, a "Foshan sector" on the stock market will emerge.

5. More substantial measures were taken to improve people's livelihood and forge a harmonious Foshan. Continuous efforts were made to consolidate the accomplishments of environmental protection achieved in the course of applying for National Demonstrative Cities for Environmental Protection and advance environmental protection and ecological environment construction. Since ecological environment is the most essential aspect of people's livelihood, the government

took advantage of hosting Asian Games to advocate regional joint efforts to deal with air pollution and sewage, bring forward the design and construction of "Green Roads", and strengthen the measures of energy saving and emission reduction so as to build a comfortable and environment-friendly city.

Continuous efforts were made to turn into reality the promises of the municipal government to complete the ten key projects related to people's livelihood, such as building affordable houses, implementing new rural endowment insurance systems, policy-based agricultural insurance and subsidies for basic farmland protection, refurnishing and repairing primary and secondary school buildings and housings for poor families, strengthening the capacity of providing public health service, and increasing basic pensions for enterprise retirees.

Continuous efforts were made to further improve the integration of urban-rural employment service systems and build incubator bases to encourage the initiation of businesses so as to promote employment, especially the employment of university graduates and people in poor conditions and in financial difficulty.

Finally, more government support was given to various social undertakings, such as culture, education and sports. Supervision was strengthened to monitor law and order, social administration, food safety, work safety, and epidemic prevention and control. All these efforts helped build a harmonious society.

4.4 Taking Active Steps to Construct the Modern Industrial System

The increasing scarcity of such production factors as land resources, the continuously limited supply of work force, the rise of production cost, the increase in industrial upgrading difficulty and the limitations of natural resources and environment deem it highly necessary to transform the mode of economic growth from scale expansion to structural upgrading and to optimize resources allocation.

One of the most important aspects of transforming the mode of economic growth and maintaining scientific development is to promote industrial upgrading. For years, Foshan took advantageous opportunities to actively optimize and upgrade the industrial structure so as to construct a modern industrial system, which displays peculiar features of Foshan as well as conforming to the international practice.

1. No efforts were spared to nurture and develop advanced manufacturing industry. The most important aspect of establishing the modern industrial system is to improve and heighten the standards of manufacturing industry. Aiming to upgrade its industrial structure, cluster its industrial enterprises and intensify its factors of production, Foshan established three world-class industrial bases, i.e. "the household appliances center", "the industrial base for flat panel displays", and "the city of ceramics", and nine unique national industrial bases, such as the base for professional machinery equipment and the base for medicine and health-care products.

All these were of great significance for updating the technology of traditional industry and cementing and elevating the status of pillar industries. In financial terms, 100 million yuan arranged in the municipal fiscal budget was spent in supporting the application of information technology to industrialization so that information technology would be integrated with advanced applicable technology. The development of advanced manufacturing and the upgrading of traditional industry helped Foshan raise its position in the world industrial manufacturing system.

2. Every effort were made to accelerate the development of modern service industry, which was crucial for upgrading industrial structure and fostering new strains of economic growth. Foshan, as a "CEPA demonstrative city of the Ministry of Commerce" and the CEPA pilot city of Guangdong Province, took the chance to strengthen its cooperation with Hong Kong and Macau, develop with great efforts modern logistics (especially TPL, third party logistics), speed up the construction of China-Singapore Modern Logistics Park and South China Purchasing and Distribution Center, and accelerate the construction of the modern logistics hub so that better conditions would be created to attract more enterprises.

   The integration of innovative industry with traditional industry were encouraged, and the construction of industrial parks and bases, such as Chancheng Innovative Industrial Park, Nanhai Animation and Virtual High-tech Business Incubator and Shunde National Industrial Design and Innovation Base, were accelerated. What's more, financial innovation was propelled, especially the construction of New Guangdong High-tech Financial Service Center, so as to provide financial backstage service. Exhibition resources were also employed to prepare for international professional exhibitions.

3. The capacity of self-initiated innovation was enhanced. As Foshan's economy entered into a new stage of growth, one of the important tasks of transforming the mode of development was to shift from "resource-driven" to "innovation-driven". More support and priority was given to enterprises with their own name brands, stronger competitiveness and greater capacity of self-initiated innovation so that they would become bigger and stronger.

   The special fund for economic and technological development was utilized for 100 enterprises to build technological innovation platforms, help small and medium enterprises in technological renewal and innovation to make their technology "high", "new", "special" and "excellent". Foshan established joint projects with the Ministry of Science and Technology and Guandong Province to co-build Foshan National Torch Innovation High-tech Business Incubator. Assistance was provided to large and medium enterprises in industrializing new and high technology through self-initiated research and innovation so as to expand into the world's high-end market.

   The government quickened the construction of public innovation platforms, establish regional and industrial innovation service systems, such as industrial clusters, specialized townships and industrial bases, and set up and improve industrial innovation platforms covering five major industrial lines like product research and development.

   "The Ten Billion Program for One Thousand Projects of Technological Renovation and Innovation" was being implemented with a view to establishing key projects of self-initiated innovation, helping enterprises renew technologies and developing new products. Foshan Incubation Center for Industrial Technological Innovation was set up to promote the application of self-initiated innovations and their commercialization and industrialization. Foshan, as the demonstrative city of national intellectual property, encouraged enterprises to participate in the research and establishment of industrial technological standards. In order to build a first-class incubator in China, Foshan accelerated the construction of the national park for new and high technology consisting of "one zone and six industrial parks" and its incubation system. What's more, the integration of production, teaching and research were promoted so as to solve the bottleneck of key technology. Enterprises were supported and encouraged to develop name brands and implement the brand-driven strategy. Competitive enterprises developed their national or international brands.

4. Industrial structure was adjusted and optimized. The increasing scarcity of such production factors as land resources, the continuously limited supply of work force, the rise of production cost, the increase in industrial upgrading difficulty and the limitations of natural resources and environment deemed it highly necessary to transform the mode of economic growth from scale expansion to structural upgrading and to optimize resources allocation.

   To enhance the comprehensive competitiveness of industries, the Foshan government took a series of measures, such as removing labor-intensive enterprises at the low-end of industrial lines and with low added values out of the Pearl River Delta and building industrial parks in Qingyuan City and Yunfu City, to make more room for high added-value businesses from both home and abroad, such as advanced manufacturing industry, new high-tech industry and modern service industry. The Foshan government planned to spend no less than 100 million yuan annually from 2009 to 2013 of newly added fiscal revenues or general budget expenditures to co-build industrial transfer parks, coupled with the implementation and improvement of the policies and mechanisms for "double transfer".

(First published in *The People's Daily*, December 22, 2009)

4.5 Optoelectronics Industry: The Newly Emerging Sector of Foshan's Industry

Foshan, as the new national demonstrative base for industrialization, will develop itself in the way consistent with the national strategy for development and the plan of Guangdong Province to quicken the transform of modes of economic growth and the adjustment of industrial structure. In a new round of development, Foshan draws up the plan of development in advance, seizes the opportunity of financial crises to initiate industrial restructuring, focuses on and supports the development of new strategic industries such as optoelectronics industry so that Foshan's economy will grow on a sound base.

March 25, 2010 witnessed the launch of the construction project of Guangdong New Light Source Industry Base.

Previously, a joint venture of SemiLEDs corporation, one of the three biggest global LED chip manufacturers, was founded in Foshan. Thus Foshan was awarded the title of "The New National Demonstrative Base for Industrialization". LED, lighting and PV industry, which emerge unexpectedly and have developed from scratch, are now Foshan's new strategic industries and have become the envy of the world, which has not happened by accident.

Judging from the national and international situations and the status quo of China's economic development, it will be an issue of primary importance in the Twelfth Five-year Plan (2011–2015) to quicken the transform of modes of economic development, which is also the demand of the national strategy for economic development, particularly owing to the demand of modern industrial structuring and development subsequent to the 2008 international financial crisis. Foshan, as the new national demonstrative base for industrialization, will develop itself in the way consistent with the national strategy for development and the plan of Guangdong Province to quicken the transform of modes of economic growth and the adjustment of industrial structure. In a new round of development, Foshan draws up the plan of development in advance, seizes the opportunity of financial crises to initiate industrial restructuring, focuses on and supports the development of new strategic industries such as optoelectronics industry so that Foshan's economy will grow on a sound base.

So far, over 230 lighting enterprises have been set up in Foshan whose annual output value reached 20 billion yuan in 2009. The fact that international lighting corporations, such as OSRAM and America's SemiLEDs, one of the world top class LED enterprises, provides solid proof that world-class enterprises with first class technology have shown an especially keen interest in Foshan.

The former lighting enterprises in Foshan, which were mostly located at the lower end or the middle part of the industrial line, together with the newly introduced upper-end enterprises, form an orderly chain of lighting industry. Besides the two listed lighting companies—Foshan Electrical and Lighting Corporation and CnLight, Foshan NationStar Optoelectronics Corporation also joined in the chain in 2010. All this demonstrates the bright prospects of lighting industry as well as the strength of Foshan. The Semiconductor lighting industry in Foshan is of considerable scale and advanced and well-developed enterprises take up a considerable proportion. There is great hope that the lighting industry in Foshan will be developed and expanded to the greatest extent possible once combined with capital market.

Let's turn to the LED industry. According to a survey, only five enterprises in the world are capable of producing the 7.5-generation OLED (organic light-emitting diode) LCD panel. ChiMei Innolux Corporation in Nanhai District of Foshan has been trying to introduce this high technology. The OLED project, which is launched by Guangdong Sinodisplay Technology Corporation together with Hong Kong University of Science and Technology, is now in operation in Nanhai. IRICO Group, which produced the first CRT in China, has also established its OLED project in Shunde, and the project is now under operation.

Three top class LCD and OLED enterprises have set up their branches in Foshan, whose annual output value reaches 25 billion yuan in 2010, an increase of 18% over the previous year. It shows that LED industry in Foshan, aiming to be the first class LED base in the world, not only possesses the most advanced technology in the world but also forges an orderly and stable industrial line and cluster.

Comparatively speaking, PV industry in Foshan, which focuses on film solar energy, is still in its infancy. However, with supporting infrastructures and strength, Foshan will introduce a lot of big projects of PV industry and accelerate the development of upper and lower lines of film solar energy industry in clusters so as to form a complete line of PV industry which will be the powerful engine of the whole Foshan industry.

The industry of LED, lighting and PV in Foshan boasts not only world-class technology but also industrial clusters and lines. Foshan has a clear picture of its future optoelectronics industry: in 2012, the output value of LED industry will reach 170 billion yuan, and the output value of lighting and PV industry will exceed 80 billion yuan. By that time, the New National Demonstrative Base for Industrialization in Foshan will be the largest-scale base in China and an important global base of LED, lighting and PV industry.

The formation of business clusters and industrial chains manifests a bright prospect for the development of LED, lighting and PV industry in Foshan. However, we should not take blind pride, since optoelectronics industry in Foshan is confronted with complicated situations in its development: on the one hand, first-rate enterprises from home and abroad with world-class technology have been established in Foshan, which enables Foshan to be chosen as the national demonstrative base, on the other hand, industrial clusters are still of small scale and in their early stage of development, and private enterprises remain at the middle part or the lower end of the industrial line, while foreign enterprises or projects launched through investment from outside sources occupy the upper end.

Optoelectronic industry accounts for an insignificant part of Foshan's total industrial output value, compared with other industries. In 2009, the total industrial output value reaches 1.2 trillion yuan, 20 billion yuan of which is contributed by lighting industry and 25 billion yuan by LED industry. The total output value of the two industries only account for 4% of the total industrial output value.

What should be done to make the national industrial demonstrative base worthy of its title?

According to the municipal plan, by 2012 a three-dimensioned development pattern of LED, lighting and PV industry will be taking shape, which will highlight the development of LCD and OLED industry. The demonstrative base will cover three regions: Nanhai and Shunde mainly for LED manufacturing, Sanshui mainly for Guangdong unique PV industry base, and Nanhai and Chanchen for Guangdong new light source industry. These regions ought to further develop their existing industries, introduce relevant large-scale new projects with more radiating power and driving force, nurture local locomotive enterprises and guide them to the upper end of the industrial line so as to build unique industrial clusters. Meanwhile, three to five optoelectronic industrial clusters with considerable competitiveness in the world are to be established and two to three national industrial technology service platforms and institutions are to be set up.

It is also important that effective measures be taken to support the development of optoelectronic industry. Foshan takes pride in its admirable cooperative platforms for production, training and research. More than 100 projects have been put into operation in cooperation with the Chinese Academy of Sciences. In addition, Foshan boasts a "one region and six parks" national high-tech zone that enjoys a series of preferential policies. Moreover, Foshan has 34 specialized towns of national fame, which have all titled their names to street communities. How to make good use of all these platforms for the development of newly industrialized bases is a question worthy of serious consideration.

At the same time, relevant supplementary policies should be improved, such as policies of land use, interest subsidy or direct investment. Government at all levels in Foshan will set 1 billion yuan aside annually to encourage the advance of science and technology and self-initiated innovation. In 2009, 30.8 billion yuan was invested to guide businesses to undertake technological innovation, an increase of more than 39% over the previous year. However, only a limited portion was spent for the industry of LED, lighting and PV. Therefore, it requires joint efforts on the part of both the municipal and lower-level government to invest more money for the support of optoelectronic industry, its technology incubation and its personnel recruitment and training.

The best approach to the development of high-tech industry is the introduction, absorption and innovation of new technologies. Strenuous efforts should be made to develop and accumulate our high-tech industries so as to keep pace with developed countries.

4.6 "Predicament Release" Through Financial Innovation

The financial objectives of Foshan are set as follows: to embrace the financial radiation of Hong Kong, Macau, Guangzhou and Shenzhen and accelerate the development of financial backstage services and outsourcing services through undertaking the transfer of international financial industry so as to turn Foshan into a pilot base for innovative financial cooperation between Guangdong, Hong Kong and Macau, an important financial backstage service pivot and the advanced region for the harmonious development of national finance and economy and with strong financial service capabilities.

In 2009, when the export slipped down about 15.1%, the GDP of Foshan kept an increase of about 13.5%. Foshan was released from the financial crisis through financial service innovation. Statistics will illustrate the fact. In 2009, Foshan invested 43.659 billion yuan in the manufacturing industry, a decrease of 3% over the previous year, and 90.79 billion yuan in the tertiary industry, an increase of 19.6% over the previous year. The investment in the manufacturing industry more than doubled that in the tertiary industry. The tertiary industry accounted for 35.1%

of Foshan's 2009 GDP, an increase of 2.6% over its overall GDP. The statistics indicate that it is time for Foshan to develop modern service industry and transform the modes of economic growth in its "post-industrialization" age of highly developed manufacturing industry. Financial service should rank top and enjoy priority among all the sectors of service industry.

One important aspect of Foshan's financial innovation is to take effective measures to help small and medium enterprises remove the difficulty of financing. Small and medium enterprises, as the backbone of Foshan's economy, had special difficulties in financing due to the international financial crisis. To solve the problem, Foshan set up Financing Service Center for Small and Medium Enterprises, the first platform of its kind in Guangdong Province which provides direct online financing services for small and medium enterprises.

Meanwhile, Foshan has established and improved financing assurance systems for small and medium enterprises and developed a great variety of assurance and re-assurance institutions. By the end of 2009, assurance institutions provided assurance services for 7,000 enterprises with a total deposit of 26 billion yuan. Another major innovation is to popularize Shunde's method of establishing credit assurance funds in the whole of Foshan. What's more, the Foshan government supports financial institutions to promote new kinds of loans on credit for small and medium enterprises. Some banks promote "supply chain finance" service. China Construction Bank cooperates with Guangdong Re-assurance Company to promote "quick assurance" services and increase the ratio of asset back. Nanhai District experiments on financing by backing intellectual property. In addition, Foshan helps small and medium enterprises solve the problem of financing by equity financing.

Guangdong Financial High-tech Service Zone established in Nanhai is another good example. By now, about 100 domestic and overseas financial institutions from the sectors of banking, insurance, securities, assurance, funds and financial BPO (business process outsourcing) have come to exchange ideas and negotiated possible collaboration. Twenty-three of them have signed agreements and opened offices in Nanhai, such as the backstage service center of American International Assurance (AIA) in Asian Pacific Region, the information center of People's Insurance Company of China (PICC) in South China, and the backstage service center of Hong Kong Sun Hung Kai Financial Group and China Merchants Bank, with a total investment of 6.5 billion yuan and a total gross floor area of 1.03 million square meters.

At present, five of these enterprises, such as AIA, PICC, have initiated the construction of their office buildings. The information center building of PICC in South China has sealed the roof, and the backstage service center building of AIA is under full construction. Hong Kong Sun Hung Kai comprehensive financial service zone, China Merchants Bank and China Everbright Bank have drawn up their plan of construction. Guangdong Financial High-tech Service Zone, as a backstage service base of Guangzhou, Shenzhen and Hong Kong, will assume greater responsibilities and perform more important duties in the development of Guangdong's financial industry and play a more significant role in the strategy of building up a stronger financial Province of Guangdong.

In the 2008 and 2009 financial crisis, financial industry played an important role in releasing Foshan from financial predicament. In 2010, the focus of financial innovation was laid on the optimization of financial recourses allocation, the support and speed-up of industrial upgrading and restructuring and the removal of financial difficulties and conflicts in in-depth development.

In 2010, Foshan will work out a detailed 3-year plan of financial development with specified details of measures and tasks to be taken in terms of cooperation between Guangdong, Hong Kong and Macau, the unification of Guangzhou and Foshan, and the setting-up of rural financial systems.

First, the innovation projects, one of the three plans for financial development will be operated in an all-round way, and new innovation projects, such as setting up banks of villages and towns, debts for small and medium enterprises, and funds for talents cultivation, are to be added to the plan according to the actual situation. Insurance companies, securities and futures institutions will play a more important role in personal investment and wealth management so that more people will enjoy better financial services with greater convenience and efficiency.

Second, in order to solve the bottle-neck of financing for small and medium enterprises, it is necessary to establish an all-round financing service system by ways of innovation and standardized development. Financial means and fiscal budget measures are to be taken to encourage banks to increase loans for small and medium enterprises.

Third, Foshan will continue its reform of rural credit cooperatives and establish microfinance organizations, assurance companies, village and town banks so that the financial system will be much more diversified and optimized. It is necessary to better the management of microfinancial organizations and assurance companies as well as the construction of Guangdong Financial High-tech Zone. It is urgent to carry out the instructions of Wang Yang, secretary of Guangdong Provincial Committee of CPC so as to obtain more policy and financial support and enhance competitive edges of Guangdong Financial High-tech Zone.

Lastly, Foshan will quicken the steps of enterprises being listed on the stock market, take full advantage of the emergence of second board market to expand the “Foshan Plate” in the securities market and encourage listed companies to refinance.

Foshan will avail itself of the advantages and rich resources to achieve breakthroughs in financial innovation from four aspects:

First, thought must be given to Foshan’s economic features in its financial innovation. As small and medium private enterprises in the manufacturing industry constitute the main body of Foshan’s economy, more support should be devoted to expanding and strengthening small and medium enterprises and helping them remove financial difficulties via capital market, as part of Foshan’s financial innovation.

Second, the geographic advantage of Foshan should be brought into full play for financial innovation. As is known to all, Foshan is situated in the center of the Pear River Delta, bordering Guangzhou in the east and adjoining Hong Kong and Macau in the south. Foshan should avail itself of the geographic advantage on the one hand to cooperate with Hong Kong and Macau and introduce more financial institutions to establish offices and branches by means of CEPA, and on the other hand, to propel the unification of Foshan and Guangzhou, encourage financial institutions to set up branches in both places and unify their accountant settlements. In addition, Foshan will complete all supporting devices to actively undertake the transfer of Hong Kong financial service industry and build supporting systems for financial innovation between Guangdong and Hong Kong and backstage financial service.

Third, more policy support should be obtained from higher-level government for Foshan's financial innovation. For example, the State Council is expected to support the unification of Guanghzou and Foshan and integrate the construction of Guangdong Financial High-tech Zone into *the Outline*. The Ministry of Commerce is expected to consent that Guangdong Financial High-tech Zone will enjoy, under Guangzhou-Foshan unification, some of the preferential policies for Chinese demonstrative service outsourcing parks.

Fourth, favorable environment must be created for specialized personnel for financial innovation. The officials of Financial Bureau of Foshan are mostly graduates of finance, and two are doctoral degree holders. All of them are experienced in financial operations. An agreement has been signed with Guangdong University of Finance to establish a division in the financial high-tech zone in Foshan. A postdoctoral working station is also to be opened in the high-tech zone.

The financial objectives of Foshan are set as follows: to embrace the financial radiation of Hong Kong, Macau, Guangzhou and Shenzhen and accelerate the development of financial backstage services and outsourcing services through undertaking the transfer of international financial industry so as to turn Foshan into a pilot base for innovative financial cooperation between Guangdong, Hong Kong and Macau, an important financial backstage service pivot and the advanced region for the harmonious development of national finance and economy and with strong financial service capabilities.

4.7 The Shaping of Multi-level Capital Market System in Foshan

The Foshan municipal government has adopted the listing strategy of "some getting listed, some submitting applications, some being cultivated and some others being incubated" to encourage companies to go public through various channels and in various forms, such as domestic or overseas stock market, main board and second board or NASDAQ-style second board (growth enterprise market), IPO, backdoor listing or reverse merger. Besides, prospective companies are fostered with considerable support for possible listing in the future.

Led by the IPO of Foshan Electrical and Lighting Corporation on A-share stock market in 1993, 14 other companies in Foshan got listed by 2008. Comparatively speaking, Foshan has lagged far behind Wu Xi, also a municipal city in Jiangsu Province, whose economic volume approximates to that of Foshan but with 35 listed companies and even a well-known "Jiangyin sector" on the stock market. Jiangyin, one of the county-level cities in Wuxi, has 18 listed companies. It doesn't means that all the enterprises in Foshan have not met the standards for listing but that they are not quite aware of the importance to capital market to business growth and need to transform their ideas and thinking, in addition to just hard work.

Foshan boasts the most developed private enterprises with extremely promising prospects for going public in Guangdong Province. The growth of private enterprises generally undergoes three phases: family-style startup and management, then share-holding operations, and finally the separation of ownership from operations through directors and board of shareholders, in which stage the enterprise is managed by personnel with expertise. At the current stage, most of the enterprises in Foshan are in the transition from the first phase to the second phase, which indicates that private enterprises should integrate with modern enterprise system and grow bigger and stronger with the help of capital market.

The current brisk capital market provides a precious chance for private enterprises in Foshan to upgrade their industries. The development of capital market is chiefly determined by three factors: macro environment, the enterprise itself and social demand. Years of reform have created favorable conditions for all the three factors to be developing in a healthy, steady and sustainable way. The two listing climaxes for enterprises getting listed, respectively in the middle of the 1990s and at the turn of the century, are followed by a third wave, which started from 2006. Foshan has been taking firm hold of the third opportunity, though the previous two were lost.

Speaking from the macro-level perspective, enterprise listing facilitates the general investment environment and drive Foshan's economy to develop with great leaps. Public monitoring subsequent to enterprise listing helps enterprises to get standardized. The chain of reactions thus caused will push the investment environment of Foshan to become more internationalized and to adapt more easily to market operations and contribute eventually to the all-round development of Foshan.

The harmonious development of economy will lay a firm foundation for a harmonious society. The harmony of an economy is reflected chiefly in the reasonable proportion of the primary, secondary and tertiary industry that is congruent with the demands of the times and the specific region. The "Triple Three Strategy" proposed by the Foshan municipal government aims to foster and support more than three key enterprises in each of the three categories of industry to achieve the coordinated development of the three categories of industry and enhance their competitiveness on domestic and overseas market. Obviously, one effective short-cut to the accomplishment of the goal is to encourage and lead enterprise to make full use of capital market.

What should the government do to help enterprise to be listed? Foresighted leading is the best service that the government can provide for enterprises, for economic development and for the market. This concept has become the guideline for the Foshan municipal government.

Most enterprises have experienced great difficulties in going public owing to historical problems. These obstacles have arisen mainly from the enterprises themselves and the policies and the external environment of that time. Periodically objective analyses of the problems have been conducted on the part of the government to help remove these problems, in addition to providing help and guidance for enterprises to go through those difficulties from the developmental perspective and with foresighted leading. If the enterprises fail to free themselves from those problems, the development of not only the enterprises but also the regional economy will be seriously affected and restrained.

Since 2004, efforts have been strengthened to spur enterprises to get listed through a series of supportive policies, such as *Decisions Concerning the Promotion of Economic Growth in Foshan with the Help of Capital Market*. The Foshan municipal government has adopted the listing strategy of "some getting listed, some submitting applications, some being cultivated and some others being fostered" to encourage companies to go public through various channels and in various forms, such as domestic or overseas stock market, main board and second board or NASDAQ-style second board (growth enterprise market), IPO, backdoor listing or reverse merger. Besides, prospective companies are fostered with considerable support for possible listing in the future. Meanwhile, the municipal and district government have respectively issued a series of preferential policies for enterprise listing and reducing the cost of enterprise transformation and listing by providing interest subsidies for technological innovation, fiscal subsidies and rewards. For example, in Nanhai District, enterprises that can get listed will have no expenditure involved and will get a reward of 1 million yuan and a subsidy of 3 million yuan to cover intermediary services for listing.

In addition, a wide range of resources have been integrated to speed up the development of capital market in Foshan. In April 2009, Foshan cooperated with the United Nations to launch "The International Demonstrative City Project of Supporting Industrial Upgrading and Capital Operations". The project is now under full operation. Delegations of the United Nations Industrial Development Organization have paid frequent visits to Foshan to discuss relevant issues concerning how to make good use of capital market to promote industrial upgrading of Foshan. Both parties have initiated talks about introducing international capital for the establishment of venture capital funds and industrial investment funds in Foshan.

More supportive policies have been issued and implemented in Foshan to assist in the launch of the growth enterprise market. In August 2009, Foshan set the precedent in Guangdong Province by promulgating *Provisions of the Management of Green Path Permits for Enterprise Listing in Foshan*. The green path permit is issued mainly to enterprises which are making preparation for listing. The municipal government and relevant functional departments provide legitimate, speedy and convenient services to enterprises with such permits in going through procedures, like restructuring, counseling, application and auditing. The first green path permits have been issued to Nanfang Ventilator, Foshan NationStar Optoelectronics and other enterprises that are ready for listing.

To our delight, a work conference for listing was held in March 2007, which put forward *The Plan for Foshan Sector Formation on Stock Market*. Decisions were made to lead enterprises, especially group corporations, to be listed on the fast rack with a view to fostering "Foshan Sector" on the capital market within 3–5 years. October 30, 2009 marked the listing of 28 enterprises, including Nanfang Ventilator, on the growth enterprise board, which is a milestone for Foshan. Through years of hard work from 2004, Foshan Sector has come into shape on the stock market, which consists of 22 listed companies on the main board of Shanghai and Shenzhen stock exchanges, second board, growth enterprise market and overseas markets. Now, a multi-tier capital market system for Foshan is coming into shape.

The number of listed companies of Foshan indicates that Foshan Sector is taking shape. It is expected that clusters of listed companies in Shunde and Nanhai will appear on the Foshan Sector and will exert significant influence upon domestic and even overseas capital market with superior quality, rapid growth and high standards.

The future capital market of Foshan will assume the following features. First, the number of listed companies is great and in clusters. A number of excellent enterprises, not 3–5, but about 30–50, will be the first to go public through standardized operations on the main board, second board and growth enterprise market and play a leading role and set examples for over 300,000 enterprises to follow in Foshan.

Second, the district and industrial distribution of listed companies in Foshan is much more balanced. Three of the five districts of Foshan have enterprises listed, and with the emergence of high quality enterprises and the updating of corporate concepts, another two districts, Sanshui and Gaoming are expected to fill their blanks in due course. Besides, further balance has been achieved in the industrial distribution of listed companies. More enterprises will grow into locomotive businesses and go public, particularly those in pillar industries, such as machinery equipment, electronics, pharmaceuticals, ceramics, and in new high-tech emerging industries, such as optical-mechanical-electrical industry and new energy saving industry. Foshan's enterprises will appear one after another on both domestic and overseas stock exchanges.

Third, the majority of listed enterprises are in the manufacturing industry. Foshan is known as "world factory", and its second industry accounts for over 60% of its GDP. This situation determines that manufacturing enterprises will be the main body on the stock exchanges, but enterprises of the service and consumptive type, like Saturday Footwear, will be emerging on the stock market in successions.

Fourth, the majority of listed companies are small and medium-sized enterprises, and they are the backbone of Foshan's economy. That is congruent with the structural characteristic of Foshan's enterprises and is an inevitable option for rapid growth of small and medium-sized enterprises.

Fifth, the majority of listed companies are of an innovative type in science and technology. Foshan, faced with great opportunities for industrial upgrading, enjoys a considerable number of famous brands and powerful capabilities for research and development. Enterprises of an innovative type in science and technology will play a leading role in the construction of the high-tech "one zone and six parks" and in expediting enterprise listing on the stock market.

Sixth, the majority of listed companies have enjoyed government support and guidance. For example, the "Eagle Plan" has been put into operation in Nanhai District for several years, and credit rating has been conducted by open bidding for those "Eagle Enterprises". Such efforts have helped to foster and develop some enterprises into listed companies, and examples include Chigo, Saturday Footwear and Nanfang Ventilator.

4.8 The "Foshan Experience" in Transforming "Three Outmodes" in China

Foshan's transformation of "three outmodes" follow the following principles: establishing organizational mechanisms; planning goes first; government leading and market regulating work side by side; encourage the grass-root units to create new transforming patterns congruent with local situations; promoting demonstrative projects to extend the successful experience from one point to all areas; be concerned about people's livelihood and win the support of the grass roots and the people, and finally, active publicity creates positive atmosphere.

Since the reform and opening up, the land for construction use in Foshan has only tripled, but its economy has grown by 30 times. In 2009, the GDP of Foshan reached 481.45 billion yuan, an increase of 13.5% over the previous year. The great achievements from economic growth have also made us keenly aware that the contradiction between land demand and supply is becoming increasingly acute and has become a bottleneck for future urban development. The transformation of "three outmodes" is undoubtedly a master stroke in solving this problem.

Over recent years, great economic, social and ecological benefits have been achieved in Foshan's transformation of "three outmodes" and have won highly positive comments from leaders of Guangdong provincial government and the Ministry of Land and Resources. Foshan's experience in transforming "three outmodes" has been widely publicized and promoted throughout Guangdong Province.

Since 2007, Foshan has been taking the lead in transforming "three outmodes" in Guangdong Province. 730 transforming projects have been launched with a total land area of about 5,000 acres and with an increase of newly added construction land of 23.99 million square meters. Among all the projects, 229 were started in 2009, with a transformed land area of 2,000 acres and a new construction land area of 7.1 million square meters. The transformation of "three outmodes" has yielded substantial economic, social and ecological results, which can be summarized as follows: transformation has eased up the adverse effects of the 2008 international financial crisis and has considerably helped Foshan to break out of its economic difficulties; transformation has greatly improved urban and rural environments; transformation has substantially increased the utility of land resources and improved the structure of land utilization and industries; and finally transformation has enabled people to enjoy tangible benefits.

Experimental accomplishments in transforming "three outmodes" can be summed up in the following seven aspects:

First, organizational mechanisms must be established. The enthusiasm of government leaders and necessary organizational mechanisms are the prerequisites for such huge transforming projects. When the decision was made to start the transforming projects in the whole of Foshan, a working team was also appointed by the municipal government and headed by the deputy mayor in charge of this part of government work with relevant functional department heads as the team members, and a standing office for transforming "three outmodes" was set up with specialized staff attending to routine office work. Similar organizations were also set up in all relevant districts and towns.

Annual plans are made for transforming "three outmodes" in the whole of Foshan and are accordingly carried out in the five districts and 33 towns. Their successful implement is listed as one of the important indexes for appraising the performance of government leaders at all levels. In addition, liaison mechanisms are established to facilitate the horizontal connections of all relevant departments and the vertical connections of government offices at all levels of government.

Second, planning goes firs. In June 2007, the Foshan municipal government put forward *Decisions concerning Accelerating the Transformation of Outmoded Towns, Factories and Inside-city Villages*. Soon afterwards, a survey of the outmoded towns, factories and inside-city villages was conducted to find out a "three outmodes" area of about 41,150 acres in Foshan, followed by a special working plan for transforming "three outmodes".

What deserves to be mentioned here is that the plan is so detailed and complete that middle- and long-term objectives are carefully specified and archives of transforming projects are made. According to the types and locations of the projects, the six purposes for the use of transformed land are clarified: transforming outmoded towns, transforming outmoded villages, transforming outmoded factories and mines, transforming ecological environments, the comprehensive development of modern and urban agriculture, and the construction of cultural theme parks. After repeated appraisal and consultation, *The Special Plan for Transforming Outmoded Towns, Factories and Villages of Foshan (2009–2010)* was announced in October 2009. All this provides strong policy support for the smooth transformation of outmoded towns, factories and villages.

Third, government leading and market regulating work side by side. Efforts have been made to further standardize and spur the transformation of "three outmodes" through Guangdong Provincial Government's promulgation of and guidance on the implementation of "*Provisions on Promoting the Transformation of Outmoded Towns, Factories and Villages and the Economical Land Utilization*", in addition to other supporting polices put forward by the Foshan municipal government. Fiscal and financial support is also part of government leading. By now, 8.06 billion yuan of public finance has been invested in transforming "three outmodes" by government of all levels in Foshan.

Measures have been taken to push the transforming projects into market operation under the guideline of "government providing policies, land owners/users providing land and developers providing capital", and the operation of specific projects has been conducted by following the principle of "whoever invest in the project will reap its benefits" so as to bring the initiatives of the people from all walks of life into full play and remove the headache of capital shortage in transforming "three outmodes". So far, the on-going transforming projects have absorbed a total of 35.7 billion yuan of social investment. In 2009, 41 transforming projects were recommended at the conference of operative projects of Foshan and attracted a total investment of 18.858 billion yuan.

Fourth, encourage the grass-root units to create new transforming patterns congruent with local situations. The municipal government supports and respects the grass-root units to create new ways of conducting transforming projects. Over the past 2 years or so, at least ten patterns and models for transforming project operation have been brought into operation in Foshan. There is the Miaozhu-Donghuali model for transforming outmoded towns, the Xiaxi village model for transforming outmoded villages with collective investment of villagers who will enjoy project benefits, and the Shitou village model in which villagers contribute land to cooperate with developers. As to the transforming of outmoded factories, there is the pattern of "Foshan Creation Industrial Park" for new industries, where the outmoded factories are not pulled down but renovated in a creative way, and the pattern of "Lanshi Metal Market", which is transformed and operated by its owners.

Fifth, promoting demonstrative projects to extend the successful experience from one point to all areas. Good examples have boundless power. At the initial stage of transformation, Foshan adopted the strategy of setting good examples and taking one or two cases as examples for others to follow, which eventually led to the setup of the municipal-level demonstrative transforming sites.

Since 2009, 30 municipal-level demonstrative transforming sites have been established in Foshan, such as the Miaozhu-Donghuali Site and Foshan International Household Expo City. Efforts have been concentrated achieving breakthroughs in key projects so as to set up examples and promote transforming projects.

Sixth, be always concerned about people's livelihood and win the support of the grass roots and the people. The transforming projects are directly related to the interest of villages and the villagers. Therefore, in the transforming process, the rights and interest of the villages and their residents must be respected, and at the same time, their interest should be subject to the government's unified planning and development so as to create a mutually rewarding situation.

Two points deserve the serious attention of the government: focus on comprehensive long-term effects and benefits and avoid myopia; balance the interest of both the investors and the original proprietors. For example, the Miaozhu-Donghuali Site covers a large land area and involves a large population. However, no complaints have been received from over 30,000 affected residents, 99.7% of whom from 9,635 families have been relocated and resettled, thanks to the fruitful efforts of the government to balance the interest of all parties.

And finally, favorable atmosphere for positive public opinion is created through active publicity. The smooth progression of transforming projects is contingent on the appreciation and understanding of the grass-roots people. Governments at all levels have made good use of all possible media and propaganda means, particularly village affairs publicity and special training, to enhance the awareness of the necessity and significance of conducting three-outmode transformation on the part of all government officials, the grass-roots people and the proprietors. Focus has been laid especially on the government's supportive policies and the ways of allocating interest so as to arouse the people's concern about and enthusiasm for the transforming projects.

The year 2010 is the beginning year for the implementation of the 3-year program of "Building up a new Foshan and giving people a new look". The government has decided, on the basis of the achievements of the previous 3 years, to propel the reconstruction of Foshan with greater strength and efforts. The"532 Project" is to be launched and implemented in the whole city, aiming to renovate and reconstruct an land area of about 15,180 acres within 3 years, about 8,330 acres by 2010, 5,000 acres by 2011, and about 3,330 acres by 2012. By the end of 2012, the land under reconstruction will take up 50% of the total land area to be reconstructed and transformed so that the transformation of "three outmodes" will move towards a higher level, a larger range and better quality.

4.9 "Bigger City": The Growing Pain of the Economically Demonstrative Region

Being a bigger city means that the city will have the legislative power to enact regional rules and laws so as to lessen contradictions and problems in social and economic development and turn the achievements and experience of reform and regional features of economy into regional regulations and laws.

At the National People's Congress and Chinese People's Political Consultative Conference of 2010, I suggested that the State Council delegate more administrative power to those "bigger cities" so that Foshan would develop into a really bigger city at an earlier time. I have submitted the proposal for three consecutive years, in the hope of removing the bottleneck problems in social and economical development so that Foshan will develop in a sound and rapid way.

What should be emphasized is that to be a bigger city does not mean administrative upgrading for Foshan. The term "bigger city" is just a legal concept. The greatest advantage of being a "bigger city" lies in that the city will be entitled to enact regional laws and regulations and the legislative power can safeguard autonomous reforms. Although no quantitative criteria have been fixed for a "bigger city", it is generally acknowledged that being a "bigger city" signifies its level of development and its influence upon a region, which will be helpful for the local government to build a flexible and effective law system congruent with its actual situation and enhance the efficiency of government administration.

The Foshan municipal government has been concerned with being a "bigger city" since 2003, at which time Li Jingming, the then Foshan municipal CPPCC member, put forward the proposal "*Suggestion on Foshan's Application for Being a 'Bigger City'*". The proposal attracted the attention of the then municipal leaders and was approved for further processing. The motivation for applying to be "a bigger city" is derived from *The Legislation Law of the People's Republic of China* (short for *Legislation Law*), which stipulates that a bigger city has the legislative power to enact regional laws and has the right to lay down regional laws and regulations on certain issues according to actual needs in cases where no national laws and administrative regulations have been formulated.

Over the recent years, Foshan, following the outlook of scientific development and the target to be a bigger city, has made strenuous efforts to push forward social, economic, political and cultural development and has achieved great accomplishments through legal governance in building a prosperous and harmonious society. Foshan has outpaced some of the "bigger cities" in terms of economic capacity, city scale, regional influence, level of urban administration and legal governance.

Foshan is well qualified for being a "bigger city". Located in the hinterland of the Pearl River Delta, Foshan is one of the national or even global bases of manufacturing industry, as well as one of the most important centers of transportation, commerce, finance, science and technology, information, education, culture and tourism in Guangdong Province. In 2009, Foshan took great initiatives to meet the challenges from the international financial crisis and was among the first to have achieved successful economic breakthroughs, with its GDP reaching 481.45 billion yuan, an increase of 13.5%. The per capita GDP by registered resident population amounted to 80,579 yuan, approximately 11,795 US dollars.

Foshan has been awarded a lot of highly honorable titles, mainly National Hygiene City, National Model City of Mutual Support between Civilians and Armed Forces, National Historical and Cultural City, National Clean city, Pilot City of the United Nations Human Settlements Program (UN-Habitat), National Garden City, Excellent Tourism City of China, National Advanced City of Scientific Advancement, Brand City of China, National City of Brand Economy, Powerful Education City of Guangdong Province, Civilized City of Guangdong Province, and National Environmental Protection Model City. In the "*2009 Blue Book on Chinese Urban Competitiveness*", issued by The Chinese Academy of Social Sciences, Foshan ranked 15 among all the big and medium-sized cities in China. It follows from all this that Foshan is well qualified to apply for being a bigger city.

The successful application for being a "bigger city" will help to solve some deeply-rooted contradictions and prospective problems in Foshan's development. Foshan is a frontier city of reform and opening up in China and a demonstrative city of early economic development and transformations, accompanied by social contradictions and problems. Legislation insufficiency and even vacancy have continued to exist, as no legal support has been obtained on a number of issues concerning "first trial and first execution" in reform and opening up and economic development and administrative operations.

For example, Foshan was the first in China to have conducted the reform of administrative streamlining and approval systems so as to simplify administrative procedures and delegate power to lower levels, the transformation of "three out-modes", the rural proprietorship system reform, the reform of strengthening townships, the cross-department restructuring of government functions in Shunde District, and the comprehensive pilot reform of prefecture-level administrative powers for counties and county-level cities. Some reforms were assigned to Foshan by the central or the provincial government. All these reforms have given rise to a number of Foshan patterns or models.

All these reforms require the innovation of mechanisms and systems, without which it will be impossible to push forward the reforms. Being a "bigger city" will entitle Foshan to the legislative power to enact regional regulations and laws so as to lessen contradictions and problems in social and economic development and turn the achievements and experience of reform and regional features of economy into regional regulations and laws. Those "first trials and first executions" will set examples and provide practical experience for late-developed regions and cities to handle similar contradictions and problems in their reform and development. In addition, being a "bigger city" will accelerate the unification of Guangzhou and Foshan and the integration of the Pearl River Delta. At the beginning of 2009, the State Council issued *the Outline*, which proposed to "intensify the effects of the Guangzhou-Foshan unification and lead a well-planned, full-featured and closely-connected city cluster in the Pearl River Delta".

At present, the unification of Guangzhou and Foshan is well under way. The two cities are integrated in urban planning, industrial development and transportation infrastructure. However, complete integration is difficult to achieve due to some obvious differences in systems. For example, legislation is in effect for some social administrative issues in Guangzhou, while only rules or regulations are carried out in Foshan, which lead to differences in legally abiding power in the two cities and consequently a big policy gap, such as in the management of dump trucks and the restriction of motorcycles.

If Foshan is entitled to legislative power, system barriers will be avoided to the greatest extent. And then, the policies of the two cities will coordinate and correspond with each other, which will facilitate the seamless incorporation of the two cities. The unification of Guangzhou and Foshan will become a real breakthrough for the integration of the Pearl River Delta and enable both cities to take a leading position in this region. Nine cities are situated in the Pear River Delta Region, and only Guangzhou, Shenzhen and Zhuhai have regional legislative power. Foshan will also have legislative power when it becomes a "bigger city" and will be exerting greater influence and give its leading role a full play in its unification with Guangzhou and the integration of the Pearl River Delta.

One more reason why Foshan shall apply for being a "bigger city" is that the rights of the town (or street community) do not match with its volume of economy. Foshan's economy is well known in China for its feature of "one town, one brand". Although the comprehensive economic strength of Foshan ranks among top ten in China and the GDP of some of its subordinate towns even exceeds that of some cities, they still stay at the town-level without the rights to approve and the necessary authorities to handle some issues, which has become a bottleneck restricting their development. Under such an administrative system, Foshan's social and economic development will assume a situation of "a petite pony drawing a big heavy cart".

Therefore, the Foshan municipal government hopes to solve the problem by delegating some county-level authorities to townships. It means that the definition for the rights of government at town level should be modified in the law concerning government organization, which needs the approval of the State Council. All such problems and difficulties will be removed if Foshan becomes a "bigger city" with equal authorities to provincial capital cities and the legislative power specially approved by the State Council.

The State Council advocates streamlined government organizations in its institutional reforms so that the efficiency of government administration, operations and services can be enhanced and effective measures can be taken to solve possible problems within a limited time. However, from the perspective of local government, there should be not only horizontal streamlining of government organizations but also vertical in-depth reform and innovation of administrative institutions so as to enable economy to develop with great leaps.

4.10 The Unification of Guangzhou and Foshan: A Master Stroke in Integrating the Pearl River Delta

Foshan can be regarded as a twin city of Guangzhou, which differs essentially from a satellite city. The relation of Foshan to Guagnzhou is somewhat similar to that of New Jersey to New York and Dublin to London.

Historically, Guangzhou and Foshan are descendents of the same ancestor. It is not commonplace in China and abroad for two big cities with such a dense population to converge within 1 h distance and develop in a clustered and interwoven way. It is of historical and practical significance to build a Guangzhou-Foshan metropolitan so that the economy of the two cities will be closely linked and developed in a complementary way.

Early in 1921, Sun Yat-sen proposed in his famous work *A Plan of International Common Development of China's Industry* to build a big international port city in South China stretching from Huangpu in the east to Foshan in the west. This early plan for the Guangzhou-Foshan unification aimed to drive the development of the western region of Guangdong Province. Thus the unified development of Guangzhou and Foshan or the construction of Guangzhou-Foshan metropolitan is the long-cherished wish of our predecessors. Now a clear, specific and systematic plan has been drawn up to develop the western region of Guangdong Province by the integrated construction of Guanghzou-Foshan Metropolitan, which has been approved by the Guangdong provincial government and received enthusiastic responses from the people of both cities.

According to *the Outline*, Foshan should make good use of its own industrial foundation and unique features to expand and strengthen its own industries. Foshan should take advantage of not only its industry, particularly its manufacturing, but also its logistics, exhibition, trade and modern finance that are closely related to Foshan's industrial development so that Foshan and Guangzhou will develop in a complementary way. Foshan can be viewed as a twin city of Guangzhou, which differs essentially from a satellite city. The relation of Guagnzhou to Foshan is similar to that of New York to New Jersey, or London to Dublin.

The unification of Guangzhou and Foshan, as a demonstrative model, will lead the integrated development of the Pearl River Delta Region and upgrade the economic, social and cultural development of the region. This process will effectively integrate Foshan with Guangzhou in transportation infrastructure, technology, information, network, planning and layout and strengthen its ties with Guangzhou in education, culture, sports, technology, labor force and social pension system. In the unification of Guangzhou and Foshan, Foshan will fulfill its own duty as well as incorporate itself with Guangzhou and play a leading role in the integrated development of the Pearl River Delta Region.

According to the general law of regional development, the unification of infrastructure is the foundation for regional integration. Since 2007, Foshan has initiated the construction of urban rail transits and the first nine main roads to Guangzhou. In March 2009, Foshan signed with Guangzhou *The Cooperative Framework Agreement on the Unified Construction of Guangzhou and Foshan*, and four joint contracts of urban planning, transportation infrastructure, industrial cooperation and environmental protection. The three major regional infrastructure projects—Nansha Port, Guangzhou South Railway Station, and New Baiyun Airport—have been completed and put into service, which manifests that the sharing of infrastructure is a strategic choice in the unification of Guangzhou and Foshan. The construction of the network of highways and subways will further propel the all-round integration of transportation infrastructure of the two cities.

Most media articles describe 2009 as "the year of Guangzhou and Foshan". 2009 witnessed the substantial government promotion of the unification of Guangzhou and Foshan through the formulation of *The Key Work Plan of the Unification of Guangzhou and Foshan in 2009* and the specification of the 52 key cooperation projects. In addition, the unification of the two cities has provided tangible benefits to the public and solved a lot of long-standing problems, such as the construction of transportation infrastructure. The Huanglan highway from Foshan to Nansha Port via Panyu has been built, the Sanshan Port Bridge connecting Foshan with Guangzhou South Railway Station is under construction, and the bridge connecting Shunde and Guangzhou South Railway Station is under planning. It will take only a 20-min distance between downtown Foshan and Guangzhou South Railway Station. All these transportation projects have yielded benefits for the people of both cities not only in travelling but also in environment protection, education services and medical care.

In 2010, the construction of infrastructure has been further strengthened. At the third joint session of mayors of Guangzhou and Foshan on April 7, 2010, 69 key cooperative projects were nailed down, 38 of which were unfinished projects of 2009 and were continued till completion in 2010. The first section of Guangzhou-Foshan subway line, which has attracted considerable public attention, was put into trial operation in June 2010 and will be open to the public before the 2010 Asian Games.

According to the international norms for urban integration, transportation, logistics, finance and telecommunications are the most important issues. Obvious progress has been made in the integration of Guangzhou and Foshan in areas of transportation and logistics, but integration in the sectors of finance and telecommunications has become urgent and must be strengthened.

A great deal of work on urban integration has been tried in some cities in China as well as in the Pearl River Delta. For example, Zhengzhou City and Kaifeng City of Henan Province have proposed a detailed scheme of financial integration, Dandong City and Donggang City of Jilin Province have conducted cross-city loans and made inter-bank deposits and withdrawals possible for enterprise accounts, and mutual recognition of bills has become possible in the city cluster of Wuhan. In the Pearl River Delta, the plan for building an integrated telecommunication system in Zhuhai, Zhongshan and Jiangmen has been submitted to Guangdong Provincial Development and Reform Commission for examination and approval.

It is true that Foshan has lagged far behind other cities in the integration of finance and telecommunications, which deserves serious attention. The Sixteenth Asian Games will be a joint debut for Guangzhou and Foshan, as boxing and water ballet are to be held in Foshan, which will double the demand for inter-city telecommunications and financial services and promote the two-way flow of population and capital. Therefore, it is urgent to realize the integration of telecommunications and finance in both cities. Inter-bank deposits and withdrawals should be made possible soon, and charges for deposits and withdrawals in different cities should be canceled, and charges for telecommunications should be unified.

Comments about the balance of benefits between the two cities often appear in the unifying process, such as "Guangzhou is indifferent while Foshan is enthusiastic", or "Foshan takes advantage of Guangzhou". It is true that, for example, Foshan's transportation infrastructure is inferior to Guangzhou's, but the integration will turn out to be, in most cases, mutually rewarding to both cities. This view has been repeatedly expressed at several joint sessions of mayors of both cities. For instance, Foshan is keen on transportation connection with Guangzhou, while Guangzhou is more interested in Foshan's successful experience in environment protection. Therefore, Guangzhou-Foshan integration is mutually beneficial and will bring convenience and benefits to both cities.

It is certain that the integrating process embodies both driving forces and competitive pressure. If medical services are integrated, for example, Foshan will be confronted with great pressure, because medical services and facilities in Guangzhou are superior. What shall Foshan do? As social demands are multi-layered and multifaceted, so are the public demands of the people, which is congruent with the requirements for effective, joint and sustainable development of both cities. The progress in such areas of Guangzhou-Foshan integration will not only set a good example for other areas but also play a leading role in the integration of the Pearl River Delta.

Since Guangzhou-Foshan integration takes place in cities with independent juridical power, there will be inevitable disagreements concerning specific issues. However, all such issues have been handled with great satisfaction on both sides, as both sides are flexible as well as adhering to the principles. The construction of Jinshazhou city road is a good case in point, in which both parties made compromises that led to the settlement of the problem of dislocated joints and discrepancy in elevation. In the water-intake project from the Western River to Guangzhou, Foshan took the initiatives and shouldered some extra costs thus incurred. The utmost goal of city integration is to maximize the benefits for both cities.

4.11 Perceptions from Visits to Hong Kong

The administrative system of Hong Kong consists of three institutional frameworks: governmental organizations, quasi-government organizations and non-governmental organizations. The administrative modes are highly flexible, autonomous and efficient in performing government duties, which explains the reason for success of Hong Kong government and serves as an example for institutional reform on the mainland.

As an international metropolis and financial center, Hong Kong has accumulated a lot of experience for mainland cities to learn from in terms of government administration, economic development, city planning, environmental protection and its cooperation with mainland cities. Besides, Hong Kong is close to Foshan. It is of practical and urgent significance for Foshan to learn from and cooperate with Hong Kong, as they enjoy spatial proximity with similar social customs and cultural traditions.

With the invitation of the Hong Kong SAR Government and the arrangement of Hong Kong and Macao Office of the State Council, I paid a study visit to Hong Kong from February 21 to 26, 2005 and had direct involvement in and direct experience with the administration and development of Hong Kong. That visit gave me a lot of deep impressions and great perceptions.

4.11.1 Orientation Determines the Future

Within just 5½ days, I visited 28 departments, including the Housing and Planning Bureau, the Urban Redevelopment Authority, the Trade Development Council, the Industry and Technology Bureau, the Chinese General Chamber of Commerce, the Environment, Transport and Works Bureau, the Financial Services and the Treasury Bureau, the Economic Development and Labour Bureau, the Investment Promotion Project Officer, the Cyber Port, the Environmental Protection Department, Hong Kong-Guangdong Cooperation Coordinating Team, the Hong Kong Exchanges, the Science Park, the Innovation and Technology Commission, the Independent Commission Against Corruption, the Constitutional Affairs Bureau, the Legislative Council, the Department of Justice, the Trade and Industry Department, the Government Economic Advisor, Hong Kong Monetary Authority, the Housing Department, the City Planning and Construction Bureau, the Central Policy Unit, the Education and Manpower Bureau, the Tourism Commission, and the Department of Health.

Orientation determines the direction for development. The development of a country, a region or even a city should be oriented in the right direction. Otherwise it will encounter the embarrassing situation of "going south by driving the chariot north" or "cutting one's feet to fit one's shoes", and will hurt or prevent social and economic development.

As a busy and prosperous international financial center, Hong Kong seized the chance for further development and re-oriented itself in 2000 as Asia's World City.

To achieve this end, a series of supporting measures were taken, such as establishing the Investment Promotion Project Officer and the Innovation and Technology Commission, and strengthening the Tourism Commission, which have laid a firm foundation for the prosperity of Hong Kong.

Hong Kong sized up the situation and re-oriented itself so as to achieve sustainable prosperity, which is a good example for the mainland to learn from. However, some of the mainland cities just take city orientation as a kind of concept, and on most occasions, it is the top leaders of the city who determine the orientation of urban development without consideration of the unique regional features and history. As a result, the city will get half the results with double the efforts and be completely lost and disoriented, which is fatal for the city, because it will miss a lot of precious chances for social and economic development.

4.11.2 The Three Institutional Frameworks of Hong Kong Administrative System

Let's start from the administrative system of Hong Kong. The administrative system of Hong Kong consists of three institutional frameworks: governmental organization, quasi-government organization and non-governmental organization. The Hong Kong government finances the quasi-government organizations in three ways. In the first case, when the organization is under preparation, the government makes an appropriation for it, and after that it assumes full responsibility for its own gains and losses, such as the Urban Redevelopment Authority. In the second case, once a quasi-government organization is established, the government will bring forth certain policies to promote its development and get them closely linked to its annual performance. The Trade Development Council and its tax policy of ad valorem duty are examples. In the third case, after the founding of the organization, the government makes annual appropriations based on its actual conditions, like the Education and Manpower Bureau.

Quasi-government organizations work in the form of councils, board of directors or committees. The government will appoint two or three people to perform government duties. It can be seen that the government pushes all half-operative organizations (organizations that are related to economic development and gain economic profits in some ways) to the market and finance them according to different circumstances. The administrative modes are highly flexible, autonomous and efficient in performing government duties, which explains the reason for success of Hong Kong government and serves as an example for institutional reform on the mainland.

For the convenience of objectively and directly elaborating my reflections and perceptions concerning my visit to Hong Kong, I have classified the 28 departments I visited into five types: government administration, economic development, city planning, environment and tourism, and Guangdong-Hong Kong cooperation, though the function and responsibilities of some departments overlap to some extent.

Let's make a survey of the specific functions of the departments of Hong Kong government.

The Central Policy Unit, which consists of eight members, is directly responsible to the Chief Executive, Government Affairs Director and Financial Secretary and plays a significant role in the development of Hong Kong. Its responsibilities include studying social problems, exploring Hong Kong-mainland cooperation, making public opinion polls, handling unexpected incidents, etc.

The Legislative Council consists of 60 councilors and holds tenure-change election every 4 years (similar to the practice of U. S. House of Representatives and the House of Commons of Great Britain). Prior to 1985, councilors of the Legislative Council were appointed by the Governor. Subsequent to 1985, some of the councilors were elected directly by the legal profession, while most of the councilors were appointed by the Governor. Since 1991, 30 of the councilors are elected by constituencies and the rest 30 are elected by the legal profession. The councilors are entitles: (1) to legislate; (2) to approve government expenditure; (3) to supervise government work; (4) to appoint and dismiss Judge of the Court of Final Appeal, Chief Judge of the High Court, and to impeach the Chief Executive.

Constitutional Affairs Bureau is a comprehensive department of the government which is responsible for the promotion of *The Basic Law*, the formulation of constitutional development, election, the official accountability system and external affairs. The official accountability system, different from civil servant accountability system, is directly responsible to the three governmental departments and 11 bureaus. Since the implementation of the official accountability system on July 1, 2002, three officials of the Financial Department, the Health and Welfare Bureau and the Security Bureau have had to step down from their posts.

The Government Economic Advisor is affiliated to the Economic Analysis and Convenient Business Department and takes charge of economic analysis and the formulation of economic policies. Major current studies involve Hong Kong macro economy, unemployment, fiscal budget, housing, land, transportation, environmental protection, the implementation of CEPA, and Pan Pearl River Delta arrangement.

The fiscal year of Hong Kong begins on April 1. The Financial Services and the Treasury Bureau are mainly responsible for budgets balancing, economic stimulation, public expenditure and income growth and follow the centralized revenue and expenditure system. Its revenues come from tax revenues, government charges, and land revenues. The fiscal deficit of over 20 billion Hong Kong dollars has been basically balanced by land revenues. The performance budget is carried out by the Audit Administration and Legislative Council.

"Corruption" in Hong Kong is defined as government employees gaining benefits without the approval of the government or private employees gaining benefits without the agreement of the employer. In Hong Kong, Independent Commission Against Corruption, similar to the mainland anti-corruption bureau, is made up of over 1,250 people in three departments: Operations Department, which comprises more than 900 people and is responsible for investigation and prosecution, Corruption Prevention Department, which comprises more than 50 people and is responsible for establishing and improving anti-corruption laws and regulations, and Community

Relations Department, which consists of about 180 people and takes charge of anti-corruption publicity and education. Upon its establishment, the commission starts anti-corruption campaigns against government departments and private sectors. Its ultimate goal is to prevent corruption by all possible means and make civil servants “scared of corruption”, “incapable of corruption” and “free of corruption”. The commission falls directly under the charge of the Chief Executive.

The Education and Manpower Bureau has four ways of running schools. First, the school is completely government-run with government grants and teaching staff categorized into civil servants. Second, the government makes appropriations of certain proportions and entrusts educational organizations who recruit teaching staff and run the school. Third, the government entrusts social educational organizations to run the school and makes certain proportions of appropriation based on the annual enrollment of students. Fourth, the school is completely private, which brings the enthusiasm of social forces into full play and effectively reduces government spending.

The Health, Welfare and Food Bureau takes charge of the Department of Health and Hospital Authority. In 2003, during the outbreak of SARS, the Department of Health established the Centre for Health Protection, which comprises Surveillance and Epidemiology, Infection Control Branch, the Public Health Laboratory Service, Public Health Service, the Emergency Response and Information Office, Project Management and Professional Development as well as the Scientific Advisory Group. Health, medical care and disease prevention are the major concerns of Hong Kong Health, Welfare and Food Bureau.

4.11.3 Priority Given to Innovation in Economic Development

Innovation in science and technology is the powerful engine for Hong Kong’s economic development. To learn from Hong Kong’s economic development mode, we should, first of all, give prominence and encouragement to innovation in science and technology. The Innovation and Technology Commission was established in 2000 for the special purpose of promoting Hong Kong’s transformation of economic development mode and better boost innovation in science and technology.

The Innovation and Technology Commission is responsible for formulating strategies for innovative development of science and technology and is in charge of Science and Technology Parks Corporation, Cyber Port, Productivity Council and Designing Center, etc. Its current key projects include auto parts manufacturing, logistics, textile and garments, and nanotechnology and advanced materials. The source of investment needed for scientific research and development has been one of the hot public issues.

The Cyber Port, planned between 1998 and 1999 and built in 2004, consists of a commercial zone and a residential zone, with a total area of 24 ha, and shares some features in operations and development with the Silicon Valley in the United States: (1) It is equipped with clear intranet and information superhighway; (2) Its internal layout is just like a big laboratory, with a comprehensive network of intellectual property development, product tests, and commercial promotion; (3) It is capable of creating an entirely new multidimensional world of science and technology with all its advanced technology and wide-ranging scientific and technological products, and (4) By providing one-stop infrastructural support, including information, consultation, development, application and product promotion, the Cyber Port has attracted and cooperated with a lot of domestic and overseas mobile network operators, suppliers of equipment and information technology companies. It will be a strong force to drive Hong Kong's economy to a new height.

The Cyber Port differs from the Silicon Valley in several ways: (1) The Silicon Valley is established through private enterprises, while the Cyber Port is sponsored by the government; (2) The Silicon Valley covers a large area, while the Cyber Port covers a small floor space; (3) The Silicon Valley is not well planned or defined, while the construction and development of the Cyber Port is well designed; (4) The Silicon Valley cooperates with internet developers and focuses on commercial business, while the Cyber Port focuses on developing digitalized entertainment products, such as digital image, music, animation, and advertisement. Now, the Cyber Port has become an experimental platform of information technology.

The Science Park was put into operation in 2001, with a total investment of 12 billion Hong Kong dollars, and is owned and run by the government. It provides platforms (sometimes through leasing facilities by the hour) for domestic and overseas companies to research and develop products of electronics, precision engineering (optoelectronics, nanotechnology), biotechnology (mainly Chinese pharmaceuticals), and software and telecommunication. Meanwhile, there are three industrial parks located respectively in Dapu, Yuanlang and Jiangjunao and one center of science and technology to match it.

Founded in 1966, the Trade Development Council is financed by the government but is run independently. Its major responsibilities include: (1) to provide marketing platforms (such as exhibitions), (2) to collect and offer market information and opportunities, (3) to provide matching services for commerce. It mainly provides customized and specialized services for small and medium-sized enterprises (growth enterprises) rather than the formerly large-scale and popular modes of service.

The Investment Promotion Project Officer, founded in 2000, mainly targets trade and investment promotion. A number of enterprises from mainland China, America and Japan come to Hong Kong to conduct joint promotions. I once motioned that Shunde or Foshan, together with The Hong Kong Investment Promotion Project Officer, make an investment soliciting tour to Europe for molding and machinery industry so as to boost the development of new industries in both cities.

The Hong Kong Exchanges, which consists of the main and second board markets, provides IPO services for mainland enterprises. It is advisable that enterprises in Foshan and Shunde be listed on the second board market in Hong Kong, for there is no special requirements for corporate earnings and no restriction on industrial categories. However, there is the basic requirement that leaders of the listed enterprises remain in office for two consecutive years, with their corporate governance structure to be improved after listing, and that no less than 30 million HK dollars be raised. China Securities Regulatory Commission places no special restrictions on enterprises' IPO on the second board in Hong Kong.

The Trade and Industry Department, similar to the Foreign Trade and Economic Cooperation Bureau in the mainland, performs such duties as multilateral negotiation (such as the negotiation of WTO, APEC), bilateral negotiation, and services for the development of small and medium-sized enterprises. The government has established special guarantee fund, training fund, market promotion fund and development fund to boost the development of Hong Kong's 300,000 small and medium-sized enterprises.

4.11.4 Much Space Remains for Promoting Pillar Industries

The industry of Hong Kong has gone through several stages of development: from the 1960s to the 1970s, manufacturing industry is the main stay of its economy. Starting from the 1980s, finance, logistics, tourism and specialized services become the four pillar industries. In the meantime, Hong Kong started to invest in high-tech and knowledge-based industries of high added-values at the beginning of the twenty-first century, which represents the tendency of Hong Kong and world economic development. The management and operation mechanisms of high-tech and knowledge-based industries as well as their financial input (such as the establishment of Cyber Port, Science Park and Innovation and Technology Commission) are well worth our serious attention and consideration.

Much space remains for the promotion of pillar industries of Hong Kong.

Finance, as the leader of its pillar industries, has consolidated Hong Kong's status as the international financial center and has provided impetus to the development of other industries. However, Hong Kong's finance faces fierce competition form its neighbouring regions and countries, and the Hong Kong Exchanges ranks only eighth in the world stock market. Moreover, it is likely that Hong Kong's financial industry may linger around owing to its inadequacy of financial resources complimentary to the mainland in its development strategy of financial industry and lack of specific effective measures to make it one of the top five international financial centers.

Of the four pillar industries of Hong Kong, I focused on logistics and inquired the Economic Development and Labour Bureau about infrastructure, geographic locations, service networks and legal systems. What counts most in developing logistics is to build service networks, including customer sources, information flow, cross-boundary transportation, warehousing, cargo agents (inclusive of the third- or fourth-party logistics), DTTN (digital trade transportation network) service, and one package service. To ensure effective operation of service networks, it is of primary importance to provide good facilities and timely information flow, to help small and medium-sized enterprises with their financing, and to attract talents to heighten logistics standards. The biggest headache for Hong Kong's logistics industry is its high costs and its lack of ease of passing through the Customs to the mainland.

4.11.5 Scientific and Foresighted Urban Planning

As the saying goes, an inch of land in Hong Kong is worth an inch of gold. With limited land and dense population, Hong Kong suffers from the pressure of traffic jams and housing shortage, which tests the wisdom and capabilities of the government. The Hong Kong government is resourceful enough to remove barriers through scientific and foresighted urban planning and turn pressure into development opportunities. Hong Kong is one of the cities in the world with the greatest population density, but scientific and foresighted urban planning has guaranteed smooth traffic flow and the success of "Home Ownership Scheme". The setup of institutional structure has shown that the government pays special attention to housing for residents and both the Housing and Planning Bureau and Housing Department has been established to take charge of housing issues. In addition, flexible operations of urban construction and planning have provided effective solutions to the problem of construction funds.

The Housing Bureau and Planning Bureau were combined into the Housing and Planning Bureau in 2002, which is responsible for housing planning, land registration and earthquake prevention. Its most remarkable achievement lies in that it has made successful plans for urban construction, such as roads, streets and underground traffic network, and formulated the successful scheme for building, selling and leasing public houses. Unfortunately, the land in the New Territories is not included in the plans for historical reasons.

The greatest success of the Housing Department resides in its successful implementing of the public housing scheme concerning building, selling and leasing. That not only ensures the success of "Home Ownership Scheme" but also solves the funding problem for the building of public housing and community shops.

The Urban Redevelopment Authority is financed by the government but runs independently. It mainly performs the duties of reconstructing, preserving, repairing and renovating urban housing. The fund for construction comes from government support, bank loans, independent operations, investment and cooperation, and housing ownership. Its contract management, flexible operation and ratification of expenditures according to revenues highlight its success.

The City Planning and Construction Bureau is able to meet both ends meet and cover the losses resulting from subway operations by combining the construction of subways with the development of real estate connected to subways.

4.11.6 Environment Protection Goes with Tourism

Air pollution is one of the most thorny problems that should be urgently addressed in Hong Kong. The sewage of the Hong Kong Island is drained directly into the sea. It was not until 2002 that the solid waste was simply sorted manually. The number of landfills is far from enough, and the disposal of garbage is not efficient.

All this exercises negative influence upon Hong Kong's image as an international metropolis.

The Environment, Transport and Works Bureau is responsible for environmental protection, including air, water, waste and ecology. Air pollution has become the main topic throughout Hong Kong. The government has taken measures to treat automobile emission, power emission and enterprise emission. Measures have also been taken to cooperate with Guangdong to deal with the problem of "Air Basin". One of the reasons why Hong Kong has lagged behind other developed cities in sewage treatment and garbage landfill is that it is hard for the government to coordinate the interest of the masses (for example, increasing sewage treatment charges). A visit to the Environmental Protection Agency gives me the impression that its functions overlap with those of the Environment, Transport and Works Bureau.

The promotion slogan of the Tourism Commission is "Asian's World City". Hong Kong's tourism resources should be further integrated and promoted, with equal importance attached to tourist facilities, travel services and tourism promotion. In addition, "family tourism" has great market potentials. Now, a lot of tourism projects have been developed, such as the Disney Land, Big Island Shandong Chung Crane Engineering, Wetland Park, Multimedia Lighting and other diversified places of interest. A friendly environment will boost the development of tourism, which should be more closely linked to environment protection so that they will complement each other.

4.11.7 Great Prospects for Cooperation Between Guangdong and Hong Kong

Closer ties have been forged between Hong Kong and the mainland since the reform and opening up, and there are broader prospects for such cooperation. The cooperation of Guangdong and Hong Kong has penetrated into more profound economic and cultural areas and manifests a highly promising future.

The Coordinating Team for Hong Kong-Guangdong Cooperation, which was founded in 1998, consists of 17 task groups. The Chief Secretary for Administration is responsible for Hong Kong's cooperation with Guangdong, Shenzhen and the "9 + 2" Pan-PRD. The Financial Secretary takes charge of Hong Kong's cooperation with Shanghai and Tianjin. The Team focuses on the implementation of CEPA, mainland enterprises' investment in Hong Kong, Pan-PRD cooperation, the exchange of sci-tech professional resources, environment protection, port development and etc.

The Chinese General Chamber of Commerce, which I also visited, plays an important role in Hong Kong-Mainland and Hong Kong-Guangdong cooperation. It was established in 1900 and tops the four big chambers of commerce in Hong Kong (the Chinese General Chamber of Commerce, The Chinese Manufacturers Association of Hong Kong, Federation of Hong Kong Industries and Hong Kong General Chamber of Commerce). It is an association and non-profit organization of local Chinese firms, businessmen and professionals, with more than 6,000 members.

Zeng Xianzi is the former chairman and now the honorary chairman. It has built a bridge between Hong Kong government and the mainland and has contributed a lot to enhancing the position of Chinese businessmen.

Hong Kong and Guangdong should make full use of geographical, cultural and institutional advantages to cooperate in industry, economy, urban construction, environment protection. Foshan, as well as Shunde, should take advantage of Hong Kong's service platforms for finance, logistics, tourism, science and technology, and specialized services to develop local and regional industries.

(Written on March 12, 2005, as standing member of Foshan Municipal Committee of CPC, executive mayor of Foshan Municipal Government and secretary of Shunde District Committee of CPC, Foshan)

Chapter 5
Meeting the Press: Let the Light of Capital Shine over Industrial Highland

5.1 CCTV2 Program *Dialogue*: Foshan, a Top-Notch Blue-Chip

A program themed "Foshan's Transformation" was broadcasted on CCTV2 *Dialogue* on the evening of June 29, 2010. Chen Yunxian, the then secretary of Foshan Municipal Committee of CPC and mayor of Foshan, was invited as special guest, stating that Foshan's 2009 GDP reached 481.45 billion yuan. He commented that where houses exist, there must be Foshan's household appliances and that where construction exists, there must be Foshan's building materials. He pointed out, however, that Foshan must restructure and upgrade its industry and that capital must be injected to invigorate its industrial enterprises.

5.1.1 Why Foshan Must Restructure and Upgrade Its Industry

Chen Weihong (host of CCTV2 *Dialogue*, hereinafter referred to as "Host"): In the jargon of stock market, Foshan should be a top-notch blue-chip. Do you agree with that?

Chen Yunxian: I could not agree more. The 2009 gross industrial output of Foshan exceeded 1.2 trillion yuan, with imports and exports over 38 billion US dollars, which has further strengthened its domestic and international competitiveness.

Host: Foshan's GDP has kept growing at a rate of 15% over the past 30 years. Why does such a top-notch blue-chip need transform?

Chen Yunxian: Foshan's private enterprises and traditional industries are its greatest advantages, but they also turn out to be its serious disadvantages. For example, crude management and labor-intensive operations are concomitant with the development of traditional industries, resulting in high costs, high energy consumption, high pollution and comparatively low efficiency. Private enterprises, which are the foundation of Foshan's development, are originally family-owned and will remain so if they do not transform. They would eventually lag behind and be washed out if our innovation of system, technology and organization failed to keep pace in the process.

Y. Chen, *Foresighted Leading: Theoretical Thinking and Practice of China's Regional Economic Development*, DOI 10.1007/978-3-642-35368-0_5,

In the course of *Dialogue*, Liang Fengyi, president of Guangdong Shaoxin Group Co., Ltd., and Zhang Qikang, president of Guangdong Monalisa Ceramics Co., Ltd., talked about their early stage of transformation. Lu Chuqi, president of Guangdong Vanward New Electric Co., Ltd., started from his experience of his entering the industry, discussed the price war between businesses, how it seriously affected many enterprises and why his enterprise took the initiative to transform.

Ding Li (director of Competitiveness Assessment Center in Guangdong Academy of Social Sciences): Dongguan and Shenzhen have been the focus of Guangdong over the past 30 years, while in the 30 years to come, the focus will be shifting to the west bank of the Pearl River, especially Foshan, because of its sound and solid foundation of private economy and manufacturing industry. It must be noted that most enterprises have been trying to fight with costs and prices and earning money mainly by sweat over the past 30 years. What is to be transformed? Transformation has to be made from earning money by sweat to earning money through wisdom and intelligence. Anyway, this transformation is painstaking. Countries like Japan and Korea spent two to three decades for economic transformation.

Host: There are a great variety of approaches to such transformation. What approaches has Foshan taken?

Chen Yunxian: The following three strategies have been simultaneously implemented: restructuring and upgrading traditional industries, cultivating advanced manufacturing, and making full use of capital to develop enterprises.

5.1.2 Satisfaction with Minor Accomplishments Will Lead to Backwardness

Host: What makes enterprises in Foshan reluctant to be listed?

Zeng Shaowu (deputy director of Foshan Financial Bureau): When I approached them and discussed with them, they said that they are not short of money and that their businesses rank among top ones in the industry. So why bother?

Ding Li: This is typical of the mentality of being satisfied with minor accomplishments. If one can make money on his own, why should one go public and share with others? There is another problem. At the early stage of their development, they might have had some law violation, which may not be heinous crimes but probably just some petty ones, or just breaching the laws slightly. However, it is illegal act and might impair their listing. Thus, barriers have to be removed before the enterprises apply for listing. How to wash white might be a problem which Secretary Chen has also been thinking about.

Chen Yunxian: How to solve the problems of minor violations of law properly and by legal means requires joint efforts of various relevant departments and national policies. We would try to settle the problems by coordinating with relevant departments. It is indeed a bottleneck that prevents some of Foshan's enterprises from getting listed.

Host: What do you expect enterprises to benefit from listing?

Chen Yunxian: Seemingly, it is the collection of funds of one or two billion yuan. However, the process of listing will help to achieve a more important objective of establishing modern business management system. In the 1990s, three household appliances enterprises had similar scale in Shunde District, and one of them, Midea, which is familiar to us all, transformed itself into a joint-stock corporation between 1993 and 1994 and thereafter established the modern management system. It is certain that Midea's output in 2010 will exceed 100 billion yuan. Compared with Midea, its former competitors lost the opportunity of their combination with capital market at that time and have fallen behind.

Host: What have those listed enterprises actually benefited from listing?

Bian Cheng (general manager of Guangdong Keda Industrial Co., Ltd.): Enterprises must find a new growth point after getting listed.

5.1.3 How to Control the Risk of Merger and Acquisition

Zeng Shaowu: There are no less than one hundred locomotive enterprises in Foshan, with quite a lot of opportunities for merger and acquisition in future.

Host: How would merger and acquisition, combined with capital market, serve as a driving force to transformation?

Chen Yunxian: I should say it provides a new platform as well as serving as a good approach to transformation. Merger and acquisition are important strategies and approaches that entrepreneurs can adopt to strengthen and expand their companies.

Host: Nowadays in Foshan, people tend to avoid mentioning Gu Chujun, then head of Greencool, who controlled the local Kelon Electrical Holdings Co., Ltd. by capital operation. However, he was sentenced to jail for fund misappropriation and false registration in 2008. What should enterprises do to manage and control the risk in the combination of capital and industry?

Chen Yunxian: Firstly, enterprises must build solid foundation and set up sound mechanisms. Secondly, they should take precautions against being trapped in mergers.

Host: Let the light of capital shine over Foshan's industrial highland. Does it mean that Foshan's industrial highland is devoid of the shine of capital or does not enjoy enough of it?

Chen Yunxian: In order to integrate capital into enterprises effectively, both "internal" and "external" approaches have been adopted. Internally, "Financial 3P", i.e. the three financial development plans, has been put forward: the "463" program for enterprise listing, the plan for cultivating venture capital funds, technology innovation funds as well as small and medium-sized enterprises guarantee funds to help enterprises in need, and the plan for a variety of financial innovation, including village and town banks, petty loan companies and others. More importantly, the State Council provided policy support to make Nanhai Qiandenghu (One-Thousand-Lantern-Lake) Garden of Foshan a High-tech Financial Service Center of Guangdong. Externally, support is solicited from the United Nations Industrial Development Organization to designate Foshan as China's only demonstrative city for industrial clustering and effective capital market operations. Banks from outside, including foreign banks, have moved into Foshan.

Host: Today, I have brought with me a book called *The Correspondence Theory of Risks and Returns* by Mr. Chen Yunxian. When we see the light of capital has become one of the driving forces for promoting the restructuring and upgrading of Foshan's industries, we would like to know whether it is the best timing from your point of view?

Chen Yunxian: I should say, enterprises should follow the national guidelines for industrial restructuring and upgrading and take full advantage of capital market to strengthen and expand themselves and undertake effective merger and acquisition via capital market. It is a good timing, not just for now but in the "Twelfth Five-Year-Plan" as well.

Host: Can we know what other lights will shine over Foshan's industrial restructuring and upgrading, as we have seen the light of capital already shining over Foshan's industrial highland?

Chen Yunxian: We are now in the late stage of industrialization or the initial stage of post-industrialization. At this stage, we must amalgamate informationalization with industrialization, urbanization and internationalization. That is why Foshan Municipal Committee of CPC and Foshan Municipal Government launched "Intelligent Foshan via Fourization".

5.2 *Guangzhou Daily*: Knowledge Economy Is Contingent upon the Intelligent Mind

Chen Yunxian, secretary of Foshan Municipal Committee of CPC, received a joint exclusive interview with central and provincial media on September 3, 2009. He talked about the transformation of Foshan's economic development modes, the building of city image and the profound implications of "Intelligent Foshan via Fourization". With regard to Foshan's development orientation, Chen Yunxian put it in a nutshell, "Natural economy is contingent upon the capricious sky, market economy is contingent upon the invisible hand, while knowledge economy is contingent upon the intelligent mind."

During the interview, Chen Yunxian commented emotionally, "China's intellectuals of our generation have learned a great deal from books and have practiced quite a lot for long. In addition to practical work, we feel obliged to think about economic evolutional patterns and achieve breakthroughs in economic theories."

5.2.1 Great Emphasis Should Be Placed on Inward Quality Rather than Outward Appearance

Journalist: The practice of integrating industrial development with city development in Foshan leads us to a new interpretation of "intelligent" in "Intelligent Foshan via Fourization". Is it correct to say that you want to endow industries with a new soul beyond production factors?

Chen Yunxian: In the 1980's, when I was studying as a PhD candidate at Peking University, I had already conducted researches into the development mode of China's capital market. Upon my graduation, I was often praised and given a lot of fancy titles, like "pioneer" and "fill the blanks in some areas in China". However, controversy concerning the nature of capital market, i.e. whether it is socialist and capitalist, was still lingering. I was already standing at the forefront of China's capital market and began to study decipher issues relating to traditional economics.

For example, production factors in traditional economics are lands, production instruments and people. But will it work with the exclusion of capital? Of course not. Capital is as important to today's economy as blood to human body. When we perceive a person, we can only see the muscles and the outward appearance but not the quality of blood inside. We cannot decide whether he has "three-highs" (high blood pressure, high blood lipid, and high blood glucose) or leukemia. However, such intangible software is the essential element needed for today's economic development and urban construction. If all this is taken into account, the whole system of economics will change dramatically.

5.2.2 Knowledge Economy Is Contingent upon the Intelligent Mind

Journalist: Does it mean that we have to combine those intangible elements with economic development in the course of building up "Intelligent Foshan"?

Chen Yunxian: Foshan's economy develops at a fast rate. It is now already in the late stage of industrialization or the initial stage of post-industrialization. If focus is still laid on the hardware or the tangible aspects of economy within the traditional thinking model and the software or the intangible aspects are overlooked, we will feel perplexed at our city positioning or go astray. If so, it would be difficult for Foshan to reach a higher level of development.

Why did I recommend the book *Here Comes Everybody*: *The Power of Organizing Without Organizations*? It is well known that *The World is Flat* is quite influential, which tells people to broaden their horizons rather than being restricted within only one area. For example, a problem with high-tech service outsourcing can be removed with the help of only one computer, even though we are thousands and thousands of miles away from each other. It suggests that human mind and thoughts should be extended horizontally. *Here Comes Everybody*: *The Power of Organizing Without Organizations* also suggests that people should extend their mind and thoughts, but vertically. Natural economy is contingent upon the capricious sky, market economy is contingent upon the invisible hand, while knowledge economy is contingent upon the intelligent mind.

That is to say, not only those tangible and physical things, but also those intangible and ideological things should be acknowledged. "Intelligent Foshan" should be the result of combining its existing conditions with high-tech factors and is the crystallization of combining internets with the internet of "things" and digitalization and intelligence. It is embodied in every aspect of Foshan's industrial development, urban construction and international competition. Therefore, "Intelligent Foshan" matches with the actual situation of Foshan and manifests foresighted leading on the part of government.

5.2.3 "Birth Pangs" in Transformation Equate to the "Run-in Time" of New Automobiles

Journalist: Foshan is making its greatest endeavor possible to undergo industrial restructuring so as to transform its economic development mode. During this process, certain downward trends appear in some major economic indicators of Foshan in 2009 and the first half of 2010. Is it what we call "birth pangs" in transformation? How can we overcome them?

Chen Yunxian: A "run-in time" or a period of transition exists in the economic development, urban transformation or environment reconstruction of all regions. We can equate this to the "run-in time" of a new automobile, during which time it cannot run too fast. However, it can run faster and more smoothly once that time is over.

This reminds us that every region, whether it is Foshan or not, will suffer from "birth pangs" during its economic transformation. The pain and cost of transformation will be minimized with sufficient preparation in advance. Otherwise, there would be enormous cost. Cost in economics consists of actual cost and opportunity cost. Whatever the actual cost is in transformation, the more important thing to do is compare with opportunity cost.

From this point of view, the approach to transforming Foshan's economic development mode is in line with the demands of Foshan's self-development, which is characterized by foresighted leading on the part of government.

5.2.4 Government Should Exercise Foresighted Leading

Journalist: What is the government supposed to do in the course of transformation?

Chen Yunxian: The government should exercise foresighted leading, which is practiced in all our policy making and the accomplishment of our tasks. Enterprises are the subject of transforming economic development modes, no matter whether it is self-initiated innovation, foreign capital solicitation or construction of industrial highlands by financial means. It is the obligation of government to exercise foresighted leading and provide supporting measures in accordance with laws and regulations, and rules of market economy.

Foshan, especially Shunde, is a role model for "government foresighted leading" in regional economic development, and Singapore is another example if viewed from the national level. It must be made clear that what is meant here by foresighted leading differs from administrative intervention in the age of planned economy and is based on rules of market economy and the framework of laws and policies.

Journalist: Does "foresighted leading" contain your reflections about government behavior?

Chen Yunxian: Looking back upon the evolutional characteristics of economics, we first see Adam Smith's theory of "invisible hand", and then Keynes' theory of macro-level government supervision. From here, economics diversifies into microeconomics and macroeconomics. China's intellectuals of our generation have learned a great deal from books and have practiced quite a lot for long. In addition to practical work, we feel obliged to think about economic evolutional patterns and achieve breakthroughs in economic theories.

Adam Smith and Keynes were mainly concerned about intervention and adjustment during or after market malfunction. Why not exercise foresighted leading so as to effectively reduce the losses incurred from actual cost and opportunity cost? This is my major theoretical contribution to the question of how to achieve theoretical breakthroughs in studies in economics and its evolution in the light of my government work for many years.

5.2.5 Heighten Foshan's Image with "Venturing into Southeast Asia"

Journalist: An expert team has been invited to Foshan to study its city positioning and image building. How do you portray Foshan?

Chen Yunxian: Foshan's city positioning and image building ought to be a dynamic process and should match each other. Recently, a middle-ranking official from Beijing Municipal Government came to Foshan to work for some time. He felt elated at the sight of city clusters in Foshan, which are rare in China. In reality, Foshan is a combination of two cities and five districts, which is covered by a three-dimensional transportation framework with expressway and underground railway networks, an airport and transportation to sea ports.

Therefore, Foshan is a place which you cannot see through at first sight, but you will find it lovely with the passage of time. Indeed, Foshan is a dynamic city with "hidden dragon and crouching tigers". It is hard to characterize Foshan with just a few words. For example, Kang Youwei and Li Xiaolong (Bruce Lee), are both born in Foshan and famous at home and abroad. Li Xiaolong is an influential international figure, and his martial arts have become popular with many westerners. However, all these are just some aspects of Foshan. Further in-depth studies must be conducted if a picture of it is to be drawn in its entirety.

Journalist: How should Foshan improve its city image and enhance its popularity?

Chen Yunxian: The movie *Tangshan Earthquake* shows the revival of post-disaster Tangshan and has achieved good publicity effects. Foshan stands at the forefront of China's reform and opening-up, but people outside know little about it. I think it is due to lack of proper government leading and effective publicity.

Foshan has a registered population of 3.65 million, but their overseas folks amount to over 1.5 million, with over 0.8 million residing in Hong Kong. Many of Hong Kong's millionaires are natives of Shunde, and several high-ranking officials are from Nanhai. Just as I have mentioned many times, people from Shandong Province have promoted themselves with "Venturing into Northeast", and people from Shanxi Province with "Venturing beyond West Pass". There is no justification that no stories have been written about people from Foshan "Venturing into Southeast Asia" (Going to Nanyang), which can be considered a theme and make it sound loudly. Certainly, it will require greater efforts and wisdom.

(First published in *Guangzhou Daily*, September 6, 2010)

5.3 *China Securities Press*: Facilitating "China Created" with Multi-level Financial Service Systems

5.3.1 To Guard Against Risks, Enterprises Must Initiate Self-innovation, and Government Must Exercise Foresighted Leading

Journalist: In 2008, Foshan enjoyed the fastest rate of economic growth in Guangdong Province though the impacts of the international financial crisis persisted, which contrasted sharply with the regions on the east bank of the Pearl River. As mayor of Foshan, what do you think hides behind this?

Chen Yunxian: Under successive attacks of cost rises, appreciation of exchange rate and the 2008 financial crisis, Foshan's economy displayed its strong anti-risk capabilities. In 2008, its GDP amounted to 433.33 billion yuan, an increase of 15.2% over the same period of the previous year, its total industrial output value reached 1.165831 trillion yuan, an increase of 20%, exceeding 1 trillion yuan.

Two patterns for manufacturing industry in the Pearl River Delta region have emerged—the east bank pattern and the western bank pattern. The former, represented by Dongguan, focuses on the processing industry, is typically characterized by its "external" features, i.e., raw materials being purchased from overseas and products being sold overseas. The latter, represented by Foshan, Zhongshan and Zhuhai, has its own lines of industries, name brands as well as marketing networks, and most enterprises are privately owned and have grouped into industrial clusters, with their products mainly sold on domestic market. The privately-owned industrial feature and self-initiated innovative capabilities explain why Foshan has maintained a strong and steady momentum for economic development.

The two patterns resulted in variations in economic performance during the 2008 financial crisis. The root causes for such variations are as follows:

First, in terms of industrial structure, Foshan's secondary industry accounts for around 65% of its GDP, with industrial manufacturing as its foundation. Its industrial structure highlighted by its real economy generates strong competitiveness.

Second, Foshan's economy is powered and driven by the two wheels of private enterprises and foreign-invested enterprises. Confronted with the financial crisis, its private enterprises have performed as pillars of its industries with extraordinarily strong capabilities to guard against risks and crises.

Third, Foshan boasts over 2,200 enterprises whose output value exceeds 100 million yuan, over 250 enterprises whose output value lies between 1 billion and 10 billion yuan, and six enterprises whose output value exceeds 10 billion yuan. All these enterprises are not seriously affected in the crisis, thanks to their large scale.

Fourth, entrepreneurs in Foshan have grown up through hardships and possess enough intelligence to cope with difficult situations.

Fifth, Foshan proposes the strategy of five-stage development for enterprises. During the first stage, a solid foundation is to be laid, during the second name brands are to be developed, during the third patents are to be registered, during the fourth standards are to be established and recognized as industrial, national or even international standards, and during the fifth brands, patents and standards are to be franchised for OEM (Original Equipment Manufacturer) by other enterprises.

Up to now, Foshan enjoys 25 Chinese well-known trademarks and 65 Chinese famous trademarks, which ranks it among top Chinese cities.

Journalist: As mayor of Foshan, what policies do you think should be adopted to help traditional industries resist internal and external risks?

Chen Yunxian: Speaking from my own experience, government should exercise foresighted leading and take the initiatives under current circumstances. It has been proved that the "invisible hand" of liberal economy could malfunction on some occasions, while government intervention in Keynes' theory comes only during or after the economic process. It is my belief that government should play an essential role in making up for the drawbacks caused by the "invisible hand" and government intervention that comes only during or after economic activities. The government should actively exercise foresighted leading, which means that the government should take the initiatives to lead micro-enterprises via foresighted thoughts and policies in accordance with laws of market economy and help them develop in a healthy way without paying too much actual cost or opportunity cost. The Foshan government has taken the following measures:

First, in-depth investigations were conducted to have a clear picture of the actual situation. In 2008, principal leaders of Foshan municipal government held consultation conferences with entrepreneurs from 81 varieties of businesses and visited more than 130 enterprises. It became apparent from the investigations that three types of enterprises, namely export-oriented ones, small and medium-sized ones, and enterprises in real estate industry, were seriously affected by the economic crisis. Consequently, a series of measures were carried out to help them go through the crisis.

Second, industrial transformation was accelerated. Rigorous measures were taken to close down enterprises of high pollution and high energy consumption. Efforts were intensified to undertake the "two transformations and one reconstruction" of traditional industry to make full use of its advantages and propel its transformation from labor-intensive to capital and technology-intensive and from low-level to high-level processing through innovation and technological upgrading. In addition, a series of industry-related enterprises were introduced into Foshan to form industrial clusters and were led towards building a modern industrial system.

Thirdly, a package of policies was implemented to encourage self-initiated innovation on the part of the enterprises.

Fourthly, international trade platforms were set up to help enterprises expand into domestic and overseas markets, especially the Middle East market, Russian market, ASEAN market, South African market, South American market and so on.

Finally, more financial support was provided to enhance technological innovation and upgrading in small and medium-sized enterprises. Enterprises were encouraged to take advantage of the national value-added tax (VAT) reform to increase investment in research and development, purchase new equipment and advanced technology to transform traditional industry. Government subsidies were arranged for the enterprises that purchased sophisticated equipment.

Journalist: What innovation has the government launched in financial services?

Chen Yunxian: One of the government's innovations in the financial service system is the establishment of "credit guarantee fund for small and medium-sized enterprises". The credit guarantee fund is based on the principle of "government leading, market operation, and risk sharing." The government provides funds from its fiscal revenues, trusts via bidding the funds with specialized guarantee agencies and banks that will administer them. The government offers a suggested list of eligible enterprises which are to be audited by guarantee agencies and banks and are granted loans in accordance with the principle of market operations, with guarantee fees kept under 2%. Risks are shared by the government, guarantee agencies and banks. The government assumes the responsibility of no more than 30% compensations. This mode has changed the practice of "all enterprises getting some proportion of government financial support" and increased the efficiency of financial capital operation.

Over 250 million government revenues have been set aside for credit guarantee funds, through which 51 small and medium-sized enterprises have obtained loans, which exceed 300 million yuan. Over the past 5 years, a total of around 18 billion yuan has granted through Foshan's credit guarantee fund for small and medium-sized enterprises to over 5,000 small and medium-sized enterprises. The credit guarantee fund has been operating well and the compensatory loan rate remains lower than that of Guangdong Province and the whole country for five successive years.

Foshan will collaborate with China's National Development Bank to provide joint guaranteed loan and financing assurance for high-quality enterprises in the industrial park.

Meanwhile, high-quality enterprises have been encouraged to get listed on the stock market. Two venture capital firms have so far been set up in Foshan, and another two are in preparation. Capital from these firms has mainly been invested to the high-quality local businesses. The government will be opening the green channel system for enterprises to go public. The municipal government will coordinate with relevant departments to help enterprises remove problems if they stand in line with the direction of Foshan's industrial development, meet environmental requirements and are free from illegal operations.

Recently, the United Nations Industrial Development Organization has chosen Foshan as "the international demonstrative project for supporting Chinese industrial clustering and capital operation (Foshan)". The work focus of the first and second quarters of 2009 for Foshan municipal government would be on promoting the introduction of industrial investment capital and investment funds and the construction program for capital operations and industrial optimization and upgrading so as to speed up the development of industrial clusters, improve the quality of capital operation, optimize industrial structure and enhance Foshan's core competitiveness.

5.3.2 Promoting "China Created" with Multi-level Financial Service Systems

Journalist: As a representative of National People's Congress (NPC), you once suggested that China must undergo the transformation from "China Made" to "China Created". What role do you think the financial market system should play in such transformation?

Chen Yunxian: Economic and enterprise development forms the basis for the transformation from "China Made" to "China Created", which cannot do away with the powerful support of financial market. There is great necessity for the establishment of a multi-level financial service system, which consists of at least the following four aspects:

This system, first of all, should be a comprehensive banking system that can provide a complete set of financial services, possess superior innovative abilities for financial services and financial products and provide direct services to enterprises. It is especially important that this system can create innovative products catered for those small and medium-sized enterprises.

Second, it should be a multi-level capital market system with the capability of allocating high-quality resources effectively and encouraging high-quality enterprises to achieve leapfrog development via capital market, including expediting the development of growth enterprise market, venture capital industry, industrial investment funds, futures market, etc. If policies permit, efforts will also be made to establish bond market to increase financing returns and open more financing channels.

Third, it should be a financial service system with supporting policies for local enterprises. A variety of financial services have been provided in Foshan in the recent years: an institutionalized subsidy mechanism is set up to support financial service institutions and small and medium-sized enterprises by means of tax preferences, financial subsidies, and loans, etc.; a financing assurance system is under improvement; financial innovations are encouraged and venture capital funds are developed. It is predicted that ten venture capital institutions will be set up in Foshan to provide investment to 100 local enterprises in the 3 years to come, with 5 billion yuan of fund-raising.

Full play is to be given to the potentials of property rights of trading market, and explorations are to be made for the establishment of petty loan companies, village and town banks, and financial leasing companies to bring private capital into sunlight. Financing methods, such as industrial investment funds and small and medium-sized enterprise collective bonds, are also being explored to help some high-quality small and medium-sized enterprises to raise funds through bonds and provide them with necessary capital support in their medium and long-range investment projects.

The Financial Industrial Development Plan of Foshan (*2008–2015*) was issued in 2008 with a clear idea of Foshan's financial orientation. It is proposed in *the Outline* that Guangdong High-tech Financial Service Center be supported for construction to expand backstage financial service industry and to build the backup service base for modern financial industry covering the whole Asian and Pacific region. About 100 enterprises are already negotiating the terms for their entering the center, with 11 enterprises already settled down. The office buildings for South Information Center of People's Insurance Company of China (PICC) and Asia-Pacific Backup Center of American International Assurance Company, Ltd (AIA) are already under construction. Eight other projects, including Sun Hung Kai Financial Group and Guangdong Santai Electronics Technology Co. Ltd, are being designed or processed for government approval.

In the course of financial innovations driving forward economic growth, capital market development and direct financing are determined as breakthroughs with emphasis laid on the implementation of the Financial 3P, i.e., the plan for financial innovation to promote financial market development, the guiding plan for venture capital funds, industrial investment funds and credit guarantee funds and the "463" program for enterprise listing. So far, all the projects in the three plans are under proper well arrangement and operation, and some of them have borne fruit.

Journalist: What reform and innovation should be undertaken for capital market in order to promote business development? What do you think of the launch of growth enterprises market?

Chen Yunxian: At present and for a considerably long period of time in future, "new innovation plus retracking" is and will remain to be the basic feature of China's capital market. The future capital market should be facilitated from the following three aspects. First, steady reform and innovation should be pushed forward so as to consolidate its foundation. Second, risks are unveiled and made known to the investing public, who should be equipped with more comprehensive knowledge and stronger awareness of risk prevention and law abiding through capital market education. And lastly, monitoring and legal enforcement should be intensified so as to maintain market order.

Within such a general framework, it is of primary necessity to do the following work so as to achieve efficient capital market resource allocation. The first thing to do is make better use of financing functions of capital market, such as bettering the initial public offerings (IPO) inquiry system, launching growth enterprises market as soon as possible, reforming the refinancing system and constructing bond market. The second thing to do is to promote merger and acquisition and encourage listed companies to achieve leapfrog development by means of capital market.

It is a good time for merger and acquisition. Those listed companies can make plans to enter capital market through shell purchasing or merger by various means to achieve rapid growth. Third, work should be done to improve upon the market stabilizing mechanism, such as launching stock index futures and cultivating more investors. The last thing to do is to associate with domestic and overseas capital markets, such as launching the Hong Kong Stocks fast track in due course, promoting mutual recognition of qualifications for specialized personnel from home and abroad, and providing domestic enterprises with easy access to domestic and overseas stock exchanges and so on.

People are concerned about the launch of growth enterprise market. The success or failure of a capital market is, in my opinion, determined by three core-factors: macroeconomic policies, the state of microeconomic development, and the balance of supply and demand of social capital. Currently, macroeconomic policies are favorable to the launch of growth enterprise market, for they are oriented to stimulate economic growth and expand domestic demand. At the microeconomic level, some small and medium-sized enterprises possess self-owned brands and core technology, which are potential resources for growth enterprise market. The real concern lies in the balance of supply and demand of social capital. However, the launch of growth enterprise market is bound to be a success if there is sufficient capital flow and bank savings will be transferred to investment. Other risks are common to all kinds of market and therefore are left out of consideration here.

5.3.3 The Global Economy Is Developing in a U-Curve and Will Reach Its Bottom by the End of the Year, While the Chinese Economy Is Developing in a V-Shape and Will Enter into Its Trough

Journalist: As a financier, what do you think about the development of the global financial crisis and the impacts it would make? What should the Chinese government, the financial sector and enterprises do to cope with the crisis?

Chen Yunxian: As far as I can see, this financial crisis has its root causes in the direction changing of western financial monitoring ideology in the 1980s and is by nature the result of the intensification of interest struggles among nations. As a result, China's global economic status would be heightened but that would not affect the status of the United States.

Speaking from the perspective of world economy, the first half of 2009 would be more severe than 2008, for problems occurred mainly on American market between January and September in 2008, and problems began to occur on the European Union market in the last quarter of 2008. In the light of economic cycles and historical experience, the economy will stagnate or even bog down into recession every 2–3 years. America's sub-prime crisis happened in the second half of 2007 and it lasted just 1½ year by the end of 2008, so the economy will not be changing for the better in 2009. The mortgage crisis in European Union began in the last quarter of 2008 and will deteriorate in 2009. It will turn for the better until the second half of 2010. Therefore, it can be concluded that the world economy is developing in a U-curve and will get to the bottom in 2009.

Journalist: What do you think of the impacts? Is there any sign of trough in the Chinese economy if viewed from the forefront of the economic development of the Pearl River Delta?

Chen Yunxian: Both similarities and differences exist between domestic economy and international economy. On the one hand, the dependency rate of China's economy upon imports and exports reaches up to 40%, which indicates that the situation of international economy will affect China's domestic economy. On the other hand, the adjustment or change of China's economy in 2008 is not necessarily the result of impacts from the international financial crisis but the result, to a large extent, of impacts from the national policy of macro adjustment and control upon traditional industries. Ten major measures, including 4 trillion yuan investment, have been adopted by the Chinese central government to promote economic growth. Accordingly, Foshan allocated an investment of 180 billion yuan and implemented ten important measures to expedite steady economic growth.

According to the statistics of February 2009, there is an obvious revival increase in electricity generation, personnel recruitment, orders, and transactions in real estate. The statistics shows that 100 billion yuan has been invested into about 1,000 enterprises. All this indicates that China's economy will develop in a "V-shape", with its trough coming between the fourth quarter of 2008 and the first quarter of 2009, and will undergo a slow gradual revival. China's economy has gone through its hardest time and will turn for the better in just a few months. Thus, there is no need to panic.

Journalist: As a former president of an investment bank, do you think it is a good time for Chinese enterprises to conduct takeovers on Euro-American markets?

Chen Yunxian: Since the global economy is expected to revive in the second half of 2010, I don't think now is a good time to do that. Domestic enterprises should conserve their strength until an appropriate opportunity comes. However, it is quite a different case in Foshan. Many high-quality enterprises in manufacturing industry have already stepped out of China and set up their factories all over the world to carry out their global strategic deployment, which shows their courage and insight.

(First published in *China Securities Press*, March 10, 2009)

5.4 *The Twenty-First Century Business Herald*: Boosting Domestic Demand Through Greater Industrial Consumption in Rural Areas

Foshan is the central region of China's manufacturing industry and one of the key cities in the Pearl River Delta. Chen Yunxian, an National People's Congress delegate and mayor of Foshan, paid visits to more than 130 enterprises before he came to Beijing to participate in the Third Session of the Eleventh National Committee of the Chinese People's Political Consultative Conference and the Third Session of the Eleventh National People's Congress) in 2009.

During the interview, he said, "There is a great deal more the government can think about and do to help export enterprises out of the financial crisis."

Chen Yunxian, on the basis of his previous investigation, put forward three proposals at the Third Session of the Eleventh National People's Congress in 2009. They are: *On the Expansion of the Preferential Policy of Rural Consumption of Industrial Products*, *On the Improvement of Current Export Rebate Policy* and *On the Restoration of Export Rebate Rate of Some Metal Products and Aluminum Extrusions*.

5.4.1 Boosting Domestic Demand Through Greater Industrial Consumption in Rural Areas

Journalist: What are your motivations for putting forward the three proposals regarding the difficulties export enterprises face?

Chen Yunxian: To boost domestic demand by consuming more industrial products in rural areas, the preferential policy of "selling more household appliances to rural residents" should not be limited to only household appliances. Its scope should be expanded to include materials needed for house building, such as ceramics, furniture and aluminum extrusions.

In order to control economic overheating, the central government cut down export rebates of some products years ago. But it is high time to expand exports, which needs the restoration of export rebates, and it needs only a period of 2–3 years.

Another point is related to the policy of export rebates. As a matter of fact, the elevation of export rebate in 2008 did not benefit domestic enterprises. Rather it was considered an indication of decrease in Chinese export trade cost, and foreign importers demanded that Chinese enterprises reduce their prices. Such being the case, subsidies for export enterprises should be considered as a means of replacing export rebate.

Journalist: The central government has implemented the preferential policy of "selling more household appliances to the countryside" to boost domestic demand. Why do you propose to extend the range of industrial products in this policy?

Chen Yunxian: Under the current context, the largest potentials for domestic demand reside in rural areas. According to the statistics, China has over 800 million farmers, accounting for 70% of its total population, but they consume only one third of total industrial output. The data from the National Bureau of Statistics show that a one-yuan increase in rural consumption expenditure will bring a two-yuan increase of national consumption demand.

The successive 4 years of "selling more household appliances to the countryside" will stimulate consumption up to 920 billion yuan on an accumulative basis. However, its impetus to China's economic growth is limited because it fails to satisfy the diversified demand of farmers. Thus, in addition to household appliances, the range of industrial products should be extended to include materials closely related to farmers' life, especially construction materials like ceramics, coating products, furniture, and textile and garment. The inclusion of these products into the preferential policy will be considerably conducive to China's social and economic development.

Journalist: Is it of great significance for boosting domestic demand and facilitating domestic investment-driven economy?

Chen Yunxian: Yes, it is. The central government has previously proposed a series of industrial revitalization programs. In addition to more effective supporting policies for credit, taxation, and innovation and the like, their focus should also be laid on the sale of industrial products that is intimately associated with their revitalization and development.

The inclusion of those industrial products in the preferential policies of "selling more household appliances to rural residents" will expedite the development of household appliances industry and its related industries and eventually maintain rapid, steady and sustainable economic growth.

The development of domestic investment-driven economy can fortify the foundation of national economy and improve its capability of risk resistance. Products like household appliances, construction materials, furniture, textile and garments fall into the category of high-quality traditional industries in China, most of which have their deep roots in private enterprises and are of primary importance to regional economy.

The inclusion of those products in the list can not only meet the demands for production and living in rural areas but also help to extend their marketing network in urban areas to cover 2,800 counties all over the country, thus enhancing product popularity, expanding market coverage, create more employment opportunities and speeding up the development of the whole industry.

Journalist: Foshan enjoys a good number of famous brands of household appliances. What do you think needs to be improved in implementing this policy? Do you have specific suggestions in relation to rural consumption of industrial products"?

Chen Yunxian: To my mind, stronger support should be given to rural consumption of industrial products that are closely related to housing construction. Only in this way can domestic demands be effectively expanded.

Beyond that, products of self-initiated innovation should be added to the preferential list and should be placed on the top of the list, which will inspire the enthusiasm for domestic enterprise innovation, help to foster world famous brands and promote the transformation and upgrading of industrial products, as well as stimulating national economy.

Journalist: It has been more than half a year since the implementation of the policy, but the supporting facilities and measures in some rural areas are not in line with its implementation.

Chen Yunxian: Yes, it's true. I suggest that the bidding enterprises should be multi-leveled. The regional development in China is uneven. Consumption level and capacity vary greatly with different rural areas. Diversification of consumption must be considered in bidding for enterprises, which will cater for the demands for both high and medium-grade goods in the developed southeast coastal areas and low and medium-grade goods in the underdeveloped mid-west areas and border areas.

The sales network should be expanded with good after-sale service, as the number of sales outlets is extremely limited and after-sale service is rather poor. Thus, more sales outlets should be established to cover all villages with good after-sale services and quality supervision.

In addition to that, more subsidies should be granted to cover more industrial products. At present, the subsidizing standard is only 13%. Many farmers complain that the subsidy is too low with only a limited coverage of products, and there are too many formalities for application. All this has reduced the enthusiasm of farmers' purchasing the products.

5.4.2 Export Rebate Does Not Really Benefit Enterprises

Journalist: What responses and effects have the export promotion measures, including export rebate, brought to enterprises in China?

Chen Yunxian: The export rebate rate for products, like textile and garment, electrical products and chemical products, had been on the increase for five successive years since 2008. The total exports of those products covered by export rebates amounted to only 48.55 billion US dollars by January, 2009 with a decrease of 11.1% compared with the same period of the previous year and a lower-than-17.5% decrease of China's total exports, and accounted for 53.7% of the total exports compared with the same period of the previous year. Although the export value of those export rebate products continued to decrease in January, 2009, the total export value increased by 15% over the same period of the previous year, despite the influence of the Spring Festival. It follows that the increase of export rebates has exerted positive influences upon China's export.

However, the increase or expansion of export rebates has a counter effect. Foreign enterprises consider it a reduction of export costs and thus request that our export enterprises lower the prices of their products. The original intention of the export rebate policy is to benefit domestic enterprises by decreasing their costs, but advantage has been taken by foreign enterprises.

Under such circumstances, some flexible forms of subsidies can be adopted, such as the multi-level government subsidies, which may be a good way to extend the space of fiscal subsidies, because it is more flexible and brings more benefits to domestic enterprises, and there is no ground for foreign enterprises to lodge anti-subsidy complaints.

Journalist: What is your suggestion then?

Chen Yunxian: We should adopt other forms of subsidies to help exporting enterprises.

The present export rebate policy will terminate by the end of 2009. The export rebate range should be stabilized within the limits of two third of the total export rebate in 2010, which may be acceptable to both domestic and foreign enterprises. This part of export rebate should be used to lower export prices and boost domestic enterprises' competitiveness of similar products on the overseas market. The remaining one third of the total export rebate should be granted after exporting enterprises fulfill their orders and collect all earnings through application to the local government who check and assess their exporting performances.

The subsidies take various forms, for instance, in the form of government return of employees' social security cost paid by enterprises, in the form of supporting policies and funds, in the form of incentive funds for exporting, or in the form of property and real estate tax returns. These diversified forms of subsidies can really benefit domestic enterprises because they must fulfill the requirements for the subsidies, and foreign enterprises will have no justification for their request for price reduction.

(First published in *The twenty-first Century Business Herald*, March 10, 2009)

5.5 *Nanfang Daily*: Guiding the Development of Chinese Financial Industry

The establishment of "Guangdong High-tech Financial Service Center" in Nanhai District has brought Foshan into the general configuration Guangdong's development of financial industry, which means a great deal to Foshan, a base for traditional manufacturing.

Chen Yunxian, mayor of Foshan, a Ph.D. in economics and GF's former chairman, is a widely recognized expert in finance. He was recently interviewed about how he will guide the construction of "Guangdong High-tech Financial Service Center" and put the plan into operation.

Journalist: "Guangdong High-tech Financial Service Center" has settled in Nanhai, Foshan, which can be interpreted as a major move on the part of Guangdong Provincial Government to enhance economic cooperation between Guangzhou and Foshan. How do you think financial industry will develop against the background of the integration of Guangzhou-Foshan economy?

Chen Yunxian: The development of financial industry requires not only main transaction bases, such as Shanghai, Shenzhen and Guangzhou where numerous international financial organizations gather, but also backup centers with high technology, like "Guangdong High-tech Financial Service Center", which is under construction in Foshan. There is a similar case in America: New York is the center of American financial industry, but its backup centre is situated in New Jersey. A financial layout like this is compact, reasonable and scientific.

With China's entry into WTO, China's financial industry has become increasingly integrated into international financial circles. If Guangdong attempts to attract international financial magnates, it must build a backup centre. Strictly speaking, this backup centre should be settled in a place other than financial centers. The setup of Guangdong High-tech Financial Service Center in Nanhai is a strategic decision made by Guangdong Provincial Government in accordance with the scientific outlook on development and paves a good way for further developing Guangdong financial industry.

With regard to the development of High-tech Financial Service Center, there are existing models to follow from home and abroad. The primary condition is the backup centre of information technology. What comes next is the information analysis center which relates to the primary condition, then the research and development center, and finally the financial industrial innovation center. The first three work as the base for the central functions of the main financial industry, and the last one develops gradually into an industrial cluster of financial industrial systems, including banking, trust, securities, funds, insurance, futures and so on.

Guangdong High-tech Financial Service Center will, first of all, function as the high-tech backup centre for financial industry and extend this function into research and development, information analysis, financial innovation and so on. The more importance thing is to give full play to these functions so as to form an industrial cluster of financial systems and eventually lead the development of financial industry in Guangdong and even in China.

Journalist: This center is not only the backup center of Guangdong Province but also Foshan's financial foreground. What is your interpretation of "Foshan's financial foreground"?

Chen Yunxian: Guangdong High-tech Financial Service Center is designated as the backup center of Guangdong's financial industry. "Foshan's financial foreground", which you have just mentioned, is considered from the perspective of its tertiary industry. Foshan's 2006 GDP had reached 292.6 billion yuan, with tertiary industry taking up only 34.4%. Japan's tertiary industry exceeded 62% in 1979, tertiary industry in Taiwan 80%, and Hong Kong 90%. All this suggests that the proportion of tertiary industry is likely to surpass the total amount of the primary and secondary industry in the post-industrialization period. The tertiary industry should be the powerhouse of Foshan's economic development, as Foshan is now in its transformation from the middle stage to the late stage of industrialization. There should be at least 10%–15% space for increase in Foshan's tertiary industry, judging from both domestic and international experience.

In addition to non-production services, the focus should be on the industry in between secondary and service industry, such as financial industry. What are the advantages of Foshan's developing a high-tech financial center? There are many economic underpinnings for it in Foshan that are well suited to its development. More than 267,000 enterprises are registered with Foshan Industrial and Commercial Bureau, about 90% of which fall into the primary and secondary industry, and most of them are small and medium-sized private enterprises which are in great demand of capital. The total bank savings of Foshan amounted to over 440 billion yuan in 2006 and rose to 460 billion yuan in the first half of 2007, despite the attractive booming stock markets. It suggests that not only enterprises but also the public with surplus capital form the sources for Foshan's financial industry.

Foshan boasts prominent regional advantages, which, together with industrial strengths and sufficient social capital, contribute to its financial development. Besides, Foshan is the national advanced city with digitalized administration, and Nanhai is the model city of e-government.

Journalist: As a project planned by Guangdong Provincial Government, how will the High-tech Financial Center operate in accordance with the market principles? What will Foshan do to provide a suitable environment for the development of financial industry?

Chen Yunxian: Our guiding principle is "government leading, enterprise participation, and market operation." This calls for Foshan's continuous efforts to conform with international financial industrial norms and to attract international financial magnates to settle in Foshan.

Planning should go before any practical work, especially the enforcement of major measures. This center, though located in Foshan, will cover Guangdong Province and the whole of South China as well. It is hoped that the national financial authorities and relevant authorities of Guangdong Province will provide more support and provide us with guidance in planning and performing its functions with a view to effectively boosting China's financial industry, particularly banking, trust, securities, fund, insurance and other relevant businesses.

As far as I can see, a complete financial market should contain spot goods, futures, interest rate and exchange rate. But what China opens to market remains only to be spot goods—stock and bond. Other kinds of business are almost next to nothing. China's financial industry has only developed for more than 10 years, and there is a great deal of space for spot goods, futures, interest rate and exchange rate to be marketized and internationalized. Guangdong, especially the Pearl River Delta, which is adjacent to Hong Kong and Macao, can learn from their experience and do its bit to further develop financial industry.

Journalist: What support do Foshan city and Nanhai District expect to get from Guangdong Province in the course of constructing the high-tech financial center? What preferential policies will be provided to solicit investments?

Chen Yunxian: There will be a series of problems to solve in the course of its construction. For instance, network communication for such a center requires not only network application software but also wide-band communication, network channels and other supporting facilities. We must first solve the problem of technical facilities. We hope that Guangdong provincial government will provide preferential policies for these problems to be removed and that those financial organizations in the center will get easy and quick access to network communication.

We also hope that the provincial government will provide assistance to the financial institutions, both domestic and overseas, so that they can get settled and start their operations in the shortest possible time. Meanwhile, joint efforts must be made for the construction of expressway networks in Foshan, their connection with those in Guangzhou, and the coordinated enforcement of law and so on.

To sum up, our objective is to create conditions for the High-tech Financial Service Center to start operation as soon as possible so that financial enterprises in the center can reap early benefits.

Journalist: What are your thoughts about how to solicit financial projects of foreign investment in the High-tech Financial Service Center?

Chen Yunxian: After the opening up of financial industry, Foshan municipal government decided that one of the first financial tasks in 2007 was to introduce a foreign bank to set up its branches in Foshan. A promotion conference about foreign-capital financial service sector and investment environment in Foshan was held in June 2007 to introduce the High-tech Financial Service Center to over 40 foreign banks and insurance companies. Favorable feedback was received from such institutions as Hang Seng Bank and American International Assurance Company, which conducted their field investigation in the High-tech Financial Service Center. Continuous efforts will be made to attract more foreign-capital financial institutions into the center, and the first foreign-capital bank is to be settled in the center to set a role model.

Journalist: Judging from your experience of working in financial industry, what difficulties do you think Nanhai may have in developing financial service industry?

Chen Yunxian: The lack of financial specialists is the greatest difficulty. After all, as a city of traditional industry, Foshan's financial industry has been lagging behind and its financial talent pool is limited. Foshan is making a medium- and long-term plan for talent cultivation and will work together with universities such as Sun Yat-Sen University, South China University of Technology and Jinan University to train specialized financial personnel. Meanwhile, recruitment will be made of those with financial experience, especially of financial specialists from Hong Kong by means of Closer Economic Partnership Arrangement (CEPA). High-quality and efficient services will be provided to those financial personnel of high-caliber and those employed by financial enterprises so as to form large teams of financial talents and meet the human resources requirements for the High-tech Financial Service Center. The municipal government has implemented a supporting policy to offer special allowances and income tax reduction to these high-level talents and senior administrators and preferential channels for residential registration and for their children to be admitted into school.

Besides, supporting facilities are to be built for other types of tertiary industry to integrate into the High-tech Financial Service Center and create an atmosphere of a modern metropolis for them. With all the supporting facilities completed,these competent financial talents are expected to not only bring their skills into full play but also settle down in the High-tech Financial Service Center.

(First published in *Nanfang Daily*, August 1, 2007)

5.6 *Foshan Daily*: The Instant Eruption of "Financial Magma" in Foshan

"To make a comparison, I liken Foshan to a 'volcano', and financial industry is its scorching 'magma'. Once the blazing magma breaks through the surface, its huge quantities of erupted energy will shake the whole world." Chen Yunxian, secretary of Foshan Municipal Committee of CPC, told a journalist of *Foshan Daily* in an exclusive interview. The financial industry will release huge quantities of energy to propel Foshan on its track of leapfrog development. In 2010, Foshan municipal government will launch six financial innovation programs, including the establishment of rural financial systems and regional financial cooperation.

5.6.1 Finance Must Be a Leader in Building "Intelligent Foshan"

Journalist: The financial sector was heightened to a new level at the "Two Sessions" of Foshan in 2010. Everybody knows that you have devoted quite a lot to developing Foshan's financial industry. What benefits do you think the financial industry will bring to Foshan?

Chen Yunxian: To answer your question, we have to start from the basic features of finance. We all know that finance plays a crucial role in allocating resources and selecting the fittest for survival in economic development. No aspects of social development can do without financial support. Foshan Municipal Government put forward the developmental notion of "Intelligent Foshan via Fourization" in May 2010, which requires financial antecedence and finance to take the leading position in building up "Intelligent Foshan".

I compare Foshan to a "volcano", and financial industry is its scorching "magma". There is only silence before volcano eruption, but its huge quantities of erupted energy will shake the whole world once its blazing magma breaks out of the surface. The development of financial industry will enormously facilitate Foshan's popularity and competitiveness. Fourteen companies have gone public since 2007 in Foshan, more than doubling that of the past decade, which turns Foshan into a focus of the media.

The development of financial industry has also expedited Foshan's transformation of economic development mode and its adjustment of industrial structure. In the past decades, Foshan has accomplished the transformation from an agricultural city to an industrial city. In the future decades, the tertiary industry will achieve unprecedented development with the support of financial means and will catch up and match with the secondary industry.

Thirdly, the development of financial industry can help to strengthen and expand enterprises so as to build up more brands for Foshan. Take Midea Electric Appliances Group for example. The benefits it has gained from capital market enable it to develop at a surprising speed into a well-known international brand, with its output value well exceeding 100 billion.

Finally, the development of financial industry has brought more material benefits and convenience to the general public in Foshan. "Intelligent Finance" is a basic part of "Intelligent Foshan". Through "Intelligent Finance", the public can obtain such substantial benefits and services as "all-in-one" cards, online-banks, deposits and withdrawals, etc. In the next few years, Foshan will put in more funds and technology into the construction of the system of "Intelligent Finance".

5.6.2 This Year's "Six New's" of Financial Development

Journalist: Under the context of "Intelligent Foshan via Fourization", Foshan's financial circles have paid unusual attention to financial innovation. How should financial innovation be carried out in Foshan? What specific thoughts do you have? Where may the breakthrough be achieved?

Chen Yunxian: In terms of financial innovation, differences exist between enterprises and the government. The former focuses almost exclusively on business innovation and service innovation, while the latter pays considerable attention to how to adjust and guide its development so as to meet the demands of social development today.

In 2010, the "six new's" approach was put forward to financial departments of all levels of government in Foshan:

1. New breakthroughs in the construction of rural financial systems,
2. New development in the construction of the High-tech Financial Service Center,
3. New progress in enterprise listing and capital market,

4. New measures in cooperation of regional finance,
5. New highlights in financial reform and innovation, and
6. New mechanisms in standardization of financial development.

Efforts were made in 2009 to successfully introduce HSBC, the Bank of East Asia, Hang Seng Bank and Wing Hang Bank into Foshan as a result of the addition of the article into Supplementary Agreement VI of CEPA that the foreign banks which have set up their its branches in Guangzhou shall be permitted to open new branches in other cities of Guangdong Province. Although Foshan has not been included into the first batch of pilot cities for cross-border trade payment in RMB, relevant transactions between enterprises and banks have been booming, with its cross-border trade payment in RMB ranking in the second place in Guangdong Province. Midea Group successfully put 20 million yuan overseas loans into operation via China Bank Hong Kong Branch and became the first to practice overseas loans in RMB. It can be concluded that only with innovation can we take the first step and obtain priority. Next, stronger support will be given to the employment of financial talents and the setup of new financial institutions so as to provide a sound external environment for the development of financial industry in Foshan.

5.6.3 Five to Eight Enterprises to Be Listed This Year

Journalist: You have got a very famous remark, "Let the light of capital shine over Foshan's industrial highland." It is one of the major obligations of financial industry to enhance industrial transformation and upgrading in Foshan, and the primary method is to promote enterprise equity financing. Four enterprises got listed in 2009. How many are planning to go public in 2010?

Chen Yunxian: With those listed companies serving as role models, more and more entrepreneurs and government officials have come to realize that enterprise listing is not only an effective means of financing from capital market but also an opportunity for enterprises to build new platforms and mechanisms for standardized and sustainable development and better corporate governance.

Accordingly, Foshan Municipal Government decided in 2010 that the municipal government leaders be associated with key towns of enterprise listing and that some enterprises in Nanzhuang Town, Chancheng District be recommended as the first to be prepared for listing so as to set an example for others to follow. Ten enterprises have been encouraged to apply for listing, and five to eight will successfully go public in 2010.

So far in 2010, five enterprises in Foshan have got listed on domestic and overseas stock markets. On April 12, 2010, Debao Property Development Co. Ltd went public on Singapore stock market, followed by China Liansu Group Holdings Ltd, which was listed on Hong Kong Exchanges on June 24, 2010, and then Guangdong Shenglu Telecommunication Tech Co. Ltd and Foshan NationStar Optoelectronics Co. Ltd, which landed on A-share minor enterprises board on July 13, 2010 and July 16, 2010 respectively. Shenglu Telecommunication is the first listed company in

Sanshui District and fills in the blank. Asia Ceramics Holdings PLC got listed on growth enterprises market of the London Stock Exchange on September 27, 2010. Until now, there are 27 listed companies in Foshan, amongst nine from Shunde, nine from Nanhai, eight from Chancheng, and one from Sanshui. In addition, Guangdong Vanward New Electric Co. Ltd has applied to China Securities Regulatory Commission for listing. Another four to five enterprises are ready to apply. Ten enterprises have successfully undergone their guided corporate reform, over 20 enterprises are making preparation, and over 80 enterprises have expressed their inclination.

Meanwhile, Foshan is endeavoring to become the pilot city for the "new tertiary board", which, if approved, will open new channels for local businesses to strengthen themselves through financing and achieve standardized development.

5.6.4 Private Capital Possesses Huge Potentials

Journalist: Foshan takes great pride in its private capital. Now attempts have been made in financial innovations, such as the petty loan scheme, financing assurances, and rural banks. What is to be done to further tap private capital by such innovative means of financing in the future?

Chen Yunxian: Foshan has a population of 6 million, with bank savings of its residents exceeding 400 billion yuan, about 80,000 yuan per person. This is a good indication of folk wealth. But for quite a long time, the ratio between savings and loans has remained at about 60%. This comparatively low ratio reveals that a large amount of idle capital has not been effectively utilized. Although some new financial institutions, such as petty loan companies, guarantee companies and rural banks, have been established in the recent years, there has been less than 2 billion yuan of registered capital, with six petty loan companies taking up 990 million yuan, guarantee companies about 800 million yuan and one rural bank 200 million yuan. It is obvious that a great deal of potentials await to be developed in private capital by innovative financial means.

The innovative financial means include:

1. Seek more supporting policies so that more petty loan companies are established to provide help in removing the financing problems with small and medium-sized enterprises and with farmers and agriculture-related businesses, as petty loans are safe, quick and time-saving;
2. Expand the number of pilot rural banks. Drawing on the experience of the Industrial and Commercial Rural Bank of Shunde setting up Gaoming Shunyin Rural Bank, we will set up more rural banks and encourage local rural credit cooperatives to transform into industrial and commercial rural banks and set up branches in different locations;
3. Private capital is to be encouraged to be invested in local enterprises. Venture capital firms are to be established to select good-quality small and medium-sized enterprises, which can utilize private capital to develop and expand themselves so that the society, enterprises and investors can reap win-win benefits;

4. Work is to be done to encourage the establishment of such institutions as finance companies, consuming finance companies, and financial leasing companies so as to pool financial resources for major undertakings;
5. Wealth management activities should be encouraged, and wealth management centers should be set up so as to create more social values.

(First published in *Foshan Daily*, September 21, 2010)

5.7 The News Conference of Guangdong Provincial Government: Taking Full Advantage of Policies and Opportunities to Achieve Breakthroughs

The News Conference on Implementation of *the Outline* by Foshan, Guangdong

Time: September 21, 2009

Theme: The News Conference on Implementation of *the Outline* by Foshan

Speaker: Chen Yunxian, mayor of Foshan City and deputy secretary of Foshan Municipal Committee of CPC

Host: Li Shoujin, deputy chief of the Publicity Department of Guangdong Provincial Committee of CPC and director of the Information Office of the People's Government of Guangdong Province

Host: Good morning, everybody. The fifth session of the news conference on implementation of *the Outline* is to be held here by the Information Office of the People's Government of Guangdong Province. The guest We have invited today is Chen Yunxian, mayor of Foshan City and deputy secretary of Foshan Municipal Committee of CPC. He will briefing on Taking Full Advantage of Policies and Opportunities to Achieve Breakthroughs with the latest introduction about the implementation of *the Outline* in Foshan and will be answering questions from news reporters. The conference will last about one hour.

Let's welcome Mayor Chen to give us a briefing.

5.7.1 Leading Foshan to Sustainable Development by Implementing the Outline *as Turning Point*

Chen Yunxian: Ladies and gentlemen, on this special occasion of the celebration of the 60th anniversary of the People's Republic of China, I'm delighted to have this opportunity to brief the provincial government officials, the public and media friends on the latest development of Foshan and discuss with you various issues in relation to the further improvement of our work.

As is known to all, Foshan is located on the east bank of the Pearl River Delta, covering a total area of 3,800 km^2 with a population of 5.93 million and comprising five administrative districts: Chancheng, Nanhai, Shunde, Gaoming and Sanshui. At least three unique features can be highlighted in the course of Foshan's development. As a neighbor to Guangzhou, Foshan enjoys an advantageous geographic location.

It takes only 1 h to the center of Guangzhou and less than 1 h to the Baiyun Airport, Nansha Port, and the Guangzhou New Railway Station. It takes 1 h and 50 min by boat or 2 h by coach to Hong Kong and 1½h by coach to Macao.

Second, Foshan has a long history and rich cultural precipitation. In the ancient times, Nanhai Town of Guangzhou was one of “China’s Four Renowned Towns”, together with Jingde Town in Jiangxi Province, Hankou Town in Hubei Province, Zhuxian Town in Henan. The unique Lingnan culture, such as Cantonese cuisine and the art of lion dances, has been developing rapidly in Foshan. Bruce Lee and Wong Fei Hung are the city’s cards with international fame.

Third, strong industrial clusters are formed in Foshan, with a solid foundation of industrial economy as a result of China’s 30 years’ reform and opening-up. Foshan’s GDP is 433.3 billion yuan in 2008, an increase of 15.2% over the previous year. The primary industry takes up only 2.2%, the secondary industry, which is the main part of the total industrial output, 65.6%, and the tertiary industry 32%. Foshan has become a city of industrial economy. The private sector accounts for 57%, the foreign-invested sector 36%, and the remaining 7% comes from the state-owned enterprises.

So far, more than 337,000 enterprises have registered with the industrial and commercial authorities of Foshan. Among them, over 1,800 enterprises have their output value exceeding 100 million yuan, over 250 enterprises 1–10 billion yuan, and another six 10–100 billion yuan, thus forming an economic mapping with small and medium-sized enterprises as its base, coupled with large- scale enterprises, which are getting strengthened and expanded in Foshan.

The foreign trade takes up 42.2 billion US dollars of the total trade volume in 2008, with the general trade exceeding 53%, and the processing trade about 46%. The primary market in America and European Union takes up 14% and 18% respectively, and 22% are traded through Hong Kong ports mainly to America and European Union. So nearly 55% of the total foreign trade is conducted with America and European Union, which is an obvious feature of Foshan’s foreign trade.

Throughout this process, Foshan Municipal Government has made continuous efforts to exercise foresighted leading, encourage enterprises to grow larger and stronger and helps them resist possible international financial risks and crises. The implementation of *the Outline*, which was promulgated by the State Council, is not only a challenge but also an opportunity for further development. Therefore, we take the initiatives and work hard for the unification of Guangzhou and Foshan, the integration of the Pearl River Delta and the in-depth cooperation between Guangdong, Hong Kong and Macao with a view to achieving continuous and sustainable development in Foshan. From January to August 2009, Foshan’s GDP exceeds 300 billion yuan, with an increase of 12.6% over the previous year. The encouraging news is the increase of the output value of the tertiary industry from 32.2% at the end of 2008 to 33.9% in August 2009, and the decrease of the output value of the primary industry from 2.2% in 2008 to 1.9% between January and August 2009. The remaining 64% is the output value of the secondary industry.

It can be concluded that Foshan’s economy is chiefly based on its industry and manufacturing, which mainly fall into the private sector. Its economy runs on the two wheels of private enterprises and foreign-invested enterprises. Its small and medium-sized enterprises occupy a dominant position. Foshan ranks among top cities in Guangdong in the total foreign trade volume.

A series of measures have been taken to offset impacts from the international financial crisis, to lead Foshan develop on its right track of continuous and sustainable development through implementing *the Outline*. Thanks to all these efforts and measures, Foshan's economic growth headed the list in the Pearl River Delta in the first three quarters of 2009 again after 2008. I would like to take the opportunity to express our thanks to the provincial government for their wise leadership, to the general public for their concern and support of Foshan, and to our media friends present today for your attention and support. Now please allow me to give a brief introduction about the future development of Foshan.

We will do our bit to build Foshan into a modern manufacturing base, an industrial service center, a famous city of Lingnan culture, a beautiful and prosperous homeland. We need to make more efforts to overcome the difficulties incurred by the financial crisis and strive conscientiously toward our objective. That is Foshan now and Foshan in the future. Thank you.

Host: Thank you very much for your brief introduction, Mayor Chen. He is a PhD degree holder in economics, as well as a famous figure with the media. Before the conference, we decided to set aside more time for questions and answers. Now we have about 40 minutes to go, for questions.

5.7.2 *Resisting Crisis: Early Awareness, Prompt Action and Good Accomplishments*

Journalist from *Nanfang Daily*: Good morning, Mayor Chen. It is said that the growth rate of Foshan's GDP from January to August in 2009 has increased by 12%, and the proportion of the tertiary industry has increased for the first time. According to your experience, does it mean that Foshan's economy has achieved breakthroughs in some aspects? On what standards is your judgment based? What benefits has Foshan gained in this process? In what other aspects should we continue to make efforts to make breakthroughs? Thank you.

Chen Yunxian: As I mentioned just now, I enjoy interacting with the media. Now let me return you a question first: what's the standard for breakthroughs? It is clear to us that we should take both short-term and long-term measures to fight against the international financial crisis. The American sub-prime crisis began in August or September 2007, and it had been almost one and a half year by the end of 2008, while the mortgage crisis in EU began in the fourth quarter of 2008 and lasted only for one year by now. It may be safely assumed that the trend of the international financial crisis should be U-shaped. As a region of China's economy, Foshan was early aware of the crisis, took prompt action and made good achievements in its fight against the crisis. It achieved a growth rate of 12.6% of GDP from January to August in 2009 after an increase of 15.2% in 2008 and an increase of 12.2% in the first half of 2009, which is an obvious manifestation that our measures have taken effect in fighting against the international financial crisis and in ensuring Foshan's continuous and sustainable development.

More importantly, no matter what trend the international financial crisis or China's economic development takes, it remains a highly controversial and heated topic whether the current international financial crisis has come to an end or whether it would come again. What we are more concerned about is what our local government should do in the post-crisis era after achieving short-run sustainable and steady progress in Foshan's economic development, which we take pride in. We would take advantage of this post-crisis timing to establish our modern industrial system, strengthen our ecological environment protection and promote the urban-rural integration. Our people, our social causes and welfare undertakings should benefit from the achievements of reforms and opening-up. This is what we are doing and will continue to be our objective in the post-crisis era. We need more effective measures to achieve more substantial effects. Thank you very much for your good question.

5.7.3 First Trial and First Execution: Establishing Modern Industrial System and Exploring Ways for Institutional Reform

Journalist from *Guangzhou Daily*: Good morning, Mayor Chen, may I ask you two questions? Foshan is standing at the forefront of China's reform and opening-up. What will Foshan first try and execute according to *the Outline*? My second question is, Shunde's cross-department organizational restructuring was launched last week. What implication will it bring to Foshan's municipal-level restructuring of government functions, and when would Foshan start this reform? Thank you.

Chen Yunxian: Your first question is about "first trial and first execution". Let us talk about this beyond the question. In what stage of economic development is China at present, and also Foshan? As indicated above, Foshan is a city based on industrial and manufacturing economy. Today China's manufacturing and industry is still in the middle stage of industrial economy. Although Foshan has take one step ahead, it remains in the transition from the middle to the late stage, far from the post-industrial period. The urban-rural integration is holding back our urbanization, which is a stumbling block we have to remove or a key problem we will endeavor to settle.

For example, Foshan has a registered population of 3.65 million and about 49% are rural residents and take up 54% of Foshan's 3,800 km^2 of land resources, with the whole agricultural sector accounting for less than 2%. All this indicates that problems relating to agriculture, rural areas and farmers deserve immediate solution, including the urban-rural integration, the narrow-down of urban-rural dual structuring, etc. As a forerunner of China's reform and opening-up, Foshan, especially Shunde and Nanhai, is marching along the road of internationalization through continuous participation in international competition, gradual penetration into more domestic and foreign markets, is promoting the development of private and foreign-invested enterprises and improving our policies and measures to conform with international market rules. These are all areas where first trial and first execution will be practiced in accordance to *the Outline*.

As a starting point, it is of utmost importance to establish Foshan's modern industrial system on the basis of its orientation specified in *the Outline*. Foshan will continue its efforts to transform and upgrade its traditional industries, introduce and develop new high-tech enterprises and forge a strong modern industrial system, which can be summarized as "three promotions and one maintenance" according to the guiding principles of Guangdong Provincial Government. Endeavor will be made to promote self-initiated innovation, promote industrial transformation and upgrading and promote the establishment of modern industrial system on condition that economic stability and well-coordinated development are to be maintained. We hope to go first and try first in these areas.

Secondly, *the Outline* has designated Foshan, Zhongshan and Huizhou as pilot cities of urban-rural integration. Ways must be worked out to narrow down the gap between urban and rural areas and realize substantial urban-rural integration. It is essential for Foshan to fill in the urban-rural gap on its way to industrialization and urbanization. We hope to go first and try first in this area so that rural residents can really benefit from the achievements of reform and opening up.

Thirdly, the question of how to achieve further internationalization requires us to think about how to forge brand names and depend on self-development, on one hand, and how to effectively connect with the international market, on the other hand. Part of the answer, which is provided in *the Outline*, is the further development through the unification of Guangzhou and Foshan, the integration of the Pearl River Delta regions, and the more extensive in-depth cooperation between Guangdong and Hong Kong, and Macao. Foshan will go first and try first in this area, too.

More importantly, Foshan will also take bold steps to practice first trials in government administration, systems and policies, approaches and measures in conformity with the direction of the central government and in the light of the actual situation. Only in this way can we achieve further development. And that leads me to your second question about the current municipal-level restructuring of government functions.

Respecting the cross-department administrative restructuring in Shunde, breakthroughs have been achieved in at least the following aspects: a new approach has been formed in the transformation of government functions; a new approach has been formed in optimization of organization structures, which extends from district administrative organizations to district party organizations with the number of departments reduced from 41 to 16; a new approach has been formed in flat management through simplifying unnecessary procedures and formalities to achieve higher efficiency, as directors of these 16 functional departments are also district-level government leaders; a new work mechanism has been established, where the rights to decide, to know and to monitor are clearly clarified and administrative and party organizations can coordinate and function efficiently; a new approach has been formed in expediting reforms in supporting policies.

All these "first trials and first executions" will throw illuminating light upon the reforms not only in Foshan but also in Guangdong Province and even the whole country as well. A region's government restructuring is deemed to succeed if it contributes to the development of productivity, if it benefits the general public and contributes to the economy, and if it contributes to a stable, sustainable harmonious society.

The functional restructuring of the government is well under way in Shunde now. Last Thursday, principal leaders of Foshan Municipal Government, together with chiefs of Shunde District, convened a conference of cadres from all levels of Shunde, where the reform program, its facilitating measures, department responsibilities, and personnel arrangement were all announced. It is expected that all the arrangement will be in place by the end of October and that the reform will be going as planned.

5.7.4 Developing Tertiary Industry: Expediting Financial Industry and Exhibition Industry and Deepening Cooperation Between Guangdong, Hong Kong and Macao

Journalist from *Ta Kung Pao* of Hong Kong: Foshan's tertiary industry is reported to reach 40% of its GDP by 2012. It is only three years to go and there is still some distance from that target. By what means can Foshan reach this target? My second question is, it is well known that service industry is the most competitive pillar industry in Hong Kong. How will Foshan cooperate with Hong Kong in this area? What opportunities have you discovered in such cooperation in Hong Kong? Thank you.

Chen Yunxian: Good question. Foshan's tertiary industry is rather weak compared with other cities. And its proportion to GDP is the lowest in the 21 cities of Guangdong Province. How to expedite and strengthen Foshan's tertiary industry? The tertiary industry mainly consists of productive services and other varieties of service. The breakthrough is to be made in productive services and financial industry. I am sure everybody present here knows the news of the establishment of Guangdong High-tech Financial Service Center in Nanhai.

I will deliver a special speech this Friday afternoon at The Asia-Pacific Economic Forum, Guangzhou, which focuses on financial development. In line with institutional arrangements, the establishment of Guangdong High-tech Financial Service Center in Nanhai will serve as the powerful base for backup services that will be connected and matched with the demands of the financial industry in Shenzhen and Hong Kong. Foshan's industrial output exceeded 1 trillion yuan by the end of 2008, and Foshan has become one of the top cities in terms of industry and economic strength among the 21 cities of Guangdong Province. It is our firm commitment that continuous efforts will be made to enhance the development of logistics on both domestic and overseas market so that the logistics system will match with and provide strong support for Foshan's modern manufacturing industry.

Exhibition industry is also very important. As is known to all, there are supply, production, and more importantly, consumption in the whole industrial chain. The entry into domestic and international markets by means of consumption chain is reflected not only in tangible and visible consumption but also in e-commerce. Thus, our exhibition center will be actively establishing ties with various industries, as exhibition industry, which plays a significant role at home and abroad in such areas as high-tech service and industrial design service. Take Midea Group for example. It enjoys an output value of over 100 billion yuan and wants to further expand into both domestic and international markets. Are the specifications and quality of its products are in line with those of the domestic and international markets? What should Midea do to have a larger share of the international market? These problems are to be removed via RFD tag identification.

To sum up, in the development of tertiary industry, focus will mainly be laid on financial industry, trade industry, exhibition industry and other related service industries. In addition, Foshan is well known to be a famous city with rich cultural heritage, such as Cantonese opera, Foshan cuisine, tourist attractions and intangible Foshan culture. Measures have been taken to synergize these tourist resources so as to achieve maximum effects. I am confident that once all these are put into actual operation, Foshan's tertiary industry will be enjoying rapid and sound development.

The question of how to cooperate with Hong Kong effectively is well worthy of our serious consideration. The effective enforcement of CEPA has turned out to be the most desirable way in deepening cooperation between Guangdong, Hong Kong and Macao, especially the CEPA Supplementary Agreement VI, which has just been promulgated and will take effect in October 2009.

A package of agreements was signed the first time I went to Hong Kong, together with Song Hai, deputy governor of Guangdong Province, to hold promotions about Guangdong High-tech Financial Service Center in Foshan, and good accomplishments were also made the second time I went to Hong Kong as part of the delegation headed by Wang Qingliang, deputy governor of Guangdong Province, to hold promotions about Foshan's foreign trade.

I will be going to Hong Kong again, together with principal chiefs of Guangdong Province, to have another promotion in relation to the enforcement of CEPA in a few days. Previous to this, 23 project agreements were signed in areas of finance, logistics, trade, exhibition, scientific and technological service, industrial design, law, accounting and others to reinforce the enforcement of CEPA. Hopefully, these major measures will bear fruit under the framework of CEPA. I hope to pass on all this news to our friends in Hong Kong through friends present here. We sincerely welcome you all to come to Foshan and find your opportunities there.

5.7.5 Conducting Orderly Institutional Reform Throughout Foshan

Journalist from *Southern Metropolitan Daily*: Good morning, Mayor Chen, it was made public last week that Ronggui Town and Shishan Town will be the pilots in the reform of "stronger township with more authority delegation" in Foshan. What is the main idea of this reform? Will this reform be moving in the direction, as you proposed, of granting strong township county-level administrative power. Another question, reform means breaking the existing pattern. Some comment that Foshan has been sort of fumbling around recently for having undertaken a series of system reforms. What do you think of this? How can coordination be achieved between taking the initiative and maintaining stability so as for reforms to go smoothly? Thank you.

Chen Yunxian: Speaking of the issue of granting more authority to strong townships, I would like to cite Ronggui, one of the towns in Shunde District, as an example. Ronggui's gross industrial output value approximates 100 billion yuan, and its GDP exceeds 20 billion yuan. Its disposable financial revenues amounts to over 2 billion yuan. It shows that the growth rate of the economic aggregate of this small town exceeds that of a prefecture-level city in an underdeveloped region, hence the question of how to further promote the development of such strong towns as stand on the forefront of China's reform and opening up.

The selection of Ronggui and Shishan as the pilot towns in exploring ways of "granting more authorities to strong towns" intends to remove part of the administrative relations incompatible with social and economic development, namely, relations of production should conform to the productive forces. The whole development must accommodate the needs on the part of enterprises and people and benefit their development.

As for the question what its final positioning should be, it needs gradual experimentation and clarification. That is why only two out of 33 towns in Foshan have been selected for first trial. It is true that Foshan is conducting a comprehensive government functional restructuring, covering the township-level of Ronggui and Shishan's "stronger township with more authority delegation", the county/district-level reform of Shunde's cross-department organizational restructuring, and the municipal-level reform of urban-rural integration and of "two divisions and two replacements". All the reforms are well under way from trial to all-round step-by-step execution. As long as we make continuous efforts and promote the reforms effectively, we will certainly achieve the desired effects.

5.7.6 Promoting Company Listing: Collecting Hong Kong Funds and Standardizing Small and Medium-Sized Enterprises

Journalist from *New Express*: I have got three questions. First, is there any difference in government restructuring reform between Shunde District, Guangzhou and Shenzhen? Second, Foshan has performed extremely well in fighting against the international financial crisis, and small and medium-sized enterprises in Foshan have played a vital role. What supportive measures have been taken to push their listing on the Hong Kong Exchanges? Third, from my interviews with some financial institutions in Hong Kong, I was told that they were planning to set up branches in Foshan. What has the municipal government done to help them carry out their plans? And how are their plans going on? Thank you.

Chen Yunxian: As to modes of the administrative system reform, Shenzhen has announced its focus of reform on the government function. The reform in Zhuhai is under way with its focus mainly laid on the district- or town-level administrative modes. The reform in Shunde, as it was announced, is a comprehensive government restructuring through interaction between government and party organizations and merging 41 departments into 16, which has displayed its obvious differences from that of Shenzhen or of Zhuhai. To some extent, it is more comprehensive and more functional. Steady steps have been taken to propel the reform and continuously improve it till real effects are achieved, so that it meets the needs for the development of productive forces, the needs of people and the need for social harmony.

When it comes to the small and medium-sized enterprises, I'm delighted to inform that Nanfang Ventilator Co. Ltd. of Foshan is the first among the seven companies approved for listing on GEM board by China Securities Regulatory

Commission (CSRC). Small and medium-sized enterprises in Foshan have made formal registration with GEM board, and some of them have already obtained admission into it, such as the newly listed Foshan Saturday Shoes Co. Ltd. and Foshan Jin Yi Metal Products Co. Ltd. Similar measures have also been taken in Shunde and Nanhai, and at least 40 enterprises have submitted their application. We hope to take advantage of this opportunity to establish a modern enterprise system and help small and medium-sized enterprises gain access to more domestic and international markets.

We will strengthen our cooperation with Hong Kong in promoting the development of small and medium-sized enterprises mainly in two aspects. On the one hand, huge amount of small and medium-sized enterprise investment fund and start-up fund in Hong Kong have been absorbed into Foshan to promote their cooperation with small and medium-sized enterprises and help them grow larger and stronger and eventually go public in Shenzhen or in Hong Kong. This is one important aspect of our work, and another aspect is to invite specialists of financial institutions in Hong Kong, especially brokerage firms, law firms and accounting firms, to help small and medium-sized enterprises to standardize their development and build a modern industrial system on the basis of common international practices and rules. That is our current cooperation with Hong Kong.

Hong Kong has displayed special interest in the implementation of *the Outline* and attached great importance to its financial institutions settling in Foshan, especially its involvement in the construction and development of Guangdong High-tech Financial Service Center. I'm delighted to disclose that at least two or three financial institutions from Hong Kong, in particular banking institutions, have planned to settle in Foshan by October 2009, following the office opening of Sun Hung Kai & Co., Ltd. in the Center. Various financial institutions, such as banking, insurance and funds, will open their offices in the Center, and you will soon see the formation of a large cluster of financial industry.

5.7.7 Unifying Guangzhou and Foshan Through Better Interactive Mechanisms and Joint Project Promotion

Journalist from *Yangcheng Evening News*: Guangzhou-Foshan cooperation is the top priority in *the Outline*. I would like to ask what Foshan has done for its people's livelihood in the process, such as medical care and social pension. Will it benefit people of both cities? Also, there are reports about the development plans and projects in relation to the unification, such as the Pearl River Bridge, but what we have seen is the construction of factories in the Pearl River Delta, and there is no sign of the bridge or other projects getting started. Is there a definite timetable for such projects? When will they be completed?

Chen Yunxian: Speaking of welfare undertakings, especially medical care and social pensions, our "Big Brother" Guangzhou has done a great job in some aspects, while Foshan has gone ahead in other aspects. Both cities are working together and learning from each other to improve our work. Take medical care for example. Besides medical insurance for major diseases, Foshan has taken the lead in practicing clinic medical insurance in

Guangdong Province, and it is the first city to have conducted free pre-martial check-ups and antenatal care, which brings benefits and convenience to the Foshan people and to those migrant workers as well.

The monthly sum of social allowances for those families who live below the lowest living standard was raised in recent years from 310 to 350 yuan per person in districts of Chancheng, Nanhai and Shunde and from 280 to 310 yuan in districts of Gaoming and Sanshui. More importantly, the standard for medical care and social pension was also increased.

We spare no efforts to help those difficult families reach the standard and are conducting thorough investigations with the intent to standardize medical care and social pension throughout Foshan. Financial subsidies have been granted on the city-, district- and town-level to those families in particular difficulty to help them go through hard times. In doing so, the general public, especially those in the greatest difficulty, can enjoy the achievements of reform and opening up. Though Foshan has gone ahead in some areas, there is a great deal to learn from Guangzhou's experience. We hope that an interactive mechanism can be formed between Guangzhou and Foshan and be constantly improved and heightened during the unification.

Concerning the joint projects in the unification, a decision has been made by the two-city coordinating team headed by Zhang Guangning, mayor of Guangzhou, and me that among the 52 must-do projects of 2009, 19 projects be completed by the end of this year, 17 complete their formalities and the remaining 16 be launched. I'm pleased to tell you that all the planned projects are going on as scheduled, including the construction of the Pearl River Bridge you have mentioned just now.

I'm honored to announce that the major issues concerning the second consultation conference of mayors on the unification of Guangzhou and Foshan were discussed and agreed upon by Mayor Zhang Guangning and me last Friday morning. This conference will be held in Foshan, and I will be the host. The construction of the Pearl River Bridge is one of the projects to be further discussed at the conference. We intend this bridge to provide convenience for athletes and tourists to enter Foshan before the Asian Games. Leaders of both cities lay great emphasis on the integration of the Pearl River Delta regions, and the unification of Guangzhou and Foshan has been a good example. Thus, there is every reason for us to push ahead all the projects that will benefit both cities.

5.7.8 Financial Innovation via "463" Program to Absorb Domestic Risk Mortgage Fund

Journalist from *Wen Wei Po* of Hong Kong: We have been following the latest development of the Guangdong High-tech Financial Service Center of Foshan and feel encouraged by its admirable accomplishments. We have also noticed Foshan's neighbors like Guangzhou and Huadu District are competing for the projects, too. How will Foshan gain advantages in its competition and cooperation with other cities in the Pearl River Delta? Also, Foshan is working its way towards the setup of Foshan Financial Innovation Experimental Zone, with its focus on the financial cooperation between Guangdong, Hong Kong and Macao. What else is to be done to further open up space for cooperation between Guangdong, Hong Kong and Macao?

Chen Yunxian: According to *the Outline*, Guangdong High-tech Financial Service Center is formally settled in Nanhai District of Foshan, so its development will be following the guidelines in *the Outline*. Under this arrangement, it is of primary importance to avoid unnecessary costs from market competition and institute a mechanism of government leading, enterprise participation and market operation, which is in line with the direction of financial development. We hope that driven by this Center, an orderly pattern of planned development will be established with the Center acting as the engine and the backstage training center, the information center and the financial innovation center as the backup facilities.

Financial experimentation is closely related to foreign trade services, especially financial outsourcing services. Approval must be obtained from the Ministry of Commerce for financial outsourcing services. While submitting application to the Ministry of Commerce, we will take the opportunity of Guangzhou being designated as a model city of outsourcing services to expedite the development of the Guangdong High-tech Financial Service Center as a provider of foreign financial services in accordance with the requirements of the unification of Guangzhou and Foshan. In both cases, it is essential to get support from both the central and provincial government. We also hope that progress can be made in other experimental promotions, like the RMB experimental model city. Apart from all this, I'd like to take this opportunity to announce the launch of Foshan's Financial "463" Program.

We are considering whether financial banks or small clearing units can grant fund to the agricultural sector through insurance guarantee or grant industrial fund in the capacity of industrial manufacturing bases. At least 16 enterprises have been associated with Foshan for domestic fund raising, including risk mortgage fund, venture capital fund, S&T fund, etc. Continuous support has been provided to assist enterprises in listing, and I'm glad to say that more than six enterprises in Foshan have gone public on Hong Kong and mainland stock markets since 2008, which is really a substantial achievement considering the impacts of the international financial crisis. Now we have at least six enterprises on the Hong Kong Exchanges and over 15 on the mainland stock market. We hope that the "Foshan sector" will appear on both Hong Kong and mainland capital markets with extraordinary performance. So much for the measures we have taken in the process of financial reform and innovation. Thanks.

5.7.9 Modern Logistics: Combination of Logistics, Circulation Industry and Financial Industry

China Business News: Mayor Chen, just now you've mentioned logistics, and we all know that it is important to manufacturing. What plans has Foshan made for logistics and new energy industry?

Chen Yunxian: Logistics in Foshan can be categorized into three types: logistics as the base for transits, logistics based on industry (mainly household electrical appliances), and the third, what is called modern logistics, which is linked to the whole production process and the whole industry. We are now trying to introduce Taiwan Misaki Electronics Co. Ltd. into Foshan's logistics system to facilitate the development of logistics under the concept of modern logistics and through integrating logistics into circulation and financial industry. Currently, with the three types, Foshan has become a well-equipped logistics base.

By new energy, I believe you mean wind power generation, solar power generation or the like. We have an adequate supply of solar power generating products in our country, but the core technology is in the possession of foreign enterprises. Thus, in the promotion of solar power generation and new energy, Foshan focuses not only on new materials but more importantly, at least two enterprises in Foshan have been producing machine tools of generators that transfer solar energy into electric energy.

So there is a great deal of room for the development of new industries in Foshan, like new materials, biological pharmacy, information industry and environment protection. The development of new industries will combine with modern logistics in accordance with modern logistics concepts, which will be progressing and improving step by step. It is believed that Foshan will continue to take the lead in Guangdong Province or even in China in the development of new energy, new materials and logistics bases.

Host: That's the end of today's news conference. Thank you, Mayor Chen, and thank you all, and thanks to friends from the media.

Chen Yunxian: My thanks, too, for your kind support of Foshan.

5.7.10 Comments from On-site Assessment Expert of the News Conference: Chen Yunxian's Impromptu Answers Deeply Impress the Media

Yesterday, the news conference lasted for only 1 h, but nearly 50 min were spared for interaction with the journalists, which received highly favorable comments from the media. "No matter whether he was citing statistic figures in introducing Foshan or answering questions from the journalists, Chen Yunxian kept speaking impromptu, without referring to any prepared documents, but with grace and relaxation," commented one assessment expert. "Yesterday was the fifth session of the news conference in relation to the implementation of *the Outline*, and what impressed everyone present was the longest time duration for answering questions from the journalists."

(First published in *Nanfang Daily*, September 22, 2009)

5.8 Davos 2009 (1): The Increase of Number of Foshan's Enterprises Against the International Financial Crisis

The Third Annual Meeting of the New Champions of the World Economic Forum ("The Summer Davos") was held in the Dalian World Expo Center, China on September 10–12, 2009, with over 1,400 guests from 86 countries, including 100 important political leaders. The theme of this annual meeting was "Summer Davos: Re-launching Growth". As an official network partner, Tencent.com made a third live broadcasting of the grand event. The following is an exclusive record of the dialogues between Dr. Chen Yunxian, Mayor of Foshan, Guangdong, and Luo Qiping, the hostess from Tencent.com.

Hostess: Good afternoon, friends, we are honored to have invited Dr. Chen Yunxian, Mayor of Foshan, Guangdong, to have exclusive dialogues with Tencent.com this afternoon. Welcome, Mayor Chen.

Chen Yunxian: Good afternoon, dear net friends.

5.8.1 Confronting Difficulties: Guiding Enterprises in Self-initiated Innovation and Solving Financing Problems

Hostess: Well, let's begin from today's hot issue. The Obama Administration has just announced it will impose a special tariff of 35% on Chinese tires for the first year. We know that Foshan has its market share in the tire industry. Do you think this policy will make some impacts on tire manufacturing enterprises in Foshan?

Chen Yunxian: If trade protectionism is practiced in one country, it will certainly exert negative influences upon the open world market. Foshan's total volume of imports and exports was over 42 billion yuan in 2008, with 14% of its target market in America, 22% via Hong Kong mainly to the American market, and the remaining part to the EU market.

It is clear that Foshan's major target markets for imports and exports are America and the EU countries. That special tariff is sure to make impacts on Foshan's tire exporting. The first anti-dumping case, or we can call it a case of trade protectionism in international trade frictions with China happened to fall upon Shunde District of Foshan around 2004 or 2005. The concerned private enterprises directly reported this case to the Ministry of Commerce and lodged an appeal for protection.

I think similar cases will happen. What should be done is to resort to legal means and lodge appeals for protection. We will also continuously push forward foreign trade in accordance with international practices so as to achieve gradual expansion of intentional markets.

Hostess: There's also a special session for small and medium-sized enterprises on Tencent.com. We know that there is a large number of such enterprises in Foshan. Under grave financial circumstances and possible revival of trade protectionism, Mr. Mayor, what measures would you propose to help these enterprises?

Chen Yunxian: The international financial crisis has seriously affected America and the EU, and it has also made great impacts upon our enterprises. On the one hand, our government has continued theirs to help these enterprises expand into such new markets as the Middle East, ASEAN, South America, and South Africa. On the other hand, efforts have also been made to help them to open up new domestic markets in an attempt to boost their development.

Regarding the development of small and medium-sized enterprises, effective measures have been taken from two aspects. One is to spur small and medium-sized enterprises on their road to self-initiated innovation through science and technology and through knowledge to consolidate their foundation, create their own brands, register patents and turn their product specifications into the standards accepted by domestic or even international industries so that they can expand into larger domestic and international markets in the capacity of OEM providers for overseas enterprises and eventually grow larger and stronger.

The other is to solve financing problems for small and medium-sized enterprises that are confronted with fund shortage. Banks know little about these enterprises and do not feel quite confident about them. In addition, there is not a sufficient supply of capital in guarantee companies, which requires our government to help banks and guarantee companies to set up guarantee funds and loan money to the enterprises in accordance with market operating rules.

By the end of 2008, the number of registered enterprises reached 324,000 and in 2009, it amounted up to 337,000, excluding those closed-down enterprises in the first half of the year. Now, our small and medium-sized enterprises are under favorable development.

Hostess: It is really not easy to achieve all this under such unstable and competitive context.

5.8.2 Government Interaction with the Public to Promote Development of Industrial Associations and Enterprises

Hostess: Successful interaction of the government with industrial associations is one of the highlights of Foshan, the so-called government-business interaction. A lot of such good examples have been found in foreign countries. Mr. Mayor, could you please give us an introduction about the interaction between government and industrial associations?

Chen Yunxian: Intermediary agencies, especially industrial associations, are well developed in Foshan. They have been helping enterprises move forward. Foshan is one of the first cities in China to conduct reforms and open up to the outside world. In terms administrative system, there is a clear demarcation of roles and functions between government, enterprises and industrial associations, which has contributed considerably to industrial development.

The industrial associations have assumed their responsibility for helping enterprises to expand into new domestic and international markets, which started as early as the 1990s. The well-developed industrial associations can now provide guidance to enterprises, help them to solve some problems, and report their problems to the government. It is highly commendable for government, industrial associations (intermediary agencies) and enterprises to work together for economic enhancement and growth.

5.8.3 City Operation: Managing a City as Resources

Hostess: We have noticed that Mayor Chen has been a successful entrepreneur before. Your performance in GF impressed us. And we also know that you have some private intellectual assets. Do you manage the city of Foshan from the perspective of an entrepreneur?

Chen Yunxian: I should say I have drawn on my experience as an entrepreneur and the mode of market economy to look at, operate and manage the city. In the early days of 2003 and 2004, I proposed a rather comprehensive and systematic conception of city operation, that is to say, managing a city as resources, which can be divided into three categories: operative resources, semi-operative resources and non-operative resources. Operative resources can be opened to the society with government leading, enterprise participation, and market operation. Non-operative resources, which mainly involve part of social and public welfare undertakings, are developed completely through governmental funds.

In the case of semi-operative resources, like school education and medical care, part of the resources relating to education and special medical care can be pushed to the market or allow private enterprises to get involved and operate, on condition that education and health welfare are guaranteed for the general public. This is what we have been thinking about and doing in Foshan.

Six promotion conferences have been sponsored in relation to urban operative projects since 2004. Every year over 20 billion yuan of domestic and foreign capital is invested in operative projects and semi-operative projects in Foshan, which has substantially improved Foshan's development. We think it an important concept.

I specialize in finance, and with my financial knowledge and background, I'm able to do my bit for Foshan, under the leadership of the municipal party committee and with the support of my colleagues and the Foshan people. Examples include the introduction of loans from the World Bank, the cooperation with the International Monetary Fund to support small and medium-sized enterprises, and the merger and acquisition of some poor-managed financial institutions so as to help them achieve healthy development.

Another example is to lead enterprises to go public so that they can become larger and stronger under modern enterprise system. We have established incubating mechanisms, such as venture capital investment funds, incubation funds for science and technology, talent development funds and the guarantee funds, to improve economic development. We have also adopted new financial instruments, such as town banks and small guarantee companies, to expedite the development of financial industry, including agriculture and industry. All this has helped in one way or the other in city development and economic management.

5.8.4 Developing Economy: Let People Enjoy the Greatest Benefits from Reform and Opening Up

Hostess: My final question, the Summer Davos Annual Meeting is a great platform for you to communicate with industrial leaders from all over the world. What inspirations have you got from this three-day meeting? What will you do first when you go back to Foshan?

Chen Yunxian: I am here is to explore some new ideas so as to set the direction for Foshan's future development. Especially at this special time of the financial crisis, we should not only think about Foshan's present but its future as well, that is what should Foshan do to promote its development? What measures should we take to fight against the crisis? This is our top priority.

We also take the opportunities to strengthen awareness and publicity of Foshan and learn how to organize such international events from the Dalian government.

Today's theme is "The Sustainable Value Chain", which is congruent with the scientific outlook on development and the idea of sustainable development. Under the guidance of the scientific outlook on development, thoughts should be given to the promotion of social undertakings, cultural undertakings and welfare undertakings, and the top priority is economic development. Development is the fundamental principle. Only in this way can the city be developed and the people's living standard be heightened. Foshan's economy and city construction have advanced to a considerably high level, and it is high time to develop social and welfare undertakings and let the people reap and benefit from the achievements of reform and opening up to the greatest extent possible.

Hostess: Mayor Chen is very much pressed for time, the time he can give us is rather limited. We have to stop here. I am a regular reporter to international conferences. I hope the next international conference will be held in Foshan so that I can meet you in Foshan. Thank you very much.

Chen Yunxian: My great pleasure.

5.9 Davos 2009 (2): The Secrets of Revitalizing Small and Medium-Sized Enterprises

Chen Yunxian, Mayor of Foshan, as a distinguished guest present at one of the Davos sessions, was invited for an exclusive interview with www.runsky.com on the afternoon of September 12th, 2009. He disclosed the secrets of Foshan's small and medium-sized enterprises breaking out of the financial crisis in quickly increasing numbers.

5.9.1 The Mechanism of Government Promotion, Multi-party Participation and Market Operation Helps Small and Medium-Sized Enterprises Out of Predicament

When it comes to the question of how Foshan has helped small and medium-sized enterprises out of difficulties, Mayor Chen said, "Foshan's small and medium-sized enterprises can be classified into two categories: those that are congruous with the direction of Foshan's industrial development and technological advancement and have considerable space for development and those that need to be closed down, merged, transformed or upgraded."

Regarding those two categories, Mayor Chen offered his own views: "On the one hand, we should provide them with guidance in determining their development orientations and become stronger and larger with their own core brands and technology. On the other hand, our top priority is to help them solve financing problems.

Banks are not feeling confident enough about making loans to small and medium-sized enterprises, and guarantee companies do not have a sufficient supply of capital. So we follow the market operation rules by binding government financial funds, funds of banks and funds of guarantee companies together and grant loans to small and medium-sized enterprises so as to achieve the effect of "achieving most through least effort."

Meanwhile, the Foshan government has been making joint efforts with financial institutions to provide guidance through the mechanism of government promotion, multi-party participation and market operation. "Last year a total of 250 million capital was raised, and 4.7–4.8 billion of funds were solicited for small and medium-sized enterprises. By the end of last year, the loans small and medium-sized enterprises obtained exceeded 18 billion yuan," said Mayor Chen with great delight.

For a more vivid illustration of the figures, Mayor Chen gave us an example: "By the end of last year, more than 324,000 enterprises registered with the Industrial and Commercial Bureau, and by the end of the first half of this year, the number rose to more than 337,000 enterprises. The new enterprises have kept appearing in spite of the shutdown, merge and transformation of some enterprises, which proves that the measures are right and have achieved the desired effects."

5.9.2 *"Two-Wheel Driving" Is the Direction for Future Import and Export Trade*

Speaking of the unification of Guangzhou and Foshan, Chen Yunxian says that a bilateral memorandum on the comprehensive development of Guangzhou and Foshan has been signed, which will push forward bilateral undertakings in transportation, industry, environment protection and long-term planning. Following international norms, urban integration involves not only the construction of transportation infrastructure but also finance, logistics, telecommunications and others. Thus, while promoting the construction of transportation infrastructure, progress should also be made in finance, logistics and telecommunications so as to form an efficient economic ring, substantially reduce transaction costs and other actual costs and enhance competitiveness and resident satisfaction of both cities.

On the one hand, efforts must be made to enhance capabilities of science and technology and self-initiated innovation so that importing and exporting enterprises possess their own brands, the core patents of their products, and more importantly, the industrial, national and even international standards based on their product specifications, which is an ultimate foothold of transformation for foreign trade enterprises. On the other hand, the optimization of foreign trade structure is not just promoted by international enterprises but by domestic market as well. It is also one of our major tasks to support private enterprises and help them to get strengthened and expanded so as to turn them into a driving force on international markets. It is another of our endeavors to make private enterprises and importing and exporting enterprises, through enhanced capabilities of science and technology and self-initiated innovation, the two wheels that will drive foreign trade ahead.

5.10 Davos 2009 (3): Green and Environmental Protection Vital to Small and Medium-Sized Enterprises

The Third Annual Meeting of the New Champions of the World Economic Forum ("The Summer Davos") was held in the Dalian World Expo Center, China on September 10–12, 2009. The theme of this annual meeting was "Summer Davos: Re-launching Growth". Chen Yunxian, Mayor of Foshan, delivered a speech at the forum of "Building a Sustainable Value Chain" on the afternoon of September 12 and expressed his view that green and environmental protection are also vital to small and medium-sized enterprises.

The following is the record of Chen Yunxian's speech.

Chen Yunxian: The local government should also assume the responsibility of protecting the environment and various other resources. Here, I would like to use two words, shareholder and stakeholder. To the shareholders, whatever the company does, its ultimate goal is to gain the greatest interest possible and be responsible to them. However, in addition to its shareholders, the company must also be responsible to its employees and clients. It must consider the interest of the public, the government and the society, and not merely short-term objectives but long-term objectives as well.

In discussing these issues, I emphasize that the government should play its role, particularly in things like environment protection and water resources preservation, and should assume responsibility for macro-economy and enterprises. The public has their responsibility, too, for the society, including environment protection. Green and environment protection are vital to small and medium-sized enterprises, and in fact to all enterprises, as well as consumers.

5.10.1 Enterprise Growth Contingent upon Modern Industrial System

The Third Annual Meeting of the New Champions of the World Economic Forum ("The Summer Davos") was held in the Dalian World Expo Center, China on September 10–12, 2009. Chen Yunxian, Mayor of Foshan, expressed his views at the forum of "Building a Sustainable Value Chain" that the building of a sustainable value chain must be based on a modern industrial system and the growth of enterprises depends on such a system.

The following is the record of his speech:

Aron Cramer: Thank you very much, Mr. Chen Yaochang. Just now, we heard President Chen's introduction on the value chain of Wal-Mart, and how they pace with the policy of the Chinese government in their purchasing. Would you please talk about it from a mayor's perspective, Mr. Chen Yunxian?

Chen Yunxian: I'll explain the building a sustainable value chain from the perspective of the local government. Foshan is located in the hinterland on the west bank of the Pearl River, covering an area of more than 3,800 square kilometers with a population of 5.9 million. Foshan's GDP was 430 billion yuan in 2008, and 230 billion in the first half of 2009, an 12% increase over the same period of the previous year. Foshan boasts the following three advantages.

First, Foshan enjoys an ideal geographic location. Neighboring Guangzhou, Foshan is close to Baiyun International Airport and the new railway station in Guangzhou, which is only 45 min distance and 2 h ride to Hong Kong and Macao.

Second, Foshan has a long history with rich cultural precipitation. Guangdong Opera, Cantonese cuisine and many others trace back to Foshan.

Third, Foshan enjoys have a solid industrial foundation. Industries, such as household appliances, equipment manufacturing, ceramics, textiles, garments, food and beverage, pharmacy and medical services, cultural creation industry and so on, are all well developed in Foshan, in addition to high-tech industries like TST and LED. It follows that the building of a sustainable value chain must be based on a modern industrial system to enable enterprises to grow, transform and upgrade, so as to form industrial clusters and meet the needs of the people and social development, which is our policy and the goal we attempt to achieve.

To achieve this end, Foshan is functionally divided into three areas. The first is the international industrial area which gathers most industrial enterprises so as to cut down costs and develop related industrial clusters. The second is the downtown commercial area in the center of Foshan so that the public can enjoy life conveniences. The third is the non-development area, which mainly serves the purpose of environment protection. By dividing our city into three functional areas, we hope to build a sustainable value chain.

Chapter 6
Internet Government

6.1 The Mayor Consults Netizens: If You Were a Mayor?

On May 4th, 2009, as deputy secretary of Foshan Municipal Committee of CPC and mayor of Foshan City, I interacted with tens of thousands of internet users via Foshan Government Net to discuss with them Foshan's scientific development.

Since it was my first interaction with netizens, I invited responsible officials of Education Bureau, Health Bureau, Economic and Trade Bureau, Labor and Social Security Bureau and five other government departments to join me with follow-ups.

The interaction began at 3 o'clock in the afternoon. I initiated the activity with a prologue: "I hope my net friends will not treat the mayor of the city as a perfect person here. What I will be talking about here may not be accurate or all-inclusive. I would like to take the opportunity to share my ideas with you and hear your suggestions and advice about how to create a more bright future for the city and its people." Almost instantly, netizens and the radio audience joined in the interaction. Within just a little over 1 h, the on-line toll of Foshan Government Net and the City Network totaled over 28,000, more than 1,000 messages were posted, and more than 500 telephone calls were received at the Foshan Radio Call Center, pushing the event into its peak.

The next day, *Foshan Daily* carried the following report:

Chen Yunxian, as both mayor and economist, exchanged ideas with netizens respecting some hot issues, such as macro economic development, financial difficulties of small and medium-sized enterprises, HIN1 influenza epidemic, and recommendations for the employment of college students. Chen disappointed no netizens by answering all their questions. It was good to see that some specific problems were solved on the spot and that some would need follow-up. What pleased the netizens most was Chen's promise to come back to them on a regular basis and make the net a regular channel for communication between the government and netizens.

Y. Chen, *Foresighted Leading: Theoretical Thinking and Practice of China's Regional Economic Development*, DOI 10.1007/978-3-642-35368-0_6,

6.1.1 The Market Demand Is the Basis for Government Support

Net friend "BGY011" from Citygf.com: As an owner of a small startup, I have encountered many difficulties in financing due to lack of property for mortgages, despite my technological innovation and unique market niches. I am wondering if the government could come up with financial innovations, set aside some money and subsidize those small and medium-sized enterprises in difficulty.

Mayor: This is currently a common problem in Foshan. What I would like to offer to you is that, as business owners, you should have a clear idea of what is to be done in your business and that your product and development should conform to the demand of domestic and international market. If your business and product fit well, there is certainly great prospects before you.

Government support is provided to small and medium-sized high-tech enterprises and enterprises whose products with great market potentials. Foshan has established a so-called Foshan National High-tech Zone ("one area and six parks") and granted preferential policies to high-tech enterprises. If your business is of high-tech nature, you can apply for registration and set it up in the zone, and then you would obtain a full-range support from the government. Moreover, government at all levels are requested to provide general guarantee funds, tied up with bank capital, to those small and medium-sized enterprises with great potentials for market demand future development.

For example, the government of Shunde District has set aside 50–100 million to tie up with bank capital. At least ten times of that amount of the tied-up capital will be loaned, but only to those businesses that conform to the demand of domestic and international market. In some other cases where small and medium-sized enterprises operate entirely by themselves and are therefore vulnerable to risks, it is advisable that they team up by industry and form partnerships and cooperatives for more market share and even greater development.

6.1.2 Taking Full Advantage of Preferential Policies for Economic Promotion

"Green life" from citygf.com: I am overjoyed by our city's performance in its breaking out of the crisis, but there is no justification for our complacency. We must remain cool-minded and figure out the bottlenecks in our economic development. Confronting the uproars all around our country, Foshan should join in and tune down our voices about our achievements so as to gain more help from the provincial and central government.

Mayor: Since the crisis, we have twice obtained national support for nine projects in the form of preferential policies, in such areas as agriculture, environmental protection, and technological innovation. We have made full use of the opportunities and policies in those areas so as to achieve the greatest effects.

The policy of "selling more home appliances to the countryside" has just been implemented. As the making of home appliances is the pillar industry of Foshan, we have utilized the policy to the fullest extent. We have formally proposed that the same favorable policies apply to the traditional industry to which more domestic market needs to be opened up, such as building materials, furniture, and paint.

I should say, we should seize the opportunity and work out ways of meeting challenges in the crisis. What counts most now is more rapid economic growth. We should continue to make full use of the favorable conditions and see from the crisis our direction and objective and our strong and weak points in dealing with the crisis. We must remain down to earth, and I should emphasize the importance of being strategically situated when discussing principles and dealing with concrete matters.

6.1.3 The Five Districts of Foshan Should Be Unified as a Whole

Netizen "Xiaoxiao": I used to work in Nanhai and Chancheng where two separate social pension systems were operating. I am wondering if the social pension systems of Chancheng District could be unified with other four districts.

Netizen "Corner Flower" from citygf.com: I am living in the north of Shunde, though I am a registered citizen in Chancheng and work there, because I can not afford an apartment in the district of Chancheng. The other day, I was injured and spent over 200 yuan on enswathement. However, my company refused to pay for reimbursement as the hospital where I was treated is not in Chancheng. I am eager to know when Shunde and Chancheng, together with their social pension systems, could be unified, as the unification of Guangzhou and Foshan and their social pension systems is well under way.

Major: Before our meeting, a citizen of Guangzhou asked me if their children could go to school in Foshan if they bought an apartment in Foshan, as housing is extremely costly in Guangzhou. That reminds me of the importance of unifying the five districts first in policies and measures prior to the unification of Guangzhou and Foshan. I urge the relevant authorities to think seriously about this issue. Only when the five districts of Foshan are unified could the unification of Guangzhou and Foshan be further promoted.

6.1.4 Encouraging College Students to Improve Knowledge Structure

Netizen "Confiding Friend": As a native of Foshan studying in a university of technology in Guangnzhou, I am wondering if some internship opportunities could be provided by certain enterprises for our college students, or if some famous enterprises could allow some college students to join in part of their operation and research.

Mayor: That is a good suggestion. Quite a few training bases or platforms have been established for the benefit of not only college students but also factory and farm workers. For example, International Clearing Center of HSBC is in operation now, and it plans to recruit 2,000–3,000 employees this year. American International Group also set up its representative office in Foshan Financial and High-tech Zone, which has got the recruitment plan of at least 2,000 new employees. Some other enterprises, including Chi Mei LCD Monitor Corporation from Taiwan, also plan to recruit a number of high-caliber staff. It is no surprise that they require candidates to possess excellent foreign language and computer skills, in addition to some knowledge of accounting and other relevant specialties.

I just want to emphasize that employment now faces not just a structural problem. For college students, it is important to acquire knowledge, but there is something more important to that, i.e. cultivating capabilities. College students should learn how to learn and continuously improve their structure of knowledge in order to adapt to the changing demand of both domestic and global market, which will eventually enable them to advance their career development in a more firm and competitive way.

6.1.5 Welcome to Keep Online Contacts

Netizen "Romance": Party Secretary Lin Yuanhe and you have both been on line to exchange ideas with us and have set a good example for the government officials in Foshan. It is hopeful that the internet act as a common platform for the government officials to communicate with the public so as for them to hear more about our ideas and suggestions.

Mayor: This is certainly a good channel for us to know more about your opinions. More attention will be paid to the network media and public opinions from that source so that the government will know better about what the people think and what they require the government to do for them. It is the government's duty to serve the people and help the people to solve their problems. And the internet can help to broaden the social horizon of the government and the vision of the general public. I hope that online communication will become a regular means for government departments to exchange ideas with the public, and that will help us to better improve our work.

Netizen: Due to time limitation, you cannot answer all the questions from the netizens. How would you handle the messages left over and arrange for follow-ups?

Mayor: Our government officials are required to log in to the government net every day to keep themselves updated about what is going on there. My assistant and I also get online quite often. We offer prompt responses to the netizens' messages and request relevant authorities to handle the problems raised online. Please do keep in touch with us online.

Netizen "Concentric": I am wondering if the online disciplinary inspection system could be established to encourage online reporting of corruption cases so as to facilitate anti-corruption work and fight corruption.

Mayor: This is a good suggestion, and online corruption reporting should be encouraged, because that will help us to monitor improper government conducts as well as corruption. As the old Chinese saying goes, merits remain after one's retirement, and public opinions arise out of chats. We hope government monitoring will make use of online chatting as well as anti-corruption rules and regulations so that our government can make sure that our rights are utilized by the people, our benefits are gained for the people, and our hearts are concerned about the people.

6.1.6 Just-in-Time Measures Have Been Adopted for H1N1 Influenza in Foshan

Netizen "Foshan Adorer": What are the emergency measures to be taken by the municipal government, as the H1N1 influenza has landed in Hongkong? And food problems are already threatening our health and life. Are there any monitoring measures and supervision for food safety?

Mayor: The municipal government has made full preparation for any emergency caused by H1N1, including publicity about H1N1, emergency measures to be taken to cope with emergencies, and effective treatment of diseases thus caused. We have got similar experiences of fighting SARS of 2003. Appropriate emergent measures are already in place for any emergency, including H1N1 influenza. More emphasis is to be given to strengthening propaganda and familiarizing the citizens with preventive measures.

Three steps have been taken by the Foshan Municipal Government to ensure the safety of drug and food, especially pork supply. The first step concentrates on the monitoring of the manufacturing process in the industry chain, particularly the sources of pork. The second step focuses on the management of the slaughtering process. Effective market supervision and quality inspection, which follow slaughtering and manufacturing, are to be the final step. These three steps form a preventive chain. What is worth mentioning here is that ten measures are to be taken to improve the people's livelihood, with emphasis put on the protection of their basic interest, especially the safety of drug and food, and currently the safety of pork supply.

6.1.7 Our Citizens Are Entitled to Clean Environment

"Guang-Fo Citizen" (Netizen from citygf.com): It has been reported consecutively by several media in Guangzhou that the Huangqi section of the Pearl River has been heavily polluted by dead hogs. Some pigsties are very bad in sanitation. What measures would the government take to control the pollution?

Mayor: Nanhai District Government will take care of this problem. In broad terms, the environmental protection of streets, towns and villages of Foshan has been greatly improved through successive years of adjustment of industrial structuring and construction of sewage treatment systems, benefiting from the strategic unification of Guangzhou and Foshan, the integration of the Pearl River Delta regions, more in-depth cooperation between Guangdong, Hongkong and Macao. Hopefully, greater achievements will be made in environmental protection before the Asian Games, and the blue skies, the white clouds, the green mountains and the clean water are coming back to the Foshan people.

Netizen "Acid Rain": What measures would the Foshan government take to monitor those enterprises that are highly pollutant and energy-consumptive, as it has got the greatest amount of acid rain here?

Mayor: Enterprises of high pollution and high energy-consumption are mainly monitored and supervised at three levels: On the national and provincial level, focus is put on the emission index of sulfur dioxide and COD, with an obligatory progressive decrease annually. It is stated in the Foshan government report that the progressive decrease of the emission index at the annual rate of 14.35% must be enforced and reached.

Secondly, environmental protection must be considered the top priority on the Foshan municipal government agenda. In the previous 2 years, 622 enterprises were closed down. Among them, 262 enterprises were involved in ceramic, printing and dyeing, cement industries. The development of industries should be boosted, but not at the ecological and environmental cost.

Businesses should, on their part, behave responsibly towards themselves, their stockholders and the whole society. They should exercise self-discipline in accordance with the relevant policies and regulations. Otherwise certain punishment shall be enforced.

In conclusion, environmental issues, especially the close-down of highly-polluted and high energy-consumptive enterprises, should be put on the immediate agenda not only on the national and provincial level but on the municipal and industrial level as well.

6.1.8 Quotations from Mayor Chen Yunxian's Interactions with Netizens

"One day, when I was walking down the streets in Chancheng District, I happened to see a bus passing by with black clouds of heavy smoke coming out of the exhaust pipe. I approached our deputy mayor in charge of transportation and director of transportation bureau. They promised to see to the problem and solve it within a given time limit."

"I put the issue other way round by telling the netizens and small and medium-sized enterprise owners, 'The prospects will be extremely bright for you if you know well what you should do, where you should be based, in what direction you should develop your business and whether your product development fits in with domestic and international market demands.'"

"The trend of national economy assumes the 'V' shape, while the global economy is depicted in the 'U' form. The trough of national economy, which appeared between mid-November, 2008 and mid-February, 2009, is over now."

"The corporate economy in Foshan, which is basically based on industrial output and privately-owned enterprises and is gaining continuous development in scale and strength in self-initiated innovation, will be the backbone of our future development. Using those advantages as new starting points, Foshan's economy will be gaining more rapid and sustainable growth through strategic and innovative leadership."

"In conclusion, environmental issues, especially the close-down of highly-polluted and high energy-consumptive enterprises, should be put on the immediate agenda not only on the national and provincial level but on the municipal and industrial level as well."

6.1.9 Online Sidelights

6.1.9.1 Netizen Consults Mayor About How to Play the Stock Market

As an economist with Ph.D. degree in economics from Peking University and Chairman of Board of GF Securities, Mayor Chen Yunxian was surrounded by various economic problems during the online interaction yesterday. Instead of questions concerning the financial crisis or the development of traditional industry, a netizen called "Caution" raised the most offbeat question about the tricks of playing the stock market. He so called himself because of his repeated panics since his stepping into the stock market.

"Caution" asked Mayor, "How do you predict this year's trend of the Chinese stock market? There has already been a rise of 5% or 10% in the stock market value in the newly emerging economies. What do you think that indicates in the mid-term, and would that be a turning point for the whole market?"

Faced with the quizzes of that netizen, Chen responded with a witty smile and in a roundabout way. "I could only help you sort out your thoughts, for your reference only," he said, "The rise and fall of the stock market depends mainly on three factors: the macroeconomic factor comes first, followed by the profit status of enterprises, inclusive of both its past and future PE, and the supply and demand of the market comes last. All the three factors have been developing steadily towards a better condition in the national economic development and in our combat against the global financial crisis."

6.1.9.2 Mayor Told About His Feelings as Mayor with a Poem

Chen Yunxian responded to economically related issues with calm and confidence and to the problems concerning people's livelihood without hesitation. However, he was stumped by "Liangshan Hero", a netizen who claimed himself to be a new member of GF.

Here is the question from "Liangshan Hero" "Heroes": "You changed your position in 2003 from Chairman of Board of GF Securities to Deputy Mayor of Foshan, and now Mayor. People say you have been performing your duty with great ease, but I have noticed you being kept busy from here to there from the media. What have you really gained from this shift of roles?"

That question caught the mayor unprepared. With a pause, he took a long breath. He asked himself what the greatest gain was and then gave a brief reply, "The greatest gain for me is to come to know about the difficulty of seeking welfare for the masses." He then made a poem as self-reflection and self-expression: to my wish Foshan's growth, to the welfare of masses internet access.

6.1.9.3 The Youth of Foshan Have a Bright Future

It was the international Youth Day yesterday and the 111th anniversary of Peking University. As a graduate of Peking University, Chen Yunxian took that special occasion and expressed his sincere blessings to the university and its alumni. He also placed great expectations on the Foshan youth.

During the interaction with netizens, Chen did not even have time for a brief relax. He was again bombarded with successions of questions from the media and asked his opinions and expectations about the Foshan youth. He commented that the youth in Foshan have ideas, great wishes and are down-to-earth and that they have the wisdom and courage to take the lead and pass down the good traditions. "I hope that the youth of the 1980s and 1990s will develop themselves, work diligently and contribute to the national development," he said, "I also hope the youth in Foshan will create good images for the people in Guangdong, in China and even in the world. I am confident that the Foshan youth will play an even more significant part in Foshan's economic development. Foshan has got a bright future, so do the youth in Foshan."

6.2 Interaction with 40,000 Netizens: "Netizens Are Political Commissioners"

On August 6, 2010, I, in the capacity of party secretary of Foshan Municipal Committee of CPC, had my first interaction with netizens, which lasted for only 1½h. However, netizens showed great enthusiasm and sent 2,291 messages by the time it was over, and the number of net viewers soared to over 42,300. I noted down every message from the netizens, which sounded sensible and constructive. Time was extremely limited, and I could not answer all the questions. I had the questions and messages sorted out and sent to relevant government authorities for further studies and turned into workable measures. I will make it a rule to communicate with netizens and come more often to chat and exchange ideas with them.

Relevant reports come as follows in *Foshan Daily*.

6.2.1 Remarks About "Secretary of People's Wellbeing"

"I come from grass-roots and will certainly be a secretary to work for people's wellbeing."

Netizen "Dongping Fisherman": You are a doctorate holder and an expert in finance with overseas background. Now you are a high-ranking government official. I guess you have never been worried about your life. Then how do you the misery of the grass-roots people? How can you work for people's wellbeing?

Chen (with a hearty smile): I am filled with mingled feelings at this message, which reminds me of a ci-poem that I learned as a child:

As a lad I never knew the taste of sorrow,
But loved to climb towers.
Loved to climb towers,
And drag sorrow into each new song I sang.
Now I know well the taste of sorrow,
It is on the tip of my tongue,
On the tip of my tongue,
But instead I say, "what a fine, cool autumn day!"

(Translated by Yang Xianyi and Gladys Margaret Tayler)

During my high school days, I often went to the countryside to practice farm work and learned a lot of farming skills. I finished high school education in 1972. The following year, I went to settle in the countryside to do farm work. I worked very hard and soon became a production team leader. After 2 years I was sent to study in the university. I left the countryside with gratitude for the farmers who gave me a three-jin (one and a half kilogram) food coupon. I must say my later life and progress were directly influenced by my experience as a production team leader. I still have fresh memories of the miserable life and hard conditions under which the farmers lived.

I come from the grass-roots and, of course, will never forget about it, though I hold a doctoral degree. The more important thing is that the foundation on which our party and government are built resides in the people. We work for the people. Here is the starting point for my work. I am determined to be a mayor for people's wellbeing and a party secretary for people's wellbeing, speaking both from the government's angle and from my personal experience.

6.2.2 *Remarks About "Restricting Motorcycles"*

There is no turning-back in restricting motorcycles, but the measures should be based on actual situations.

Netizen "Little Ant": Restriction on motorcycling started in August, but the problem is that the current transportation system cannot meet the demand of those who used to go to work by motorcycle. How long can the restriction last if this situation cannot be changed?

Chen: Good question. Viewed from Foshan's urban administration, three things, when combined, are heart-thrilling and disturbing. They are social security, traffic accidents and environment pollution. Robbery on motorcycle accounted for 40% of law-breaking activities, many traffic accidents are caused by motorcycles. In addition to restricting motorcycles, measures will also be taken to handle vehicles that fall below standards. It is certain that the government will continue to make efforts to improve and upgrade the public transportation systems.

In terms of transportation development, work must be done to restrict motorcycle traffic and to improve public transportation system. The ultimate goal is to establish the modern transportation system in Foshan.

Considering the actual needs of the people, the government has taken flexible measures. Motorcycles are still permitted for a considerably long period of time on non-main roads and streets. Strict restriction is exercised on main streets and upon motorcycles from outside Foshan and out-of-date motorcycles.

Speaking from future development, the restriction of motorcycles must be implemented. There is no turning-back. But we do it step by step. What is more important is that greater efforts will be made to develop and improve the public transportation systems, including taxis, bikes and public buses.

6.2.3 Remarks About "Intelligent Foshan"

The Foshan people and enterprises get the greatest benefits from "Intelligent Foshan".

Netizen "Secret Guy": I have heard quite a lot about "Intelligent Foshan". What I care most is what benefits it will bring to the Foshan people.

Chen (with a confident smile): The Foshan people and enterprises get the greatest benefits from "Intelligent Foshan". Let's take the integration of informationalization with industrialization. We have a common saying, there does exist outmoded technology, but no outmoded industry. The internet of things can be used to innovate household appliances to give them artificial intelligence.

Traditional enterprises can take up a larger market share and gain greater profits through technological innovation. The integration of informationalization with urbanization will bring forth intelligent transportation, intelligent social security, intelligent education, intelligent medical care, intelligent culture, and intelligent libraries. All this will bring convenience to social and public life. The integration of informationalization with internationalization will bring benefits to the people and enterprises as well.

Consequently, the Foshan people and enterprises will reap the greatest benefits from "Intelligent Foshan via Fourization", as long as policies and measures are implemented to the greatest effect.

"Intelligent Foshan" is an objective to achieve. Its core lies in the incorporation of internets, internets of things, digitalization and artificial intelligence into Foshan's construction, development and internationalization, which involves all the people and enterprises and is shown in all aspects of life and work. As long as we have done our work well, the public will understand it and support it. The more important thing is that they can get real benefits from it.

6.2.4 Remarks About "Sense of Happiness"

Choose the right direction to construct "city of happiness"

Netizen "Truth-telling": As "party secretary for people's wellbeing", you should work hard to build Foshan into a "city of happiness" to live up to the title. GDP is on the constant rise, but no rise is seen in salaries. People in the city all look like strangers to each other. Family disputes often occur at home. Smog hovers overhead. The exhaust gas from vehicles makes it difficult to breathe on the street. Social security problems appear one after another. Happiness in such a city can only be a fantasy.

Chen: Many thanks for your comments. There are two aspects to what you have said: the current situation and the future development.

Where will Foshan be heading for in the future? Let me give you an example. As far as I can see, it should be a Singapore. It should be moving towards a city suitable for living, commerce and development due to its limitation of land resources. To some extent, what you have said is right, if we look at what it is now, and that is where improvement should be made. We have seen our drawbacks and should muster up more courage and confidence to figure out the right direction and work jointly toward a "city of happiness", as you have indicated.

6.2.5 *Remarks About "Criticism"*

Many of our government policies and measures are derived from netizens.

Netizen "Dongdong": Netizens have poured a lot of their ideas and opinions. Some are quite to the point and harsh, directing their criticism at you. Have you seen those critical views? How do you feel about them? Will you continue to support netizens? What measures will be taken to guarantee the freedom of speech on the internet?

Chen (with a frank smile): To serve the people, inclusive of our net friends, is the starting point and the objective for our work. In exchanges of ideas, some netizens may be harsh in their words, but I can feel they are speaking the truth from the bottom of their hearts. They are concerned about Foshan's development. I feel grateful to them at heart. Only with support from our people, especially for their wellbeing, can Foshan face difficulties and take effective measures to remove them.

Prior to and subsequent to the Asian Games, several projects are under way or close to completion: further planning will be made for underground transportation in the light of social needs and economic power, after the completion and operation of Underground Traffic Line One; the Southern Extension Line of the First Ring will be completed by the end of this year; the first phase of renovating the Temple will be over by October, and so on. All these projects were proposed by our net friends and residents. We devote special attention to your suggestions and special efforts to solving the problems that are of common concern.

Foshan Municipal Commission for Discipline Inspection supervises internet government

Netizen: It is good that the party secretary thinks so much of internet government. I can remember clearly that drawbacks are pointed out in the 10,000-word letter concerning Foshan internet government. So far no regulations have been made regarding accountability. How will the government strengthen its internet supervision?

Chen: Good question again. Government authorities from over 30 departments are sitting beside us to hear our conversation, including officials from the municipal commission for discipline inspection. They are here especially to hear your opinions about internet government. For example, according to government regulations, responses must be given within 15 days concerning the transportation network. The officials in charge are right here and can answer your questions right away. I hope internet communication will become a regular channel. What's more, all the practical problems will be solved one by one, and by so doing we can make progress.

6.2.6 *Remarks About "City Image"*

Use cultural synergy to promote Foshan image.

Netizen "China Foshan": Foshan boosts a huge economic output and a profound cultural deposit. However, people outside Foshan know very little about it. Its popularity is limited, with a vague idea of its image. What do you think lies behind that? What concrete measures can be taken to change it?

Chen: It is my long conviction that popularity was Foshan's advantage but has now become its weak point. Foshan ranks among the "four famous towns" in China. The culture of ceramics, dragon-boating, lion dances, and so on, was originated and has developed here ever since. We should build up Foshan's fame on industrial development, social progress and what people love to see and hear.

Serious attention should be paid to how to extend and strengthen publicity. The economic output of Dongguan is 100 billion lower than that of Foshan, but more people know about Dongguan, which shows that cultural synergy must be used to promote Foshan image. Shandong people once ventured into Northeast China to make a living, and Shanxi people went beyond West Pass to do business. Why can't Foshan people "go down to Southeast Asia"? That can help Foshan to pick up its history and add to its fame. I entrust this task to our media friends and hope they can make some achievements in that aspect.

6.2.7 Quick Questions and Answers

Question: Public servant transportation service reform will soon be executed. It is suggested that a proportion of transportation service subsidies be paid in the form of public transportation card. What do you think of the idea?

Chen: That suggestion can at least serve as a good basis for us to think about how to improve our public transportation systems and how to provide better public transportation services. We will make serious studies of this suggestion to see whether it is workable. It will certainly be desirable if it can be integrated into the general framework for public transportation service reform.

Question: How will the issue of Jinshazhou be addressed in the unification of Guangzhou and Foshan?

Chen: This is one of the special cases arising in the unification of Guangzhou and Foshan. The financial unification at Dajiaodu is another. We will follow up with them. I have a piece of news to disclose to you. Government officials from Guangzhou, Foshan and Zhaoqin will probably meet again at then end of this month to discuss and solve relevant issues so as to propel the Guangzhou-Foshan unification and the integration of Guangzhou, Foshan and Zhaoqin.

6.2.8 Features on the Spot

Secretary makes apologies for "restricting motorcycles"

Netizen raised his sharp question, to which Chen Yunxian responded with a smile. Facing "severe" criticism from the netizen, Chen offered his sincere apologies. Motorcycle restriction was one of the most concerned issue, for which Chen expressed his apologies four times.

It was only half an hour after the interaction started, and the topic began to concentrate on the restriction of motorcycles, which seemed to attract the greatest attention from the netizens.

"The deadline for motorcycle restriction will come in September. So far no policies have been issued to provide more transportation convenience to the public. I am wondering what our government has done to benefit the people?" Netizen "Little Ant" was the first to "launch attacks", which led to a surge of messages from 800 to 1,500. Some of the messages sounded tough and harsh.

Confronted with questions from netizens, Chen Yunxian kept smiling and praised them for their good questions. Occasionally, he volunteered to act as host and pick questions to answer.

"I would like to take the opportunity to express my thanks to our people for their understanding and support for the restriction of motorcycles." He went on to answer with patience a variety of questions and try to remove their anxieties concerning the restriction of motorcycles.

"The restriction of motorcycles has initiated the first step in Foshan's efforts to establish a modern cubic transportation system. Foshan's transportation development requires us to restrict motorcycles and improve the current transportation network," said Chen. Considering the convenience and ease of traveling in the city, flexible policies and measures are to be taken and implemented step by step. "Motorcycles will be restricted, not forbidden, on some main streets, but on many non-main streets, they are still permitted for a considerably long period of time."

He continued to explain how Singapore has become a place suitable for living, commerce and development. He invited the net friends to participate in the discussions about the positioning of Foshan and understand the policies of "motorcycle restriction".

"I want to express my hearty thanks especially to those who travel or go to work by motorcycle," Chen said with emotions, "To be frank, a lot of people around me travel to work by motorcycle, including those who do haircut for me and who do cooking in the government dining room. I feel quite upset at the policies. How will those people go to work?" Chen could not hide his apologies.

"But that urges us to speed up our improvement of public transportation services. There is no turning-back in restricting motorcycles. We cannot retreat in front of difficulties. My thanks go to our citizens for their support and understanding again." With this, Chen concluded his over 20-min answer to the question.

How time flies. An hour and half passed by quickly. When Chen left the studio and was asked about whether there was some difference between this time and the first time and whether he felt pressure under "sharp" questions from netizens, he answered humorously, "No pressure, I have been feeling great. I was on the bright side, and the netizens were on the dark side, so they feel free to say what they want to say. I can hear them speak the truth directly, and their suggestions and ideas will throw light upon our future social and economic development."

6.2.9 Expert Views

Associate Professor Liu Ning of Party Construction Studies from Foshan Municipal Party School: Internet public opinions are incorporated into public policy making.

2009 was the beginning year for Foshan's internet government. Nearly 100 government authorities got online to meet "face to face" with netizens to exchange ideas with them. The 2010 internet interaction was launched and led by Party Secretary Chen Yunxian, which signifies that the government interaction with ordinary people by means of new platforms and channels is conducted on a regular and rule-governed basis.

"Government prospers for its meeting people's demands, and government perishes for its neglecting people's demands." In the past 2 years, government officials have been playing an active role in internet interactions with the public, thus creating a good environment for soliciting people's ideas, wisdom and suggestions and, at the same time, leading government officials to intensify their initiatives and sense of obligation via internet.

Chen commented, "Your ideas and suggestions will be treated in the same way as those proposed by political commissioners. They will be followed up and used as the basis for policy making." Internet public opinions are to be incorporated into public policy making, and the internet is undergoing a shift of roles from public affair discussion to public policy making. Judging from this perspective, Foshan government is going into the modern age in terms of its government notions and approaches.

Government officials should take advantage of this trend, open public blogs and email accounts and realize the timely transmission of information so that interviews that are usually conducted in studios are extended into improvised activities at out-of-office time and at different locations and netizens' requests can be handled in due course. An "internet consultation" office can be established to sort out ideas and suggestions from netizens that are sent to relevant government authorities to serve as the important basis for formulating policies and improving policy making. By doing so, government work is facilitated, and a long effective mechanism is established via internet to seek consultation respecting policy making and handle appeals from netizens with a view to solving problems relating to people's wellbeing.

6.2.10 Ideas from Netizens

Net friend "Wisdom": The government can be said to have the greatest wisdom if their people enjoy life, work, and their own housing, and if they can afford medical care and education, and if they are not worried about rising prices.

Net friend "Typical Foshan": I am manager of human resources in a company. Foshan's popularity does not match with its economic power. Foshan should be ranking among the top ten cities in China in terms of its cultural assets, economic output, city size and comprehensive competitiveness. However, it is not so well-known as other cities. Our company recruits people every year in different cities of the Pearl River Delta. We find that the first-class personnel seek jobs in Shenzhen, the second-class personnel seek jobs in Zhuhai, Dongguan, and the third-class personnel come to work in Foshan. We hope that Foshan will find its right "soul" and highlight its city image so that we feel proud of living in this city.

Net friend "Little Flower": Secretary Chen's responses concerning the restriction of motorcycles have removed some of my anxieties. Over the past two years, improvement has been made in public transportation in Foshan, but the changes are slow. We hope that the government will strengthen its supervision and elevate public transportation and taxi services to a new level.

Chapter 7
Chen Yunxian in the Media: Watch Before Walking

7.1 Memories of Chen Yunxian: The Founder of Guangfa

By Qin Shuo (chief editor of "China Business News")

"Only those who care for the grassroots of Chinese economy can be reckoned as the most viable stock brokers, only those who formulate future strategies with global visions can be reckoned as the most competitive, and only those who boast collective cohesion and enterprising employees can be reckoned as the most durational," remarked Chen Yunxian, the founder of Guangfa Securities Company and the then mayor of Foshan City, with firmness and confidence at the listing ceremony of Guangfa securities in Shenzhen Stock Exchange on February 12, 2010.

He said this with absolute confidence.

I watched the video of the listing ceremony and heard the above remarks while attending the celebration of the listing of Guangfa securities on Shenzhen Stock Exchange on March 17, 2010 and came to know that Guangfa securities currently enjoys the largest market value among all the listed companies in Shenzhen Stock Exchange.

On that same day, I flew from Shanghai to Guangzhou for the celebration. It was my first time to board the plane from Terminal No. 2 of Shanghai Hongqiao International Airport, and that terminal left upon me good impressions. It is spacious but not luxurious, with convenient facilities and maximal use of space, bearing some resemblance to the airports in the US in its design, which is notable for its simplicity and customization.

At that terminal, I bought a book by Kan Zhidong, entitled "*Ups and Downs*: *The Zhidong Kan Story*", a good book indeed, written from the author's personal experience and with authenticity and delicacy. Among those first-generation influential figures in the securities sector, quite a few went astray and were even put in jail. "It is no exaggeration", said the author, "that a 'general assembly' of China's securities pioneers can be collected in the prison". The book mentions the resignation of Wei Wenyuan who is the first general manager of the Shanghai Stock Exchange, the

Y. Chen, *Foresighted Leading: Theoretical Thinking and Practice of China's Regional Economic Development*, DOI 10.1007/978-3-642-35368-0_7,

author's own dismissal from the position of legal representative of Shenyin Wanguo Securities(SWS) in 1997 with a 5-year stock market exclusion, and his return to China Southern Securities in 2002 with ending-up behind bars, the sentence of Guan Jinsheng who is the founder of Wanguo Securities to 17 years in prison due to the 3–27 national bond and futures event in 1995, and many similar cases, such as Zhang Guoqing, the founder of Jun'an Securities, Xu Weiguo, the founder of Dapeng Securities, Liu Bo, once chairman of the board of China Southern Securities, Chen Haowu, the founder of Hubei Securities (predecessor of Changjiang Securities).

However, are the pioneers deemed to failure? Not necessarily so.

On the evening of March 17, I met with Chen Yunxian at the celebration in The Garden Hotel, Guangzhou. He, along with Chen Haowu and Chen Xuerong (once chairman of Xiangcai Securities), was styled as "three-Chen" in the securities industry. They all had the experience of teaching in universities and setting up securities companies in the early 1990s. But now, except for Chen Yunxian, the other two have vanished from the mass media.

Not only did Chen Yunxian establish the Guangfa and create its unique corporate culture and public image, he also made a successful and promising transition from business to politics and performed admirably well in both Foshan City and Shunde District.

I walked over and greeted him. However, he did not recognize me. After exchanging business cards, he remembered me, and said that I had put on some weight. "You wrote preliminary commentaries in each issue while you worked with the magazine *Nanfengchuang* (literally "Window of South Wind"). I read them." he said. I made an appointment with him that I would visit Foshan someday.

During my stay in Guangzhou, I had several interviews and phone contacts with Chen Yunxian. More than 10 years have elapsed since our last meeting. How time flies!

My first interview with Chen Yunxian took place in the fall of 1992, when I participated in the Pearl River Delta report tour to Shunde, which was organized by *The Chinese Merchant Times* affiliated to the China Guangfa Bank. As the tour was sponsored by the China Guangfa Bank, we went there as our first stop. I wrote a couple of articles about him after the interview, including the one in the following section. At the time of interview, Chen Yunxian acted as general manger of Securities Department of the China Guangfa Bank. The department is the predecessor of Guangfa. I can still remember that its governor made a special mention of Chen Yunxian, saying "Dr. Chen was a Ph.D. student under Professor Xiao Zhuoji of Peking University and joined our team only last year." Chen was employed from the Provincial Talent Attraction and Introduction Program and got quick promotions.

He was born in 1955 and comes from Shanghang, Fujian Province. He once worked as a farmer and a worker before he was admitted into Fujian Normal University as a MA candidate in 1983. After graduation he became a lecturer in Fuzhou University and started to study for his doctorate in economics under Professor Xiao Zhuoji in Peking University in August 1988. He came to join the

China Guangfa Bank in 1991 as a doctoral degree holder with rich work experience with the grass-roots, which made him outstanding among those doctorate holders with only academic schooling. During the initial stage, he used to ride a bicycle, carrying a water bottle and withstanding the heat of the sun, from here to there to promote the sales of government bonds. Guangfa started to develop all by itself through hard work, wisdom, and, above all, enterprise, with its first shareholders being such common listed companies as Liaoning Chengda, Jilin Aodong, and Zhongshan Gongyong, and has worked its way to today's accomplishments. That is where Guangfa got its title of "grassroots stock brokers".

By the end of 1993, companies like Baiyun Mountain and Guangzhou Lonkey had become the first batch of listed companies in Guangzhou. As I could remember, I went to interview Chen Yunxian early in 1994 in the first securities exchange office of the China Guangfa Bank. He told me that he could not talk specifically about stocks and stock exchanges. He meant what he said.

Later on, I could meet him only during meetings. Zhang Liang, a correspondent of *Nanfengchuang*, interviewed him and wrote "Chinese brokers usher in the third wave of stock impacts" in 1999. Another correspondent of *Nanfengchuang* had close relations with the Organization Department of Guangdong Provincial Committee of CPC. He once asked me whether I would like to work for enterprises, say Guangfa. My answer was that writing articles on economy and doing economic work are entirely different. What I meant was that not everyone could do well in securities.

Both Guangfa and *Nanfengchuang* staff lived in close proximity on the Shuiyin Erheng Road beside Shuiyin Primary School. It was in 2001 (or 2002 perhaps) that I sent a letter to him, together with the articles he wrote during his study in the University of Massachusetts Boston as well as Harvard University between August 2000 and September 2001. I phoned him for a chat, but he was too much engaged. He was appointed the Executive Deputy Mayor of Foshan City in May 2003 and also the Secretary of Shunde District Committee of CPC in October the following year. He was promoted to the position of acting mayor of Foshan City in October 2006 and formally mayor of Foshan City in January 2007. Further promotions were awaiting him, as people commented.

Chen Yunxian's erudition and the Guangfa corporate culture he established, including the core values of "knowledge, strength, realism, dedication", the concept of "moderation, regulation, and sustainability" for enterprise development, and the concept of "working as explorers of economic theories and practitioners of capital markets and becoming owners of legitimate material wealth and upholders of corporate ethics and morals" for talent development, have all left deep impressions on me. He recruited a good number of doctorate holders, which made Guangfa well-renowned for its "Doctor Corps" and the first financial institution boasting a post-doctoral work station. His values of "knowledge, strength, realism, dedication" carry with a strong sense of responsibility, vocations of intellectuals to serve the country, and the spirit of working in a down-to-earth way and never staying away from reality.

Let us come back to the celebration. That evening, Chen Yunxian delivered a speech. He, as an old staff member of Guangfa, cited a few lines from Xin Qiji (1140–1207), a famous ci-poet in the Southern Song Dynasty:

As a lad I never knew the taste of sorrow,
But loved to climb towers.
Loved to climb towers,
And drag sorrow into each new song I sang.
Now I know well the taste of sorrow,
It is on the tip of my tongue,
On the tip of my tongue,
But instead I say, "what a fine, cool autumn day!"

(Translated by Yang Xianyi and Gladys Margaret Tayler)

He quoted with a slight accent but full of affection. I could see from the big screen that his eyes went moist from recitation.

He went to comment about Guangfa, saying "Guangfa has three 'good's': good foundation, good size, and good staff". He hoped that Guangfa could realize "standardization, internationalization, and a shareholding group company". That target was set when he was leading Guangfa.

That night, Chen Yunxian was particularly happy, without losing his elegance and gentle character. Among his old colleagues, he could release his real feelings. All those present at the celebration could feel that. The most solid and substantial foundation for Guangfa today is its enterprising management team, which was built up by Chen Yunxian in his days in Guangfa. Right at this moment, an old Chinese saying occurred to me, "Above ten generations a family could flourish if they value morality; farming and studies, less; studies, even less; wealth and ranks, not more than three generations." Of all securities companies in China, Guangfa is the only one that has remained among the industry's top ten in its 19 years' development, and this is what Yunxian's distinctive corporate culture has left to Guangfa.

Someday I would like to go to Foshan and write about his ways of working as a mayor.

(Written on March 20, 2010)

7.2 Chen Yunxian: Abandoning Office in Guangfa for Government Post

Chen Yunxian, Guangfa chairman, was appointed Executive Deputy Mayor of Foshan City, Guangdong Province in March 2003. That news came as a big surprise to people in China's securities industry, for this shift of position from chairman of the first echelon of domestic securities brokers to local government official did appear unthinkable, and there was no sign for this shift to take place.

When Chen Yunxian pulled out of the securities industry, China's stock market was still deep in depression that began from June 2001. Only a little more than 1 year after his taking office in Foshan, the most extensive "domino effect" erupted in China's stock market and caused a considerable number of securities brokers in China to go bankrupt.

Chen Yunxian was considered lucky, because he "went on shore" in an incredibly relaxing manner before the wave struck the securities industry. Even more incredible is the fact that Guangfa, where he was at the helm, was exempted from the vortex of bankruptcy and attracted serious attention from CITIC Securities for its fine quality and good reputation.

7.2.1 Abandoning Office in Guangfa for Government Position

Seven months after took office as Deputy Mayor of Foshan, Chen Yunxian was appointed party secretary of Shunde District Committee of CPC in October 2003. Shunde is one of the key industrial towns not just in Foshan but in China as well. In 2004, Shunde's GDP exceeded 60 billion yuan, with industrial output value totaling over 150 billion Yuan. Quite a few well-known enterprises are located there, like Midea, Galanz and Kelon.

Having been a brilliant leader in China's securities industry for years, Chen Yunxian never turned his eyes away from the capital market he knows so well, though he had given up business for politics.

In August 2004, Foshan Municipal Government formed the Leading Group for Utilization and Development of Capital Markets and set up the "Listing Office". Chen Yunxian was nominated the head of the group and the office. With his many years' work experience in the capital market, he was certainly the most suitable person for that position.

On January 13, 2005, the Shunde government, which was already under Chen's charge, issued "Provisions on Necessitating Public Offering of Enterprises", which was commended as "the sunny policy" by private enterprise owners. That document comprised the establishment of institutions for enterprises' IPO, the construction of "green channels", supportive policies and measures, rewarding mechanisms and so on. According to the document, from January 13, 2005 to December 31, 2009, companies shall be awarded 500,000 yuan by the government if they successfully go through the obligatory guidance session for IPO, and another 500,000 yuan if they successfully get listed in the stock exchange (including overseas listing, reverse merger, backdoor listing at different locations but transferring registration back to Shunde).

In reality, it was not without any preliminaries before Chen Yunxian gave up business for politics.

Chen was selected by the Organization Department of Guangdong Provincial Committee of CPC for an advanced management program for senior high government officials in The University of Massachusetts between September 2000 and September 2001. On one occasion, he was invited to deliver a speech on China's stock market at Harvard University and was honored the title of "senior research fellow" due to his rich experience and extensive influence upon China's capital market.

The Organization Department of the Central Committee of CPC selected reserve cadres to study abroad in 2002. He was the only candidate recommended by the Organization Department of Guangdong Provincial Committee of CPC and was sent again to the United States for a second time.

Some preliminary work was already under way for his transfer from enterprise manager to government official.

Chen Yunxian, like his peers, has his own beliefs deeply rooted in his heart, which have remained firm and unchanged.

Chen Yunxian was born in Shanghang County, Fujian Province. He was sent, as an educated youth, to a village in Shanghang, still a poverty-stricken place even now. There, he had direct contacts with people and their impoverished life at the bottom of the Chinese society.

The farmers who toiled away without enough food and clothing were deeply imprinted upon him. The idea of "doing something to improve their living conditions in future" began to take roots in the mind of that young leader of the production team. Over three decades went by, but he held to his simple ideas without any change, while others lamented that changes were taking place all the time and so fast.

In actual reality, a government official has the power to influence the life of far more people than an enterprise leader. And this is probably one of the motivators for his shift from business to government.

7.2.2 *Chen's Days in Guangfa*

In a sense, the rise and fall of an enterprise depends on its management team and the team leader.

Chen Yunxian earned his doctoral degree at Peking University in 1991, when Guangdong Development Bank, only 3 years after its setup, recruited securities personnel in Beijing. That employment opportunity started his 13-year career in Guangdong Development Bank.

As the first doctoral degree holder in Guangdong Development Bank, Chen Yunxian's first major responsibility was concerned with bond issuance. The stock market was then a novelty in China, the leaders of the bank did not feel confident about its future. As a result, Chen did not get an official appointment and no official title. His colleagues addressed him as "Dr. Chen". He continued to be called Dr. Chen even after he earned his official title. Interestingly, Guangfa staff call each other by their academic titles now rather than by their functional titles.

Chen Yunxian was fully engaged in work at that time. In the daytime he visited numerous companies by bike, familiarizing them with the benefits of financing through issuing bonds, and during the night he stayed up very late, writing proposals of bond issuance for them. There were only a dozen employees in the Department of Bonds working under him. Those days were the toughest time in his career.

Under the context of financial markets regulation in July 1993, China's financial industry was separated in operations. Guangfa became independent of Guangdong Development Bank and started to operate by itself.

Chen Yunxian, the then Deputy Governor of Guangdong Development Bank, started to give full play to his politic talent. Thanks to his efforts, Guangfa was upgraded from a bank department to one of the most important financial institutions in Guangdong Province.

His Ph.D. advisor Professor Xiao Zhuoji commented in one of his articles, "Many students of mine are highly competent with outstanding achievements... Dr. Chen Yunxian, who graduated in 1991, is one of them. He is the first in China's economic circles to discover the interactive relations between risks and returns of securities investment. Not only has he made serious theoretical studies of investment banks, he has also been working in the investment bank. Under his leadership, Guangfa has been developing very fast and making outstanding achievements."

Few people may have known that Chen Yunxian's early experience of management came from running a rice flour mill during his stay in a little village. The rice flour mill was the only enterprise in the village, and he had to balance between the income of farmers and the revenue of the mill. It is safe to assume that that experience of resolving conflicts between institutional constraints and realistic necessities initiated his awareness and accumulation of experience in balancing the relations between government and businesses.

The mid-1990s was a special time for China's securities industry. Quite a number of securities brokers earned a huge fortune by setting up their own companies, investing on real estate and bond futures. Guangfa met with severe criticism for its "conservative" investment style. However, who knows what would happen in the future? Guangfa takes great pride in its "conservative" style now. As is mentioned on Guangfa's website, "Since its founding more than 10 years ago, Guangfa has neither been affected by such financial turbulences as national debt repurchase, bond futures, and lawbreaking financial operations, nor has it been involved in the then heated real estate investment, thanks to its foresighted development strategies, its established risk control mechanism and its standardized management. Guangfa boosts excellent assets."

The race between the tortoise and the rabbit is a household story in China. Some securities people compare Guangfa to the tortoise, who walks slowly but wins the final victory for it never goes astray.

7.2.3 Guangfa's Doctoral Corps

In China's securities industry, Guangfa is unique for its doctoral corps.

According to its website, Guangfa employs a staff of 1,690 employees, with an average age of 32. Among them, 54 are doctorate holders, post doctorates, and Ph.D. candidates, and 297 are master degree holders. Guangfa is among the first securities companies in China to have been granted approval by the Ministry of Personnel to establish post-doctoral work stations.

Under the influence of the "all-inclusive" tradition of Peking University, the doctoral corps Chen Yunxian recruited included not only those specializing in securities but also those majoring in fields entirely unrelated to securities, like geology and geophysics. It is the comprehensive backgrounds of the corps that have helped forge a firm basis for a top-class investment research team, which was created by Chen Yunxian and become a group of securities elites.

Wang Hongmao, former president of Guangfa, is now the general manager of Canton Venture Capital Co. Ltd. Ye Junying, former vice president of Guangfa, is now the general manager of E Fund Management Co. Ltd. Lin Chuanhui, former deputy general manager of the Investment Bank Department of Guangfa, is now the president of Guangfa Fund Management Co. Ltd. What's more, Zhang Hongyi, former general manager of Hainan Branch of Guangfa, is the executive vice president of PICC Asset Management Co. Ltd, and Li Shuiquan, former Chief Financial Officer of Guangfa is now the Chief Financial Officer of WanLian Securities.

When Chen Yunxian left in March 2003, Guangfa, formerly a department of Guangdong Development Bank, was already one of the top securities brokers in China and has maintained that ranking in the securities industry ever since. Between 2001 and 2003, Guangfa first controlled Jinzhou Securities, changing it into Guangfa North Securities Co. Ltd, and then controlled Huafu Securities, changing it into Guangfa Huafu Securities Co. Ltd. In addition, Guangfa Futures and Guangfa Fund are also operated under Guangfa. Guangfa also shares in E Fund Management Co. Ltd. Through years of effective management, Guangfa has started to take the form of financial holding.

Chen Yunxian is reputed to be the "New Star of the Political World" and "Tycoon of the Financial World". Here is an anecdote of a different kind about him. Once he saw his daughter off at the airport. When his daughter was passing security check, she was reminded by the airport security not to bring her boyfriend into the security gate. I was told that he was quite pleased at being mistaken as a younger man.

(First Published in *twenty-first Century Business Herald*, February 21, 2005)

7.3 Foresighted Thinking Leads Unparalleled Development

This is not an ordinary encounter but a contest between the past and the future.

This contest is led by Chen Yunxian, the new secretary of Foshan Municipal Committee of CPC, with foresighted leadership, to mark a break-up with the old development style in Foshan.

It is a contest to transform the traditional industrial key city into a newly emerging industrial center.

It is a contest to turn industrial economy into information economy.

It is a contest to change the old township into a modern metropolis.

It is a contest to shift from manufacturing thinking to creative and capital thinking.

Chen Yunxian, who has been well-known for leading Guangfa's Doctoral Corps, is now leading another "Doctoral Corps" of Foshan government leadership to make foresighted planning for Foshan and launch an unprecedented revolution in ways of government thinking.

As former senior research fellow of Harvard University and Ph.D. of Peking University, Chen Yunxian's English introduction about Foshan at the press conference took entrepreneurs, investors and the media by surprise. He is considered "the hardest-to-palter leader" by his subordinates for his foresighted thinking, prompt action and serious style.

In Foshan, government officials have entirely different comments about Chen Yunxian from ordinary people, media and foreign friends.

"It is a great delight to interview Chen Yunxian. The transcription from the interview record makes a logically perfect article," comment some correspondents after their interview with Chen. They conclude that they enjoy three things in interviewing Chen. First, Chen can cite on the spot statistic figures relating to economic and social analysis, such as the aggregate investment, export ratios, the average assets-liabilities ratio of enterprises, and industrial output, even precise to two decimal places. He is apt to figure out logical connections between the figures and the major problems that may lie behind them. Second, he has a broad vision and a clear mind. He can answer questions on the basis of observations and proofs with transparent logical connections, just like writing an article. Third, he never reads from scripts prepared beforehand. His expressiveness and eloquence makes you "feel like listening to a lecture while interviewing him", said one correspondent.

In 2009, Chen Yunxian, then Mayor of Foshan, gained the highest score among all the mayors of the Pearl River Delta region at the news conference held by the Guangdong Provincial Information Office on "Program for Reform and Development of the Pearl River Delta". Professor Zhang of Guangdong University of Foreign Studies, one of the judges at the conference, said, "The news conference of Foshan got the highest score. The reason was that, unlike other mayors who designed questions and answers beforehand, Chen Yunxian answered all questions on the spot, with confidence and elegance. He answered in a logical way, quoting lots of data without referring to materials. His performance was in line with norms of a modern statesman dealing with foreign affairs."

Chen's fluent command of English impressed people deeply. He made an English introduction about Foshan to entrepreneurs, investors and the media present at the Foreign Investment Spring Tea Party in 2009 and "Forum of Guangzhou-Hong Kong Financial Cooperation and Guangdong Financial High-tech Zone Promotion" held in Hong Kong. The correspondents were caught unprepared and asked for his speech script. The event organizer replied with a shrug of shoulders, "Sorry, Mayor Chen's speech was improvised."

"Many government officials in Foshan can communicate in English, but unlike him, no one can make an English speech without referring to the script. His English speech is fluent and free from Chinglish, in much the same style as that by English native speakers, in terms of form and diction and with intermittent additions of humor, which is not common even among the former colonial officers of Hong Kong

SAR Government," commented a manager from a Japan-funded enterprise, who frequently participated in government investment-attraction events.

Dr. Bo Murong, CEO of the Worldwide Operational Department of HSBC Group, was once amazed at his proficiency of English and commented, "It is quite out of my expectation that Mayor Chen has such a good command of English, which makes the whole negotiation harmonious and efficient," after an agreement signing ceremony for key infrastructure projects in the High-tech Zone of Foshan.

Chen Yunxian's skillful capability of handling foreign-related affairs considerably heightens Foshan's international image and sets a good example for government officials in Foshan to follow.

One more thing about Chen Yunxian deserves mentioning. Chen Yunxian impresses government officials in Foshan with his prompt action and reaction. "He is effective and efficient, the hardest leader to palter with in my experience. He never talks empty words, nor does he tolerate subordinates' verbiage at meetings or during field inspections. He has a clear idea of the progress and difficulty of each project. Therefore, vague expressions like 'speed up', 'try one's best', or 'spare no efforts' will not be accepted. He wants clear ideas," said a public servant in the local government.

What makes his colleagues upset is that, besides listening to work reports, Chen reads a wide range of newspapers and periodicals, regardless of workdays or holidays. "On many occasions, the articles from the media have not reached the relevant government departments, but Chen's instructions have come down to us, requiring us to explain to the public."

Many officials cannot adapt to his high demanding of administrative efficiency. In February 2010, during an investigation tour to New Dongping Town, he made a brief positive comment about the achievements made in construction, before he expressed strong dissatisfaction with the progress of the project, severely but tactically. He cited the successful cases, such as the declaration of Qiandeng Lake Financial High-tech Zone, the transformation of Donghuali Temple, and the construction of first-ring south-extension project. Then, he made a humorous comparison of "opportunity" to "the hair on a bald head". He said, "If you have kept it, it would be an opportunity; If not, it would never come back." "His criticism would not make you lose face, but everyone present will feel pressure, which stems from the distance in thinking between him and us," commented an official in private.

7.3.1 First and Fast: Foresighted Leading Gives Foshan Priority

The guideline of "scientific development, first execution, first trial" is a principle with rich connotation and great power. Chen Yunxian has a much more profound understanding of this principle than his subordinates. The "Foshan speed" that people have been speaking highly of in recent years results from his extraordinarily foresighted visions and the pressure of "first execution and first trial". He reiterates that Foshan's transformation must be examined and assessed against the general background of the whole nation's new industries, the Pearl River Delta integration and the cooperation of Guangdong, Hong Kong and Macao. The race in industrial restructuring and urban transformation is a fierce competition of "winner-take-all". A journalist from *People's Daily* once interviewed Chen Yunxian and asked, "What is the biggest obstacle to the development of Foshan?" "Backward thinking and slow execution," he answered without hesitation.

Chen summarized Foshan's primary problems as follows: irrational structure of the three industries, traditional factors of production still acting as the driving force for development, and lack of innovation; the industrial development not matching urban development; and short of motivation to transform and upgrade.

Chen Yunxian believes that government thinking can never fall behind and must go ahead of market and exercise foresighted leadership. With international academic researches and comparative studies of global development as background back-up, he obtained a clear sense of history and a good sense of location. He resolutely attributed those problems to the natural outcomes of the late stage of industrialization and tried to figure out solutions in no time. Not only did he try to solve the problems, he raced to be the first to solve them.

In Guangdong's industrial restructuring and transformation, Foshan has, more often than not, been the first to take full advantage of the opportunities and is often commended for its predictability, responsiveness and effectiveness.

1. Foshan is the first city in Guangdong Province to sign the strategic cooperation agreement with The Chinese Academy of Sciences, which has attracted hundreds of high-tech projects.
2. Foshan cooperates with U.S. SemiLED to develop the 100-billion "Three Opto-electronics" industry, aiming at Global Top Five.
3. Foshan has launched venture funds, industrial investment funds, fund guiding plans, and the "463 Plan", to lead the transformation of capital market services with the tactic of "achieving greatest undertakings with least effort".
4. Foshan used to be a low-class-manufacturing intensive city with underdeveloped urban infrastructure and wretched ecological environment. It has been undergoing earth-shaking changes. Three new industries have been emerging, each with over 100 billion output. The city has been rapidly upgrading itself through transforming outmoded towns, factories and villages. Decisive efforts have been made to shut down the polluting enterprises to improve the environment.

It is acknowledged that Chen Yunxian's quickness implies not only the speed of development but also the strict requirements for development quality and higher starting points. Contrary to the low starting point of grassroots economy, Foshan's transformation is foresighted and well-planned. Technological innovation connects directly with the projects of The Chinese Academy of Sciences and The Chinese Academy of Engineering. Cooperation is forged with international firms from the very beginning in the emerging industries, and international developers and international concepts are introduced into urban transformation.

People who know Chen Yunxian are familiar with his principle of "watch before walking".

As early as 2005, when he was appointed secretary of Shunde District Committee of CPC, he put forward the idea that "government should have foresighted leadership". He said, "Many cities have been developing through joint forces of the 'visible hand' and the 'invisible hand', which is only one-dimension. On some occasions, government adjustment in the middle course or afterwards cannot take effect. That is why government should exercise foresighted leading." Foresighted leading requires not only government officials' capability to make macro-level prediction and judgment and effective execution but also the courage of reform to blaze a new trail.

In the same year, he put forward an industrial development program called "The Triple-Three Strategy", which struck the vital point of Foshan. At the time that EU enforced its environment protection instructions for importing electronic products, Chen Yunxian, then executive mayor of Foshan and secretary of Shunde District Committee of CPC, pointed out that the industrial structure of Foshan depended excessively on exports and just a few industrial lines, and that most small and medium-sized enterprises were located at the low end of production chain with poor anti-risk ability.

To cope with the situation, he put forward "the Triple-Three Strategy" for industrial development and the "Five-step" development strategy for enterprise development. The former aimed at nurturing new industrial groups with strong anti-risk ability, and the latter focused on transforming the mode for enterprise development and supporting independent innovation and brand building. They later became strategies for municipal development of Foshan as a result of their remarkable achievements.

Actually, the above strategies broke the past patterns of "industries obtaining more supportive policies on the basis of more taxes and output values". The strategies changed the overall distribution pattern of government resources by establishing a multi-index system of scientific assessment and displayed greater policy orientation towards new industries with independent technology. This way of government thinking broke the Matthew effect of governments' resources distribution and led the flow of resources into innovative fields rather than accelerating the vicious cycle of putting in more resources to further expand low-class manufacturing.

Inevitably, the new system affected the vested interest of some and therefore arose a great deal of controversy. The 2008 financial crisis proved that the strategies are foresighted. After the crisis struck Guangdong, Foshan was the first to win victory in "maintaining economic growth" among the cities of the Pearl River Delta, because it had completed its adjustment of industrial structure. The newly developed industries with independent technology had stronger power to resist and survive the crisis.

When anxiety pervaded Foshan concerning the task of "maintaining economic growth", Chen Yunxian, an economist mayor, predicted boldly that China's economic development would take a V-reverse. Based on this accurate estimation of the macroeconomic situation, the Foshan government did not rush to be the "firefighting team" to help the enterprises but launched the "Three Financial Projects" policy. The government offered guarantee with small investment for the purpose of driving bonding companies and banks to grant loans to advanced manufacturing companies and eventually promoting venture capital investment. This innovation of system, which intended to “achieve greatest undertakings with least effort”, provided a breakout for capital market and led champion enterprises of different industries to go public in succession, hence the “Foshan Plate” appearing in A-share main board, small and medium-sized board, and second (growth enterprise) board.

It is really rare for all such accidental factors as the international financial crisis, policy changes, development bottleneck and industrial upgrading and restructuring to come altogether, but it is even rarer for a foresighted mayor, who has accurate insights and foresights on macro-economy with extraordinary approaches under extraordinary circumstances, to come together with the above factors. Foshan is blessed for boasting this rare arrangement.

7.3.2 Philosophy and Dreams Initiate a Revolution of Ideology

The moment that took office in May 2010 as secretary of Foshan Municipal Committee of CPC, Chen Yunxian proposed his conception of “Intelligent Foshan via Fourization” and threw new illuminating light upon the thinking of Foshan government officials. They wasted no time searching for relevant studies, like the idea of “intelligent globe”. For a considerably long period of time, it remained a hot topic how to amalgamate informationalization with industrialization, urbanization and internationalization.

However, his conception of “Intelligent Foshan” was not put into immediate operation. The draft proposal was first sent to Beijing for consultation of top Chinese experts from The Chinese Academy of Sciences, Peking University and Tsinghua University. And then, it solicited opinions through various channels from people of all walks of life. Judging from the number of serious discussions and consultations and the number of people involved and their ranks, people of Foshan began to become aware that “Intelligent Foshan” differed radically from any former measures, plans, and policies. Nor was it purely methodological approaches. It meant a revolution of ideology concerning economic development.

To put it in another way, “Intelligent Foshan” is not only a government slogan, nor merely an economic development route of a region, but more importantly, an academic issue, an issue of philosophic nature.

Behind this ideology reside rich implications that cover “self-initiated innovation” and “technical transformation” which are closely related to “things” and great emphasis upon “information”. It discloses the crucial problem that remains unsolved in the process of transformation and upgrading: what other factors are required when Foshan is positioned at the high end of the industrial chain and is equipped with high technology? To make it more concrete, what leads to the distance between Apple and Fujitsu, an OEM enterprise with high technology? Chen Yunxian reiterated the necessity and importance of OEM, but how can that come about?

Judging from this perspective, “informationalization” does not equate simply with the application of internet and IT technology nor merely data acquisition and information circulation.

During an investigation tour to Gaoming District of Foshan, Chen Yunxian recommended to the government officials a book entitled *Here Comes Everybody: The Power of Organizing Without Organizations*. The author describes the industrial age as the "firm power" and the information age "flexible power".

In the past, product economy tended to be tangible and visible, but in the future, information economy will tend to be intangible and invisible.

In the past, individual characteristics were sacrificed for achieving large scale as was implemented by the "firm power" method, but in the future, the "flexible power" method will have to be adopted so that individual differences, respect for individuals, and cultural content of products will be highly recognized and valued.

Here lies the answer to one of the key questions: "fourization" is to pump new blood and life into industrialization, internationalization and urbanization and to give dead "things" a working brain. What is meant by information? Information means difference and vitality. Information implies originality, culture, brand and trustworthiness that are greatly scarce in China's economy. It must be admitted that Chen Yunxian has got a profound understanding and a firm mastery of the core issue in China's economic transformation.

The transformation of modes of economic development does not merely mean upgrading technology from low to high and shifting production mode from extensive to intensive but also heightening such active factors as information, culture and so on. What is to be commended is not cheers for soaring GDP but a call for ideological revolution.

It comes to be found that Foshan's lighting industry has been ranking top five in the world as a result of the amalgamation of LED technology, and the ceramic and household electrical appliances enterprises, which Foshan takes great pride in, have become industrial leaders as a result of joint efforts with software industry. All this indicates that what counts most is the revolution of ideology.

Discussions and reflections regarding "Intelligent Foshan via Fourization" are well under way. There is sufficient justification that Foshan, as one of the most competitive cities in the Pearl River Delta, is well prepared for "foresighted leading". It is "foresighted leading" that positions Foshan and Chen Yunxian on the peak of the historical moment.

(First published in *Nanfang Daily*, July 22, 2010)

7.4 Chen Yunxian: Warm, Assiduous and Witty

7.4.1 Affinity: Considerate of Others' Feelings

Chen Ting, a reporter of *Zhujiang Business*, interviewed Chen Yunxian on different occasions when he was working in Shunde. She said that Chen's thoughtfulness, as well as his elegance and kindness, impressed her most.

She mentioned one of his anecdotes. She went to one of his lectures delivered to government officials in Party School of Foshan Municipal Committee of CPC.

Chen, along with several other officials, was waiting in the common room before the lecture. It was very cold. She went into the room, undid her scarf, opened a notebook and began to rub her hands to make them warm, without noticing their presence. Chen Yunxian saw her shivering and greeted her, "Chen Ting, why not come and sit closer to us; it's warmer here." Concentrating on her work, she did not hear his words. Chen repeated. That gave her a big surprise when she suddenly realized what was happening.

Warm feelings were still with her when she recalled this, "We often meet those government officials we have interviewed. They rarely take special notice of what we do. He is really warm and easy-going."

7.4.2 *Excellent Command of English: Faster than Interpreters*

It is well-known in Foshan that Chen Yunxian, who has made several study visits to America, has a good command of English. His on-the-spot interpretation left admirable impressions upon many foreign businessmen at an agreement signing ceremony for key infrastructure projects in Foshan's High-tech Zone according to a news report in December 2006. "Mayor Chen's fluent command of English, which came as a big surprise to all present at the negotiation, made it smooth and efficient," commended Dr. Murong Bo, CEO of Global Operations of HSBC Group.

A staff member of Economic and Trade Bureau of Foshan, who accompanied Chen Yunxian on a business soliciting tour to Chicago, told the correspondent that Chen was able to, on many occasions, translate some technical terms even before the interpreter due to his large vocabulary.

A subordinate of Chen's, who accompanied him on several overseas visits, said that Chen can speak English fluently, but with an accent. He jokingly commented that his pronunciation is not always very accurate and that his advantage lies in his large vocabulary power. People are impressed by his assiduity. On one occasion where he saw Shunde's specialty of "shuanpinai" (double layer milk custard), he earnestly asked people around him how to translate it into English.

7.4.3 *Responsiveness: Handle Expert Questions Tactfully on CCTV*

In October 2006, the State Statistical Bureau released China's Top 100 counties/cities of 2005. As secretary of Shunde Party Committee of CPC, Chen was invited, together with party secretary of Nanhai as two representatives from Top Ten, to the CCTV program, *Dialogue*, to answer questions by hostess Wang Xiaoya about "happy GDP". Many still have fresh memories of Chen's active performance in the program.

Chen Yunxian was the first to raise his hand to signal his request to answer questions. He opened his remarks by saying, "Shunde is the major manufacturing base for Chinese private enterprises. Our promotional slogan is *Shunde's Product, China's Pride*." He spared no efforts in his promotion of Shunde.

As a response to the concerns of a professor from Renmin University of China about whether social security and environment problems in Guangdong Province are likely to reduce people's feelings of happiness, he said, "Your question leads me to conclude that you have not been to Foshan and Shunde for long. Not long ago, I received a French delegation of more than 200 members to Shunde. When they arrived, they commented that some parts of Shunde feel even better than in Europe. I would like to invite experts present at this program, especially this professor from Renmin University of China, to visit Shunde and give us your valuable suggestions".

7.4.4 Good Memory: Accurate to Two to Three Decimal Places

With work experiences in economic areas for many years, Chen Yunxian has the habit of quoting statistic figures in his speech. At the Party Congress of CPC in 2007, he left delegates very good impressions when he made a speech as a member of Shunde delegation. He cited an example to illustrate rich cultural resources in Shunde: "Chen Clan Academy in Guangzhou started its construction in the 14th year under Emperor Guangxu's (1888) reign in the Qing Dynasty and was completed in the 20th year (1894), while Chen Clan Academy in Shunde started its construction in the 21st year (1895), only a few years later." A delegate checked the figures afterwards to find they were accurate.

A businessperson who had listened to Chen Yunxian's speeches on various occasions once described him as "having a very good memory, and he can remember figures precisely even to two or three decimal places."

(First published in *Southern Metropolitan Daily*, January 12, 2007)

Epilogue

As Chen Yunxian's doctoral supervisor, I am delighted at the news that another new book of his has come out. What makes me even more delighted is that he never loses his character as a scholar and continues to think about theoretical economic issues in spite of his shift from business to government and his extremely tight work schedule. This new book—*Foresighted Leading*—is the result of his 8 years' theoretical innovations as a government official.

How time flies. It has been over 20 years since Chen Yunxian's graduation from Peking University as a doctoral degree holder. The image of Chen Yunxian as a Ph.D. candidate 20 years ago has been imprinted in my mind: assiduous, energetic and ambitious. One cannot image how hard it was for him to be admitted into Peking University as a Ph.D. candidate. There were rigid criteria for Ph.D. candidate enrollment, and the required level of English proficiency blocked the road of quite a few students, to say nothing of other requirements. I used to joke about myself being a clodhopper, but the school of economics in Peking University adopted a complete set of "international standards" for its doctoral education. It was hoped that Ph.D. candidates of Peking University should never be inferior to those of overseas institutions.

It has turned out to be true that Ph.D. candidates of Peking University have not proved themselves inferior to those of overseas institutions. After Dr. Chen went to settle down in Guangdong, he set up Guangfa and turned it into a first-class securities company in China. He became a well-known figure in the securities industry. He was transferred from business to government in 2003 and displayed extraordinary capabilities in government administration as well. Moreover, he has persevered in his researches in economic theories and practice in the field of regional economic development. This book is a good manifestation of all the achievements he has made in theoretical generalization and practical work.

As a teacher, nothing makes one feel more pleased than hearing the good news about his students' progress.

It is often said that one's destiny is always intertwined with that of his nation and his times. Chen Yunxian represents a lucky generation. Their school days coincide

Y. Chen, *Foresighted Leading: Theoretical Thinking and Practice of China's Regional Economic Development*, DOI 10.1007/978-3-642-35368-0,

with the age in which the state and the society attach great importance to education. Chen Yunxian has taken best advantage of this great opportunity and has kept pursuing his education in eight different universities at home and abroad. After they completed their education, they have come up with the period of China's rapid economic growth, and that provides them with platforms and opportunities to give full play to their talents and expertise.

Consequently, it is not surprising that there appear in China a great number of special talents like Chen Yunxian, who can not only do practical work but conduct theoretical researches as well. They have done their bit to contribute to China's sound and rapid development.

Currently, the rise of China has been a hot topic. The Chinese government has maintained a low-key attitude towards this topic, but China's performance in fighting against the international financial crisis and the sight of Chinese tourists and products "made in China" will suffice to attract world attention. It is inevitable that scholars will probe into the Chinese experience behind China's rise.

An analysis has been made in this book. Chen Yunxian says, "In addition to enterprises, regional governments also play a major role in market competition in China. In other words, in China's development, competition exists not only between enterprises but also between governments. These two levels of competition are the 'double forces' for China to have achieved speedy sustained economic development in the course of more than 30 years' reform."

He concludes that under the context of market economy, government is an independent economic entity that not only provides services and administers public affairs but also coordinates, facilitates, and leads economic development. The dual role of local government represents its functions at both micro-level of market economy and macro-level of government leading, regulating and adjusting economic development.

Looking back upon China's previous practice under the guidance of this notion, Chen Yunxian proposes that a truly successful economic system implies that government must exercise foresighted leading by the aid of the foundations of market economy, its mechanisms and rules and employ the "visible hand" to overcome the defects and make up the margins caused by the "invisible hand".

As an economist with financial background, Chen Yunxian has positioned himself at a great height. Foresighted thinking and strategic visions are essential to the success in finance. Chen Yunxian's experience in Gunagfa Securities Co. Ltd has been solid proof for this. After taking office in local government, Chen Yunxian has applied them to regional development and put forth the regional economic theory of foresighted leading, which he defines as follows: giving full play to government functions, particularly those of regional governments, in economic guidance, regulation and warning and taking the lead in promoting scientific and sustainable growth in regional economy with recourse to market rules and forces, by means of investing, pricing, taxation, legal and other measures and through innovation in organization, system and technology.

In terms of regional economic development, what are often encountered are individual notions, for instance, "some sort of project" or "some sort of strategy", etc.

The theory of "foresighted leading" has pushed regional development from notions to theoretical heights. Judging from China's current situation of economic development, regional development should no longer be "wading across the stream by feeling stones", and it is high time that a theoretically innovative system be established for China's economics.

Chen Yunxian's researches are of great significance and value. I believe that the theory of "foresighted leading" for China's regional economic development has not only extended the research scope of economics into macroeconomics, meso economics and microeconomics but also provided the direction and approaches for the reform of China's economic system, in particular regional economic development.

Foresighted Leading is the crystallization of Dr. Chen Yunxian's years of thinking and practice as government leader. Economics, as an applied discipline, needs most the theories derived from practice. Economics needs "the academic school" and more importantly, "the practical school". Hopefully, more economists who are engaged in practical work will join in theoretical innovations in economics and make substantial contributions to "keep the tree of economic theories evergreen".

By Xiao Zhuoji

MIX
Papier aus verantwortungsvollen Quellen
Paper from responsible sources
FSC® C105338

If you have any concerns about our products,
you can contact us on
ProductSafety@springernature.com

In case Publisher is established outside the EU,
the EU authorized representative is:
Springer Nature Customer Service Center GmbH
Europaplatz 3, 69115 Heidelberg, Germany

Printed by Libri Plureos GmbH
in Hamburg, Germany